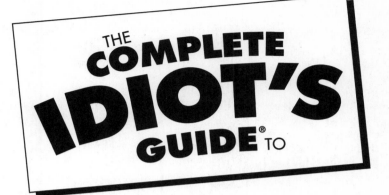

THE COMPLETE IDIOT'S GUIDE® TO

Successful Outsourcing

by Gene Marks

ALPHA

A member of Penguin Group (USA) Inc.

This book is dedicated to my father, Ronald Marks, who was outsourcing long before everyone else caught on.

ALPHA BOOKS

Published by the Penguin Group

Penguin Group (USA) Inc., 375 Hudson Street, New York, New York 10014, U.S.A.

Penguin Group (Canada), 10 Alcorn Avenue, Toronto, Ontario, Canada M4V 3B2 (a division of Pearson Penguin Canada Inc.)

Penguin Books Ltd, 80 Strand, London WC2R 0RL, England

Penguin Ireland, 25 St Stephen's Green, Dublin 2, Ireland (a division of Penguin Books Ltd)

Penguin Group (Australia), 250 Camberwell Road, Camberwell, Victoria 3124, Australia (a division of Pearson Australia Group Pty Ltd)

Penguin Books India Pvt Ltd, 11 Community Centre, Panchsheel Park, New Delhi—110 017, India

Penguin Group (NZ), cnr Airborne and Rosedale Roads, Albany, Auckland 1310, New Zealand (a division of Pearson New Zealand Ltd)

Penguin Books (South Africa) (Pty) Ltd, 24 Sturdee Avenue, Rosebank, Johannesburg 2196, South Africa

Penguin Books Ltd, Registered Offices: 80 Strand, London WC2R 0RL, England

Copyright © 2005 by Gene Marks

International Standard Book Number: 1-59257-370-3
Library of Congress Catalog Card Number: 2005926957

07 06 05   8 7 6 5 4 3 2 1

Interpretation of the printing code: The rightmost number of the first series of numbers is the year of the book's printing; the rightmost number of the second series of numbers is the number of the book's printing. For example, a printing code of 05-1 shows that the first printing occurred in 2005.

Printed in the United States of America

Note: This publication contains the opinions and ideas of its author. It is intended to provide helpful and informative material on the subject matter covered. It is sold with the understanding that the author and publisher are not engaged in rendering professional services in the book. If the reader requires personal assistance or advice, a competent professional should be consulted.

The author and publisher specifically disclaim any responsibility for any liability, loss, or risk, personal or otherwise, which is incurred as a consequence, directly or indirectly, of the use and application of any of the contents of this book.

Most Alpha books are available at special quantity discounts for bulk purchases for sales promotions, premiums, fund-raising, or educational use. Special books, or book excerpts, can also be created to fit specific needs.

For details, write: Special Markets, Alpha Books, 375 Hudson Street, New York, NY 10014.

Publisher: *Marie Butler-Knight*
Product Manager: *Phil Kitchel*
Senior Managing Editor: *Jennifer Bowles*
Senior Acquisitions Editor: *Renee Wilmeth*
Development Editor: *Jennifer Moore*
Production Editor: *Megan Douglass*
Copy Editor: *Keith Cline*
Cartoonist: *Chris Eliopoulos*
Cover/Book Designer: *Trina Wurst*
Indexer: *Julie Bess*
Layout: *Ayanna Lacey*
Proofreading: *Donna Martin*

Contents at a Glance

Contents

Part 2: **Do You Need to Outsource?**

5 **The Pros and Cons of Employees**

11 Avoiding Common Outsourcing Mistakes   121

12 Where to Look for Outsourced Help   133

Appendixes

Foreword

Everyday, fewer and fewer of the people doing work for a company actually work for that company. That, in a nutshell, is outsourcing. It's a new way of doing business that's been adopted by the world's largest companies like GM and IBM, as well as smaller businesses right in your community. And, of course, the same thing is happening in our own lives. Cleaning the house, doing laundry, repairing the car, making meals, and preparing tax returns are all examples of things my parents pretty much did for themselves that I mostly hire others to do for me.

But why? Why are businesses large and small and individuals wealthy and middle-class doing less and less for themselves? How can it be cheaper to hire someone else to do something for you that you can do quite adequately for yourself?

There's really a pretty long list of reasons, but most of them fall into three big buckets:

It's Cheaper

Let's face it, if someone does something over and over for a whole bunch of customers, they're likely to get so efficient at it that they can do it more cheaply than the customer could do it for him- or herself. The savings go up even more when you consider the "overhead" costs of equipment, maintenance, training, and insurance. And, of course, a specialist's bigger customer base gives them more buying power for supplies, which adds even more savings.

Time Is Money

Not only are you saving on the work, but think about where you or your company can now spend that time. How much better can you do the things you decide to keep doing because you can now focus more time and energy on them? Take that time and reinvest it in yourself or your customers, and the return from outsourcing can go up many fold.

Knowledge Is Power

Finally, there is a whole range of benefits that come from having a real specialist working for you. New ideas, new ways of looking at and solving problems, a flexible resource you can call on whenever you need it for just what you need it for. Their specialized knowledge, which probably took them years to develop, is on tap for you, whenever you need it—and you only pay by the drink.

Gene Marks's book is a superb resource for every business person. In clear, to-the-point prose, he takes you through the entire process—from deciding what type of outsourcing makes sense for you, to finding the right provider, to the contractual in's and out's. Just to make sure everything is covered, Gene takes you through the "off-shore" dimension—both why it scares so many people and how it might just be the right thing for you someday.

If there's one idea everyone should take away from this book, it's that outsourcing is here to stay and either you figure it out, or you watch your competitor do so at your expense. Read the book. Learn the valuable lessons shared. Make up your own mind. But, most importantly, be informed and take control of outsourcing as a business tool for your use.

Michael F. Corbett

Michael F. Corbett is one of the best-known experts in the field of outsourcing and is executive director of the International Association of Outsourcing Professionals (IAOP). Working with leading customer, provider, and advisor organizations around the world, IAOP helps companies increase their outsourcing success rate, improve their outsourcing ROI, and expand the opportunities for outsourcing across their businesses.

Mr. Corbett is also the author of *The Outsourcing Revolution: Why It Makes Sense and How to Do It Right*, which has been called "the definitive work on outsourcing."

Introduction

Outsourcing is not just a buzzword. It's an established business practice. It's an industry. It's a way to reallocate resources, reduce costs, and increase revenues.

This book introduces you to the world of outsourcing. We'll begin by looking at how outsourcing has grown through history to become so essential to business practice today. We'll also help you decide whether or not it's right for your business to outsource. We'll discuss the best practices to employ if you decide to take the leap. And we'll help you avoid some common outsourcing pitfalls.

This book is divided into four main parts.

Part 1, "The Outsourcing Environment," begins with a description of the various types of outsourcing arrangements that have been created over the years so that you can begin to consider which types of arrangements might be best suited for your business. You'll also learn about a typical day in the life of an outside service provider so that you can better appreciate the challenges he or she faces. Finally, I share with you the lessons I've learned about outsourcing in the hopes that you will avoid some of the mistakes I've made.

Part 2, "Do You Need to Outsource?" examines the outsourcing decision-making process. As you'll learn in this section, outsourcing isn't the solution for every problem, and some people should probably avoid outsourcing any process due to their personality traits and management philosophies. Chapters in this section discuss the plusses and minuses of having people on your payroll versus contracting out the work. In addition, I walk you through the seven steps for deciding whether to outsource. We then look at ideas for creating revenue and reducing expenses through outsourcing and where to look for outsourced help. Finally, I give you tips for selecting the best outside service provider for your work.

Part 3, "Outsourcing in Action," focuses on the day-to-day challenges you'll face when managing an outsourced service relationship. I start by examining the two most popular forms of outsourcing: employee leasing and information technology outsourcing. Then I tell you about the best ways to manage your service providers. I discuss the importance of creating effective service level agreements and review ways to evaluate your service provider's work. Finally, I talk about the things you need to consider before sticking your toe into the global outsourcing pond.

In **Part 4, "Staying Out of Trouble,"** you'll learn about the legal ramifications of outsourcing and how to avoid getting into hot water. I discuss how the tax authorities can affect your outsourcing relationship and, in the final chapter, leave you with some ethical considerations to ponder.

Throughout this book I've included sidebars to highlight items worthy of special consideration.

Outsourcing Insights

Here I offer additional outsourcing tips and advice.

Business Buzzwords

Here you'll find definitions of key words and terms.

Stay Alert!

These boxes draw your attention to potential areas that could land you in trouble, so watch out!

Knowledge Is Power

When deciding whether to outsource, you need all the facts you can get. Look here for unbiased information about outsourcing.

Special Thanks to the Technical Reviewer

The Complete Idiot's Guide to Successful Outsourcing was reviewed by an expert who double-checked the accuracy of what you'll learn here, to help us ensure that this book gives you everything you need to know about outsourcing. Special thanks are extended to Dave Taylor. For more information on Mr. Taylor, see www.intuitive.com.

Trademarks

All terms mentioned in this book that are known to be or are suspected of being trademarks or service marks have been appropriately capitalized. Alpha Books and Penguin Group (USA) Inc. cannot attest to the accuracy of this information. Use of a term in this book should not be regarded as affecting the validity of any trademark or service mark.

Part 1

The Outsourcing Environment

Welcome to the world of outsourcing.

People have been farming out work for a long, long time, but only recently has this type of work arrangement exploded into a multi-billion-dollar industry.

In this section, I explain the basics of outsourcing, including the various processes and jobs that can be outsourced and the types of businesses and individuals who specialize in such services. Next I encourage you to step into the shoes of an independent contractor. Looking at outsourcing from a service provider perspective will help you better manage all of your outsourcing relationships. As we wrap up this section, I share with you some of the outsourcing lessons I've learned over the years.

Our Outsourcing World

In This Chapter

- ◆ Defining outsourcing
- ◆ Exploring outsourcing's history
- ◆ Understanding the reasons why outsourcing has grown
- ◆ A review of important outsourcing lessons

Although it's gotten a lot of press lately, outsourcing is not about shipping jobs overseas. And it's not a new phenomenon, either. Also, you don't need to be a giant company to enjoy the benefits of outsourcing. In fact, almost every business today practices some form of outsourcing. The question is: Are they doing it well? And can they do it better?

But before we answer these questions, we need to spell out exactly what it means to call something "outsourcing."

Getting the Definition Down

Outsourcing means paying another person or company to do something for you that could have otherwise been done by your own staff.

Usually this work is in the form of services. That's why in this book I frequently refer to the people doing outsourced work as outside service providers.

> **Knowledge Is Power**
>
> There are approximately 138.3 million workers in the United States today out of a total population of close to 300 million.

> **Knowledge Is Power**
>
> Labor costs for call-center operators in India are about $8,000 per year, compared to more than $57,000 per year for a worker in the United States.

But lots of other words are used to describe outsourcing, including the following:

Contracting

Sourcing

Subcontracting

Farming it out

Offshoring

Freelancing

Although each of these terms has a unique meaning, they all refer to various kinds of outsourcing arrangements. What it comes down to is this: no matter what you call it, if you're not doing something yourself, you're outsourcing.

The Outsourcing Explosion

Outsourcing has become a major part of our economy, and its growth hasn't been by chance. Five factors have fueled its expansion. Each of the following sections is devoted to one of these factors.

The Rise of the Internet

With the Internet as a tool, your bookkeeper in Chicago can print out checks at your office in Miami. An e-mail message to your office can be instantly routed to a voice-mail system across the country. Your assistant can send legal documents instantaneously to a lawyer in Japan. You and your business partners can hold conversations in real time using instant messaging.

Outsourcing Insights

Think outsourcing is new? No way. People have been farming out work for centuries. Don't believe me? Then consider these key events:

100 B.C.E.   As the Roman Republic, and then empire, grows, foreign nations are used as sources of cheap labor. The manufacturing of exotic foods, silks, spices, cloths, and furnishings are outsourced abroad.

12th century C.E.   The Roman Empire falls as outsourced soldiers (called mercenaries) cannot contain the hundreds of warlords and other factions jostling for land and control.

15th century   In England, the farming of land is outsourced by the country's gentry to peasants in exchange for food and shelter.

The queen of Spain outsources the exploration of purported new lands to Christopher Columbus and his three ships.

16th century   Niccolo Machiavelli advises his Italian client kings against outsourcing the military to mercenaries or befall the same fate as those emperors before them.

17th century   The giant East India Company pioneers outsource in a way that would be familiar to modern managers (e.g., contractors, offshore factories, intermediaries, and brokers).

17th and 18th centuries   The rise of colonial America provides its owners a place to manufacture products at much lower costs than at home. England farms out the fighting of French and Spain intruders to hired Americans.

19th century   Cloth makers in India during the 1830s are unable to compete with the more efficient manufacturers in England. Much of India's clothing production gets outsourced to English makers, devastating the Indian work force.

Before Parliament repeals the corn laws in 1846, English farmers loudly complain that outsourcing farming to other countries would make the country too dependent on foreign food. They are wrong. Soon after, England becomes the richest and most well-fed nation in the world.

20th century   Beginning in 1950, the American economy outsources jobs around the world.

In 1962, H. Ross Perot starts Electronic Data Systems (EDS). The company outsources computer operations for some of the largest firms in the world. By 1998, EDS provides $16.9 billion worth of information services to clients worldwide.

In the 1960s and 1970s, larger companies begin outsourcing computerized batch processing of payroll checks and remitting payments of employee withholding taxes to financial services firms.

Congress considers bills to discourage the outsourcing of information technology and manufacturing jobs outside of the United States. Outsourcing becomes a significant issue in the 2004 presidential campaign.

The Internet, and other technologies, such as wireless devices, satellites, and software applications, have enabled companies to shift work to less-expensive locales while keeping some level of control over the process.

The Shifting and Educated Population

Children of Indian families go off to England or America, get an education, and return home to service Western customers over the Internet or phone. Government funding of education programs in Malaysia enables workers there to improve their technical skills so that European firms can outsource work to them. Across America, independent entrepreneurs set up shop in their own homes and hire themselves out to provide highly skilled outsourced services such as business process consulting, human resources management, and technical writing.

Outsourcing Insights

The 50 top information technology (IT) companies employ about 1.25 million people worldwide.

As borders open, economies flourish, and education increases, workers in many countries around the world become available to provide services that would at one time have been unthinkable. Farming out manufacturing to Vietnam? Hosting your website in Prague? Today, this is all a reality!

The Spread of English

Go to Tokyo and order your meal in English and, most likely, your waitress will understand you. Ask for directions in English while you're in Germany and the response may sound like it comes from a native American rather than a native German.

English is taught throughout the world and has established itself as either the primary or secondary language of most industrialized and developing countries. As a result, negotiating and managing overseas outsourcing relationships have become that much easier to accomplish. Of course, you don't need to be a linguist to understand the words "show me the money"—no matter what dialect it's in!

Overnight Shipping Firms

What was once a dream of Fred Smith, the founder of FedEx, is now a reality: overnight and expedited shipping. Machine parts made in Southeast Asia can be delivered to a European warehouse in days, not weeks. Key agreements can be flown from New York to London in hours. Shipping firms such as FedEx, UPS, and DHL have grown the overnight shipping business into a multi-billion-dollar industry and are another big reason why outsourcing has exploded over the past 30 years.

The Lower Cost of Travel

Maybe just shipping the part isn't enough. Maybe you want to go to China yourself and supervise the work that's being done by the company that's making the parts. It's easier and more affordable to travel now than at any time in history.

The ease and, most important, the speed of travel has enabled service providers and customers from all parts of the world to establish stronger relationships and work together face to face.

Now that we've seen why outsourcing has grown in popularity, I'd like to share with you a few of my own experiences and what I've learned by outsourcing.

Outsourcing Lessons I've Learned

In the past 20 years, I've seen a lot of companies, both large and small, practice the art of outsourcing. I've seen these relationships succeed and fail. I've watched and participated in many long-term relationships, both as an outsourcing company and as a service provider. And along the way, I've learned quite a bit. Many of these concepts will be more fully developed in the rest of this book, but what follows are some key lessons about outsourcing.

> **Knowledge Is Power**
>
> The U.S military outsourced $18.2 billion of their work in 2003.

Lesson 1: Everyone Outsources Something

The world is full of specialists. It's nearly impossible to be an expert at everything. It usually makes more sense to outsource a task to a professional rather than taking on the responsibility yourself. This is why most of us outsource something.

Don't believe me? Take a look around. Few businesses have the expertise they need to complete their own tax returns, so they outsource the job to an accounting firm. Many companies find it easier to have another company "host" their website for them rather than train their employees to operate it. We can manage much of our own legal work, but most of us prefer to farm this out to a lawyer.

Lesson 2: You Can Save Money *and* Make Money by Outsourcing

Most people think of outsourcing as a means of reducing costs. When you read about a company "offshoring" their customer service to another country, they usually cite cheaper labor as the reason for the move. Although some companies do outsource labor to cut costs, many companies also outsource work to generate revenues.

As you'll see in Chapter 9, there are many ways to generate new revenue opportunities through outsourcing. Turning a profit off of the work done by hired guns is a big reason why people outsource. Don't think of outsourcing only as a way to reduce your costs. Think of it as a way to expand your business.

Lesson 3: Outsourcing Is an Industry

Outsourcing is a big, big business that generates billions of dollars each year. Thousands of firms perform outsourcing services, and equally as many home-based and self-employed professionals do the same.

The outsourcing industry has trade organizations, political action committees, industry associations, specialized publications, thousands of websites, and dozens of worldwide conferences each year. Such corporate giants as IBM, Dell Computers, Microsoft, and Ernst & Young provide outsourcing services for their customers. A lot of resources are available to anyone interested in finding out more about outsourcing.

Lesson 4: There Is No Outsourcing "Threat"

The recent explosion in outsourcing has struck fear in some people. They see the loss of American jobs to foreign countries. They fear the demise of American manufacturing to other locations. They sometimes view those companies that outsource work overseas as unpatriotic or selfish. I don't agree with these characterizations.

Outsourcing Insights

More than 70 percent of the outsourcing done in this country occurs right here in this country! Don't fall for the myth that the help you need resides only overseas.

There is no outsourcing threat. Companies do what they can to remain profitable. Outsourcing a menial task to a Chinese company helps an American firm grow. Through their growth, they hire more people and fuel the economy. The rise of outsourcing has provided opportunities for hundreds of thousands of entrepreneurs to farm themselves out, work from home, spend more time with their families, and make more money.

Lesson 5: Outsourcing Is Not for Everyone

It takes a certain type of person and organization to be able to successfully outsource a task. Outsourcing necessarily involves some loss of control. It may require a large outlay of cash at the outset. It takes many hiring decisions out of your hands.

Outsourcing Insights

According to one survey, 30 percent of companies saw no cost reductions or actually saw increased expenses as a result of outsourcing.

Before deciding to outsource any aspect of your business, you need to make sure doing so makes financial and emotional sense. Outsourcing needs to fit in with your company's culture. Don't outsource without a clear reason for doing so, and make sure you're up to the task.

Lesson 6: There Is No Single Form of Outsourcing

When researching this book, I came across words that I've never heard of before. I've discovered they all have important meanings. In the next chapter, for example, we discuss the buzzwords of co-sourcing, co-opetition, transformational outsourcing, and multi-client shared services. We discuss independents (both full- and part-time), hobbyists, consultants, tinkerers, and partners.

You'll learn what all these terms mean later in the book. For now, all you need to know is that there is no typical outsourcing arrangement. Farming out a task to a third party means forming a relationship. Each relationship is unique. Outsourcing is not a cookie cutter kind of thing.

Lesson 7: Your Service Provider Has a Challenging Job

As you'll come to learn in Chapter 3, your service provider must overcome a lot of challenges. It isn't so easy doing what they do. The idea that a high-priced consultant sweeps in, has three-martini lunches, and sends a large bill at the end of the project is only partly correct. The bill will always be large!

Nowadays, however, outsourced service providers take responsibility for transforming entire warehouses, reshuffling operations, and administering human relations. They're abused by their clients, have to fight to get paid what they're worth, and go from one problem to the next.

It's important to treat your service providers with respect and understand where they're coming from. Your relationship will succeed if there's mutual respect and courtesy toward each other.

Lesson 8: The Decision to Outsource Is Not Just Quantitative

True, there might be a very clear dollar-and-cents reason to outsource. (See the calculations in Chapter 7.) You might determine that an outside payroll firm can reduce your administrative costs. You calculate that having a job shop manufacture a part for your assembly will increase your margin by a couple of points. You figure that outsourcing a technical service to an expert can provide another source of revenues for your company.

But there are other factors to consider, too. What will your employees think? How will your customers respond to a subcontractor? Is your resource reliable? Are they using the best practices? Could there be quality problems?

Outsourcing is not just a financial decision. It's a commitment. It's an attitude. You'll learn in this book about evaluating all of the factors that affect an outsourcing decision.

> **Knowledge Is Power**
>
> Employee services, which include employee leasing, human resources, and payroll, are one of the top forms of outsourcing around. Worldwide human resources outsourcing reached $46 billion in 2003 and has been growing between 15 to 20 percent each year since 2001.

Lesson 9: There Are Plenty of Places to Look for Outsourcing Help

Thinking of farming out a job? Don't worry, there's no shortage of resources. We discuss them all in Chapter 12. You'll find out all about the sorts of resources available on the Internet and through traditional resources, such as the Yellow Pages and good old-fashioned references.

Your decision to outsource shouldn't be hindered by finding the right firm or person. Don't worry, you'll have a lot to choose from.

Lesson 10: Service Level Agreements and Contracts Are a Must

Don't farm out work without a contract. Too many people rely on a handshake and suffer unfortunate consequences. The outsourcing industry has spawned a new generation of lawyers who protect their clients against violations of service commitments, confidentiality, and the hiring away of employees.

An outsourcing arrangement covering services, privacy, and security issues, no matter how big or small, should always be well documented and signed off on by both parties. For more on contracts and service level agreements, see Chapters 17 and 21.

> **Knowledge Is Power**
>
> The IT industry—programming, computer services, Internet services—accounts for billions of dollars of outsourcing work. The average value of an IT outsourcing contract is $47 million, and the average contract length is 6 years.

Lesson 11: Outsourcing Creates Liabilities and Ethical Problems

When you enter into an outsourcing relationship, you're putting your trust in the service provider. If the service provider violates that trust, you could be in big trouble with your customers or your employees.

Outside parties might misuse data, steal employees, violate privacy, or disclose conflicts of interest. And in some situations, service providers don't disclose to their customers or employees that the service provider is doing outsourced work. This can create liability issues. Make sure your service provider is doing things on the up and up.

Lesson 12: Outsourcing Involves a Leap of Faith

You go through all the analyses and calculations. You talk to a hundred references. You interview, test, and interrogate. But in the end, you're taking a leap of faith.

You're going to have to take a chance that the firm you're entrusting to make a part, ensure quality, service your customers, do your books, host your website … is competent. And loyal. And trustworthy. And that there are no hidden costs. When you're done with all of your analyses, take a deep breath, look the other person in the eye, and ask yourself, "Am I ready to take this risk?"

Lesson 13: Outsourcing Is Not a Solution, It's a Tool

Some people make the mistake of thinking that by outsourcing a job they can wash their hands of the matter and move on to something else. Not so! Outsourcing still takes a lot of involvement by management. Outsourced workers need supervision. Deadlines need to be met. Problems still need to be solved.

Outsourcing is not the end. It's a means to an end. Getting a job done by farming out the work is a method, not an answer. Consider your decision to outsource not as a total solution, but as a tool for solving a problem.

These are the lessons I've learned about outsourcing. Now let's dig deeper into these and other concepts!

The Least You Need to Know

◆ Outsourcing means paying another person or company to do something for you that could have otherwise been done by your own staff.

◆ The practice of outsourcing has been around for a long time.

◆ Outsourcing has grown significantly in recent years due to advances in technology, population shifts, the spread of English, and improvements in shipping.

◆ Whether you've outsourced before, are outsourcing work now, or plan to outsource in the future, bear in mind the lessons that others have learned.

Outsourcing Arrangements

In This Chapter

◆ A comparison of outsourced service providers

◆ The risks and rewards of using different types of providers

◆ A review of popular outsourcing arrangements

Paul, the owner of a 50-person insurance brokerage firm, was really frustrated when we met.

"Gene," he said to me. "The software program you sold me works fine, but sometimes we get error messages. And we're getting error messages when we use some of our other applications, too. What's happening?"

After taking a few hours to review his computer network, I knew what the problem was.

"Paul," I began as we sat down together in his office. "Your network needs upgrading. Your server is almost out of space, and your workstations aren't running the most recent versions of your operating system. This is what's causing the problem with your software."

"I didn't realize we were in that bad of shape," Paul said with a sigh.

"Well, what does your IT guy say?" I asked.

"Oh, we don't have an IT guy," he said. "I've got a friend who comes in sometimes after hours when we've got a problem. He's got a full-time job elsewhere. He just loves working with computers."

"So you mean to tell me that you've outsourced your entire information technology support to one person, and he's not available during the day?" I asked, incredulously.

"Yup," said Paul. "Why, is that not a good idea?"

Lots of people will do outsourced work for you. And there are lots of different outsourcing arrangements you can enter into. The trick is matching your business with the right person and forming a good working relationship. Obviously, Paul's use of a "moonlighter" to support his network is not working out. But he's got plenty of other choices to consider.

In this chapter, we discuss who performs outsourcing work and how they can best work for your company.

What Are You Looking For?

Let's say you manage a 10-person company and you're sick and tired of doing your own payroll. You think it might be a good idea to outsource this time-consuming task to a company that can do it more quickly and accurately than you can. But who would best do the job? Do you send this to a payroll service company? Or should you hire an individual contractor? Before making a decision, let's review all the options.

Contract Workers

You could bring in a *contract worker* for the short term until you decide whether to continue outsourcing or hire an employee. Your outsourced contractor would not be an employee (or have the same employment costs, such as health benefits, disability pay, and vacation time), but he or she would very much act as someone on staff. Some contract workers put in as many hours as full-time workers. However, the level of employment commitment is low. The relationship demands little commitment from either one of you to continue working together beyond the stated term of the contract.

> **Business Buzzwords**
>
> A **contract worker** is a non-employee who performs specific tasks over a predetermined timeframe and in accordance with a written agreement.

A word of warning: hiring contract workers can open up a can of worms. Microsoft Corporation got into some hot water with its contract workers a few years ago. They didn't give these workers the kinds of benefits (vacation, stock plans, and so on) that the company offered to full-time Microsoft employees. A group of these contractors got together and sued the company ... and won.

There can be a fine line between contract workers and employees. In Chapter 20, I include the IRS's 20-step test for determining the employee status of subcontractors. The longer someone works for you and the more "employee-like" tools, such as a working area, you provide to them, the more likely the IRS will consider the worker to be an employee, and you may be subject to employer taxes.

Outsourcing Insights

Good outsourcing firms are made up of skilled professionals, each an expert at what they do. Not every outside service provider can assemble the level of individual experts that you may require for the job. Make sure you ask any firm you're considering about the experience of the people who will be doing the job.

Outsourcing Companies

Maybe you'll hire an outside payroll company, such as ADP or Paychex. There are hundreds of outsourced payroll companies around the country. In fact, numerous companies provide mostly outsourced services for their customers. For example, a significant part of FedEx Kinko's business comes from outsourced mailroom services, such as photocopying, shipping, and binding; and accounting firms do outsourced taxes for their clients. Big corporations used to have in-house printing and document-production facilities, but they're now obsolete because it's cheaper and easier to upload them to Kinko's and have them overnighted without fuss.

Choosing a company, rather than an individual, to perform outsourced services comes with its own advantages and disadvantages, depending on the situation and the specific firm's needs:

♦ An outsourced company will likely have more depth of personnel and knowledge. If you decide to hire ADP to do your payroll, for instance, you're going to get a company that is well versed in the most recent payroll and tax laws that could affect your business. An individual might not be able to keep up on all of the rules.

◆ An outsourced company can provide you with a better variety of experts to help you with your problem than just a single person. However, you may experience more turnover if you hire an outsourced company rather than an individual. Clients at large accounting firms often complain that they have to re-educate new staff members every year.

◆ An outsourced company may be financially more stable than an individual. Large outsource providers, like IBM, have been around a long time. As a result, you may experience a longer lasting relationship. Even so, you may gain a lot more loyalty and trust with an individual performing your work.

◆ An outsourced solution may not necessarily be the cheaper solution. It all depends on volume and the type of work. You may hire a worker to do filing from a temp firm and end up paying that person $15 an hour. If you hire an individual contractor, you might find someone to do the work for a lot less money. There's no guarantee that hiring an established firm will be more cost-effective than hiring an individual.

◆ An outsourced company may lend your business more credibility than an individual. Hiring a large consulting firm to implement your computer system may go over better with your management team than relying on one person, no matter how much of an expert he or she may be.

◆ Outsourced companies may be less flexible than individuals. Try getting someone from the company hosting your e-mail on the phone over a holiday weekend and you'll see what I mean.

Part-Time Independents

Maybe all you need to get your payroll done is a part-time independent contractor. A lot of independents work for multiple customers on a part-time basis. Unfortunately, a part-time independent may not be available when you need him or her the most. Due to financial constraints, a part-timer may take a job elsewhere to pay his bills, potentially leaving you high and dry. On the plus side, part-timers are usually flexible and often can tailor their schedules to match yours. And many are extremely competent at their chosen task.

Moonlighters

Some independents have full-time jobs but like to *moonlight*. When just starting out as a doctor, my sister moonlighted for an insurance company that hired her to visit people in their homes and conduct insurance exams. She could do this work after hours, and the extra money helped her pay down her medical school loans a few years ahead of schedule. The insurance company got to farm out a necessary procedure to a doctor whom they paid only when needed.

Moonlighters are a good outsourcing option as long as you're able to cope with the idea that they already have a full-time job. If you have questions about your payroll, you may have to wait until they get off work to discuss it with them. Also, you could get yourself into a pickle if you're relying on a moonlighter to get something finished under deadline. What if the moonlighter is given a round-the-clock project at work?

Business Buzzwords

To **moonlight** means to work at another job, often at night, in addition to one's full-time job.

Consultants

You probably wouldn't need a consultant to solve your payroll problem. Consultants are brought into a company to proffer their expert insight and opinion. They're a valuable resource because they bring an outsider's point of view (and expertise) to help figure out the issue at hand. Unfortunately, you never quite know just how "expert" a consultant is, and there's no guarantee that their advice will work.

Business Service Provider

A business service provider (BSP) combines outsourcing and consulting services. If you not only want a certain task done (such as your payroll), but also advice on how to run your entire human resources area better, a BSP can help you accomplish both. They'll provide the manpower to get the work done and the brainpower to help you improve how you're doing it.

CAUTION Stay Alert!

You may not want to put all of your eggs in one basket when using a business service provider. Many companies believe that dividing consulting and outsourcing services between two firms is more beneficial. Splitting services between more than one firm can add another source for advice and oversight to your business.

Other examples of BSPs are accounting firms that do bookkeeping work and consulting work, information technology firms that maintain your servers and recommend ways for improving security, and warehousing companies that store your products and suggest methods for improving turnover.

A good BSP is like one-stop shopping: you can get everything you need from one place.

Partners

A partner is a generic description for any outside party that shares with you responsibilities for a process. Partners open up mutual revenue opportunities for each other. Microsoft "partners" with technology companies to sell and customize its applications. An engineering firm may have a "partner" firm that specializes in a certain type of analysis and design. Partners can be individuals or firms.

> **Outsourcing Insights**
>
> Many firms like to tell their customers that they partner with others to give themselves credibility and the confidence that they have the resources available to get the job done.

The word *partner* connotes a strong relationship. But, in reality, there may be few, if any, legal ties. As a result, partner loyalties often change.

Hobbyists and Tinkerers

Maybe you know someone who just loves to design websites. Many people love the challenge and creativity involved and consider it a hobby. They sometimes offer their services to companies looking for help at a reduced price. The downside to hiring a hobbyist is their availability and commitment to the job. Just because they're passionate doesn't mean they'll do the work on time or be available when you need them!

Hobbyists and tinkerers are different than part- or full-time employees. They bring a passion to their job. Many do it for the love of the job, not just for the money.

The following table summarizes the different types of outsourced service providers and the risks and rewards of working with each type.

Outside Service Provider—Risks and Rewards by Type

Type	Risk	Reward
Contract worker	Potential tax exposure	Lower costs
	Little incentive to be loyal	No long-term commitment required
Outsourcing company	Lots of other customers	Stability/credibility
		Deep resources
Part-time independent	Not always available Potentially financially unstable	Flexibility
Moonlighter	Not always available	Lower costs
	Lack of consistency	Reduced up-front expenses
Consultant	Advises, but might not perform work	Outside point of view
Business service provider	Too many eggs in one basket	One-stop service Deep resources
Partner	Little incentive to be loyal	Credibility
	Not necessarily a legal relationship	Opens revenue opportunities
Hobbyist	Not always available	High level of passion
	Little incentive to be loyal	Lower costs

Outsourcing Arrangements

What type of outsourcing relationship will be right for you? Let's look at the most popular forms of these arrangements.

Traditional Outsourcing

Traditional outsourcing generally involves taking something you can't or don't want to do and having someone other than your employees do it for you. This is the most common form of outsourcing. Traditional outsourcing may involve any of the parties mentioned earlier in this chapter.

Co-Sourcing

Co-sourcing means outsourcing only part of a function. When you co-source, both you and the service provider contribute employees and other resources to the project. It's not like traditional outsourcing, where you don't contribute any resources.

Suppose you decide to start up a customer service call center. You might decide to outsource the infrastructure, phone, furniture, hardware, and software systems to one or more independent companies. But you provide the people who will be answering the phones and interacting with customers. Rather than your outside contractor assuming all duties of the call center, the two of you share responsibilities and each contributes an agreed-on amount of resources.

Co-sourcing might be the answer for companies that don't want to relinquish complete control of a process to an outsider. Co-sourcing is also popular with companies that want to supplement their internal capabilities with outside expertise.

Co-Opetition

Co-opetition involves entering into an outsourcing arrangement with a competitor.

Why in the world would you do this?

CAUTION

Stay Alert! _____

Even though your co-opetition partners might be "friendly" competitors, you're still competitors. Always protect yourself with nondisclosure agreements and contracts to avoid having customers stolen from you.

In some situations, it's better to get some of the work than none at all. I have a friend who sells the same software products my company does. We both have small firms, and occasionally we "borrow" each other's staff to perform services for our respective clients. This way we get the work done on time and the client stays happy. Airlines practice co-opetition. If your flight with Airline A is delayed, Airline A might arrange a flight for you with Airline B to get you to your destination on time.

Transformational Outsourcing

Business transformational outsourcing (sometimes referred to as BTO) is different from all other outsourcing because it involves outsourcing *and* significant change all wrapped up into one. It's a combination of outsourcing and consulting. Transformational outsourcers take responsibility for a specific area of a company for a period of time while they recommend and implement new systems. Then they hand back these functions to the company and move on. Companies often use BTO to revamp their information technology, fulfillment, and customer service departments.

Traditional outsourcing focuses on cutting costs. Transformational outsourcing is designed to increase value. Companies use BTO when they want to turn an existing process upside down.

Commodity Outsourcing

Some tasks have become a commodity. For example, preparing payroll, doing a bank reconciliation, and answering phones are all things that have been done pretty much the same way for many years. There's little variation or expertise needed. Commodity outsourcing involves farming out those simple things that have become a business commodity.

Multiclient Shared Services

Some outsourcing arrangements are more about sharing products or services rather than using them exclusively. These types of arrangements are called multiclient shared services outsourcing. In this type of arrangement, the service provider has something that can be rented out to many customers or clients at the same time. The customer can outsource a function by sharing a resource with someone else.

Business incubators are one form of multiclient shared services outsourcing. They rent out individual offices in a single building to small companies and entrepreneurs, who then share basic services such as copiers, conference rooms, receptionists, coffee, and so on.

Outsourcing Insights

Business incubators, a type of multiclient shared service, have helped to reduce bankruptcies among small businesses. Many successful companies have grown out of incubators. If you're just starting out and want to keep your costs as low as possible, a business incubator may be a very good thing to consider.

E-mail and many other application service providers are another example of multiclient shared services outsourcing. These providers allow many clients to use their applications or servers over the Internet at the same time. Many small and large businesses outsource their e-mail to an application service provider rather than hosting this service internally.

Multiclient shared services may be beneficial to managers and owners who need an economical solution to a problem and don't mind sharing a resource with someone else.

Business Process Outsourcing

When a company engages in business process outsourcing, it means that they're taking an entire process and farming it out elsewhere. Some insurance companies outsource their entire claims-processing operations to a third party. Some banks do the same for their loan processing.

Companies spend billions of dollars each year on business-process outsourcing. Because of the significance of this form of outsourcing, I discuss it in much greater detail in Chapter 10.

Logistics Outsourcing

Logistics outsourcing is a type of business-process outsourcing. Logistics involves things such as supply-chain management, procurement, purchasing, e-business—all processes that require many steps and coordination with multiple parties.

Chapter 10 covers this type of outsourcing in more detail.

The Least You Need to Know

- ◆ You have many options when choosing the right service provider to outsource your work.

- ◆ Co-sourcing is a good option for companies that want to maintain more control of the outsourcing project.

- ◆ Traditional outsourcing focuses on cutting costs, whereas transformational outsourcing is designed to increase value.

- ◆ Some outsourcing arrangements enable you to share costly resources with others.

Chapter 3

A Day in the Life of Your Hired Gun

In This Chapter

- ◆ An outsourcer's typical schedule
- ◆ Distractions and other annoyances that the independent contractor faces
- ◆ Issues that can arise between outsourced help and your employees
- ◆ What makes the ideal outsourcer

Mary is an outsourced bookkeeper. She's been doing this for her clients for going on 20 years now, ever since her first son was born and she quit her day job. What started out as part-time work, especially while her children were young, has turned into a full-time business.

Her office is in her home. But she also spends a considerable amount of time visiting her clients, if only to pick up documents and other items left for her. Some clients like her to do her work on-site, most others have her work remotely. She sometimes keeps her clients' financial information in her office but usually works directly with their accounting system over the Internet.

Her clients include a pet shop, a travel agency, and a 50-person sales office owned by a public company. Her job responsibilities are mostly the same at each: she enters invoices, payables, and cash receipts and prepares checks. She also makes sure the general ledger is in good shape and prepares monthly financial statements. Some clients only need her for a couple of hours a month, but her larger ones require a few hours of her time each week.

Mary gets paid by the hour. Her rates range between $15 and $30 an hour depending on the client. One great benefit about her work: she never has a collection problem. This is because she's able to write her own checks (although they always need to be signed by someone else). But her clients are very happy with her work. She saves them all the expense of hiring a full-time person and she's usually available when they need her.

This chapter is about Mary, and all the outsourced contractors like her you might hire. You are going to learn what makes a good outsourcer like Mary. You also get to see what it's like being in her shoes for a typical day, so that you can better understand the challenges that she faces. By understanding the challenges Mary and other outsourcers like her face you'll be better equipped to get the most out of your outsourcing relationships.

In addition, you're probably at least a little uncomfortable with the idea of giving an outsourced worker or company control over an aspect of your business. Getting to know a little bit about how they operate on a day-to-day basis may help you discover whether this is the right step for you.

An Outsourcer's Typical Schedule

Mary's clients are busy with their own problems. They don't really give a whole lot of thought to how she spends her workday. As an independent contractor, she's supposed to be responsible for her own schedule and shouldn't need babysitting. Unfortunately, Mary's chaotic schedule could very well impact you. Sure, she's responsible for managing her own schedule. But it's critical to understand what kind of scheduling challenges she faces in case your business is affected.

She's Got Scheduling Challenges

Today is Tuesday and Mary wakes up early. She likes to do a little bookkeeping work at dawn before her family stirs. After breakfast and sending the kids off to school, she's gets in her car to begin her journey. Today Mary is visiting four clients. The typical contractor juggles his or her schedule just like Mary.

Actually, Mary was supposed to visit only three clients. But one customer called her in the middle of her breakfast, telling her that he would be on vacation next week and asking her to come in today to cut checks. When Mary said that her day was pretty full, he said that today was the only day that would be good for him. He's the customer, of course, so she agreed. Mary wasn't happy about this. She appreciates clients who give her advance notice.

Outsourcing Insights

Don't be a victim of your contractor's schedule. Spell out expectations and deliverables in your contract. Agree in advance on a consistent day and time when the work will be done and make sure you stress how important it is to stick to that schedule.

She's Working On-Site ... and Off-Site

Mary's used to traveling, too. Her car, only 3 years old, has more than 70,000 miles on it. She sits in traffic a lot, with only her cell phone and talk radio to entertain her. She tries her best to coordinate her visits, going to clients in the same general vicinity when she can.

Unfortunately, the client who called her this morning happens to be on the other side of town from the other clients she was planning to visit. Most contractors want work wherever they can find it, and Mary's no different. As long as she doesn't have to get on a plane, she'll try and be there. Hopefully, you've considered distance challenges before hiring your contractor.

Mary returns home by mid-afternoon to meet the kids when they get off the bus, but her work day is far from over. She'll work in her home office until dinner time, and oftentimes at night. Occasionally Mary gets insomnia, so she works in the middle of the night. And as we saw earlier, she likes to get up very early in the morning, because this turns out to be the most productive part of the day for her. Some of her clients have learned her schedule, so they know the best time to reach her. You would be advised to do the same with your outsourced help!

She's On Call 24/7

Contractors almost never work typical nine-to-five days. They're expected to work whatever hours necessary to get their work done on time.

Mary is a full-time contractor. This means she's pretty much available to her clients all day (and sometimes at night, too). She didn't exactly plan things this way. In fact, when she started out, she was only working part-time. She decided to be an independent bookkeeper because she didn't want to be chained down to a full-time job, and she wanted to keep flexible hours to accommodate her young children's activities. Even with her current commitments, Mary likes the freedom of determining most of her own schedule. The more restrictions a client puts on her time, the less happy Mary is about the work.

Her clients know that she's raising three kids and serves other customers. And although she responds relatively quickly when a client calls, no matter when the call comes, there's no guarantee that she'll be available. For many outsourcing relationships it's not important to know this level of detail. You'll have to determine what information you'll need to help you manage your service provider.

> **Outsourcing Insights** _____
>
> Some clients expect their independent contractors to be available for them full-time. Others understand that they won't always have access to their contractors, especially when it's only a part-time gig. Whether you're dealing with an individual contractor or FedEx Kinko's to outsource your copying, it's important for both the customer and the contractor to have a clear understanding of each other's availability so as not to unfairly raise expectations.

> **Outsourcing Insights** _____
>
> Consider negotiating a long-term commitment with your outsourcer, even with some payments up front, in exchange for reduced rates. This gives the outsourcer some breathing room and helps their cash flow. Be careful not to commit too much cash in advance as you'll need to consider *their* longevity, too!

She Has to Worry About the Next Project

Even as busy as Mary is, she worries that she won't have enough work. She doesn't have the relative income security that an employee enjoys. Clients come and go. A few have fired her for various reasons, others she resigned from. Many times she'll lose a client for circumstances beyond her control—they'll decide to hire a full-time employee, they'll get purchased by someone else, they go out of business, and so on.

The contractor's dilemma is that when they're busy they don't have time to market themselves, which means that when they finish a job they are left scurrying to line up the next project. It's often feast or famine. If you happen to come upon a contractor during the famine stage, you may be able to negotiate a favorable fee for his or her work. Be careful that you don't take too much advantage of their situation as this could backfire on you if they garner new, more lucrative clients in the future!

Mary, like many other outsourcers, tries to earn as much as possible for doing the least amount of work. She tells a client a job will take four hours per week when she really thinks it'll only take two. She does this to cushion herself in case something she's unaware of takes more time and to do her best to increase her hourly rate. She's not doing anything immoral by padding her estimates. She's only protecting herself.

When doing business with an independent contractor, remember that he or she is most likely trying to get paid what they think is a fair fee for their work. Understanding this basic tenet of human nature will help you work better together.

She's Got Administrative Challenges

In the midst of all of this, Mary needs to take care of the paperwork required of any business. She's got to get her own invoices out and post cash receipts. Occasionally she encounters a collection problem. She has to pay her bills, too, and file taxes. And, of course, there's always filing to do. Mary doesn't have anyone working for her, but if she did she'd have payroll to worry about.

And don't forget renewing her insurance. Calling back prospects. Checking in with clients. Solving her own technical problems, such as the printer that intermittently stops printing and the computer that keeps crashing. She's got the same administrative issues that any business has.

So what do you think of Mary's day so far?

She Has to Deal with Distractions and Other Annoyances

Your contractor will probably not give you the full and undivided attention that you would expect from an employee. You should understand this fact right from the outset of your project together.

Don't care if you're the "apple of their eye?" You will if you find yourself relying on the service provider to go the extra mile for you to get the job done.

Let's look at all the distractions that Mary has to deal with during the course of her day. This way, maybe you can head off potential problems before they turn into your problems.

Her Phone Keeps Ringing!

Mary gets a lot of phone calls. She spends just about all of her driving time with her cell phone headset on. Sometimes she goes through two batteries a day! Her clients consider her to be on demand all the time. When a bookkeeping or accounting question arises, they think nothing of calling her. And they expect an almost immediate response. Because Mary is on the road a lot, most of her calls come to her cell phone. And because she doesn't have an assistant to handle her calls, she's in the line of fire, with no one to run interference. Mary does a good job of setting expectations with her clients. Does your service provider do the same?

If your outsourced contractor is serving other customers besides you, then expect that those other customers will be calling with fires to put out. And although Mary does her best to not speak to other customers when she's on someone else's time, sometimes it can't be avoided. She's essentially running a business from her car.

Her Pager Keeps Beeping!

Some of Mary's clients prefer to communicate with her via pager and, being in the service business, Mary complies. She carries a pager as well as a personal organizer that receives e-mail messages.

When she's out at clients, she frequently checks her e-mail. When at home, she does her best to keep current with the messages she's receiving. E-mail is an important part of how she communicates with her clients. Of course, responding to other clients' e-mails while on-site somewhere else can be a problem if it happens too often. But in today's web-based world, you should expect that an independent contractor will need to take time out from the task at hand to respond to another client's pleas for help, even electronically. It would be ideal to have her full attention, but sometimes this just isn't possible.

Her Family Keeps Calling!

Don't forget that Mary has a family. Like any employee, Mary spends some portion of her days talking to her husband and kids. Sick children and school vacations sometimes interrupt her work schedule.

Her husband, holding down a full-time job as a warehouse supervisor, considers Mary's day to be up for grabs because she's got her own business going. And to some extent, this is true. Mary can shuffle appointments around and make allowances that an employee generally can't.

Remember that your contractor has a personal life, too, and sometimes this life will infringe on his or her responsibilities. Flexibility and understanding on your part will help your outsourced contractor get the job done.

Her Customers Compete for Her Attention

Your understanding will need to extend to the demands of the contractor's other customers. E-mails and phone calls aside, Mary sometimes has to deal with unexpected problems her other clients experience. One client panicked when he received an audit notice from the IRS. Another client needed to get some special invoices out that week. Still another client had to deliver a set of financial statements to his banker for a needed loan.

Mary does her best to keep these distractions to a minimum and to keep focused on the task at hand. However, I'm sure if you were Mary's client and you had an emergency, you would want her to drop what she's doing and come out to help. Hopefully you'd understand if some other manager finds him- or herself in a similar predicament.

> **Outsourcing Insights**
>
> Besides e-mail, many people use instant or text messaging. Ask your contractor whether he or she uses one of the popular instant messaging services (such as AOL or MSN) and get their address. Communicating this way is quick and efficient.

The Contractor and You

Mary has kind of an odd relationship with her clients. As the person who handles the money, she's treated with a good deal of respect. But because she's charging by the hour, she's closely watched. She doesn't spend a lot of time chatting—if she did, she'd certainly hear about it later. As an outside contractor, she makes her own schedule and comes and goes as she pleases. Although she's not antisocial, she tends to avoid going to the birthday lunches, picnics, and holiday parties with her clients. She's not an employee, and she doesn't expect to be treated like one.

Is She an Outsider or an Insider?

Visiting a company for only a few hours a week puts an outsourcer in a unique position. Mary finds that her clients have expectations of her that they wouldn't have of their employees. They expect her to make fewer mistakes. They expect her to show up when agreed. They sometimes use her as an independent sounding board for questions and problems.

Just the other week, one of her clients brought her into his office, closed the door, and asked point blank if she thought he should fire one of the customer service people because of an attitude problem. Offering this kind of advice didn't come with the bookkeeping assignment, but because she was asked by the owner, and she had a good knowledge of the employee's responsibilities, Mary didn't hesitate to share her thoughts on the matter. She understands that managers and owners like the input of someone more objective than a full-time employee.

Many of her clients like to benefit from Mary's experience at other companies. "What do your other clients do in a situation like this?" she's often asked. Treating your contractor as an advisor can be helpful, but it could also breed resentment from your employees, so tread carefully in this area.

The Steady Job Is Enticing, Isn't It?

Being an independent contractor is certainly not easy, and many people don't have the personality for the challenges this kind of lifestyle presents. It's not unusual for an independent to be offered a job somewhere and suddenly give up their clients.

Mary is fully committed to her bookkeeping practice. She wouldn't run away to take a job somewhere. But not every outsourcer is like Mary. You should always have alternative plans for handling your outsourced work, just in case.

It's Her Way or the Highway

After all these years, Mary knows how to keep books. She's got her own system for doing things, and it works. One of her customers insisted that she keep two sets of books—one for each department of his company, and then combine them together. There was nothing illegal about doing this, but it wasn't the way Mary was used to doing bookkeeping. She tried it for a while and found the work to be duplicative and time-consuming.

Stay Alert! _____

When you outsource a task, you should agree on the end result and try not to micromanage how the contractors do their job. At the same time, be careful that their way of doing things doesn't unnecessarily interfere with your employees. For example, a business process outsourcer insists on a meeting of all key employees every Monday at 7 A.M., even though the work day doesn't begin until 9. This kind of demand may be pushing people too far and too quickly.

Mary, as an independent professional, didn't like being told how to keep her books. Ultimately she parted ways with the client who insisted she keep two sets of books. But Mary can't be too choosy. She's all too aware that there's plenty of competition out there.

Outsourcing Insights _____

You've got a huge advantage when working with someone independent in that it's much easier to fire that person than it is to fire an employee. And there are usually plenty of independent people or firms willing to step into your contractor's shoes.

The Ideal Service Provider

Mary certainly has her faults. She can be stubborn at times. Her schedule periodically gets disrupted. She makes the occasional mistake. She doesn't come on-site as often as some of her clients would like.

There's no perfect contractor, but if you think about all of the traits of an ideal person, Mary would come pretty close. In addition, many of Mary's weaknesses can also be found in employees, too. Here are a few reasons why Mary's a great outsourced contractor:

♦ **Mary does what's promised.** People who do what they say they are going to do are highly valued in any society. This is because so many people don't do what they say they will. Missed deadlines, inferior work, cutting corners … this is what managers and owners deal with all the time. But Mary keeps her promises.

♦ **She charges a reasonable fee.** Most of us walk around thinking we're underpaid and overworked. And we think that others are too expensive. No one would call Mary's billing rate cheap. But she's not gouging her clients, either. Her fees are within an acceptable range, and this gives comfort to the people who hire her.

◆ **She answers the phone.** Giving up control by outsourcing a task is difficult enough for most managers and bosses. But when you can't reach the contractor at a critical time … arrgh! So when her clients call her, no matter where she is, she does an extraordinary thing. She answers the phone! If she can't answer right away, she gets back to them quickly.

◆ **She takes ownership.** It's easy to wipe your hands and say to yourself "Hey, what do I care? I don't work there." This is human nature, and another reason why some people don't like to outsource work to others they don't know. Mary, on the other hand, steps up and says, "I'm in charge of your books, and if there are any mistakes, it's my fault." She's not afraid to take responsibility for her actions.

◆ **She treats her clients with respect.** Mary spends two hours a month writing up the books for a bakery and two days a month doing the same for a small manufacturer. But her relationship with both clients is the same. She's empathetic and understanding. She always puts herself in her client's shoes, asking herself "How would I feel if this were me?" To Mary, a client's ledger is extremely important, whether they're a bakery or a Fortune 500 company.

> **CAUTION**
>
> **Stay Alert!**
>
> Don't haggle over pennies. Independent contractors don't like their bills to be questioned any more than you do. If you think you're being overcharged, don't accuse and don't get angry. Discuss your concerns face to face and agree on an acceptable method for tracking the time. Of course, the best way to avoid these problems is to agree on fixed-price contracts.

◆ **She keeps it professional.** A typical employee has family pictures in his or her cube and may spend a small portion of the day goofing off (perish the thought!). Employers expect this—breaking the monotony of one's routine is therapeutic. Except when it comes to outside contractors. Mary knows that she's being paid by the hour, so she behaves professionally. While maintaining a friendly demeanor, she jumps to the work at hand and tries to get things done as quickly as possible. She dresses appropriately. She's cognizant of the fact that she's costing her customer money for each minute she's there.

◆ **She adds value to her customer.** It's pretty easy, as an employee, to get into the routine of showing up every day and mechanically going through the motions of the job. But Mary is being judged every time she visits a client. She can sense that managers and owners think to themselves "Am I getting good value for the rate I pay her, or should I replace her with someone else?" She tries to add a little something extra rather than just keeping the books.

If something seems irregular, she points it out. If there's a better of way of doing something, she makes a note to the manager. If she sees a problematic trend, she highlights it. Mary tries her best to make her clients feel that they got something a little extra for their money every time she visits.

♦ **She knows when *not* to charge.** When an employee has a task to complete and takes too much time, or makes mistakes, you're usually not going to dock the person his or her pay. You absorb it. You don't expect the same from an outsourcer. Mary knows this. Sometimes she takes longer to prepare a set of financials than she promised, or she makes an error that needs additional time to correct. Mary could charge for this time, but it would probably annoy her clients. She's smart enough to know when not to charge for time. She'll eat the extra hours to keep her clients happy over the long term.

♦ **She'll never be an employee.** It's comforting to work with someone who's got a plan. It's clear to Mary's clients that she has no desire to be employed by them, or anyone else. She's quite happy being an independent contractor and running her own business. Mary's clients don't have to worry about her considering job offers or changing her professional lifestyle, potentially leaving them in the lurch.

♦ **She's financially stable.** Mary runs a profitable bookkeeping business, and her clients know this because they have checked her credit and her references. This is not like those early days, when she was scrounging for cash and cutting corners. Now she can focus on her existing client base without a huge need to add more clients and revenues. She's not rushed to accumulate billable hours and is not tempted to overcharge. Her clients benefit from her financial stability.

Finding that ideal contractor is never easy. But hopefully our study of Mary's situation gives you a better understanding of the outsourcer's predicament a little better.

The Least You Need to Know

♦ Understanding the challenges your outsourcer faces will help you manage them better.

♦ Independent contractors often have hectic schedules that involve working with several different clients each day.

◆ Outsourced workers have the same kinds of family obligations that employees have.

◆ The ideal outsourcer has many characteristics, including doing what's promised, taking ownership of the task, behaving professionally, and adding value to your business.

Chapter 4

Real-Life Lessons

In This Chapter

- ◆ A look at some lessons that will help you outsource
- ◆ Examples of successful and unsuccessful outsourcing experiences
- ◆ Why outsourcing was the right (or wrong) decision for actual companies

The year 1999 was not a very good one at Hershey Foods Corporation, the famous candy maker.

The company had decided that, rather than fixing some of its older software that was potentially exposed to the year 2000 glitch, they would replace these systems with software that would help them better streamline their business operations.

The company tried to install three new systems at the same time. They purchased separate software applications to handle order processing, customer service, and human resources. They outsourced the work to six consulting firms, whom they entrusted to get the software in and talking to one other by spring, well in advance of the big Halloween candy season.

The results were disastrous. It is estimated that the company lost almost $150 million in sales that year alone, and some of the effects even spilled over into the next year.

What went wrong? Like any bad situation, many factors were involved, including poor project management, technical glitches, and unrealistic deadlines. But most experts agree that the biggest reason for the failure was that the folks at Hershey bit off more than they could chew.

Their service providers couldn't handle the workload. Responsibilities overlapped. Deadlines were missed. Shipments weren't made. And worst of all, the company had pulled themselves off their existing system in the process, so they were forced to work through the logistics problems as best they could with the new system.

This story has a somewhat happy ending, though. Hershey significantly reduced the number of outside service producers and made other changes that ultimately got the project back on track. But the damage to Hershey's customers' confidence levels took a long time to heal.

The lesson: when you outsource a big project, don't bite off more than you can chew.

Hershey Foods had a bad experience. Some outsourcing projects are outstanding successes. Others are miserable failures. Hershey's was not a miserable failure. But it was a good education. From these real-life experiences, we can all learn something.

In this chapter, we look at 18 outsourcing lessons real-life companies learned the hard way. What can you glean from their successes and failures?

Lesson 1: The Tone Must Come from the Top

A few years ago, American Plastics purchased a sales force automation system from my company. They realized that the system would be more work for their sales people but would also provide a significant amount of tracking data for management. Instead of installing the software and training everyone in-house, they elected to outsource the work to my firm.

The project seemed to go well. We got everything set up on the company's computer system and customized the software the way they wanted. We then conducted 5 training sessions with their 50-person sales force at various locations around the country. By the end of the training, everyone was excited about using this new software tool.

> **Outsourcing Insights**
>
> It's a good idea to have more than one "internal champion," a senior management member who is involved in the decision process well before the outside service firm is hired. Those same senior managers should remain significantly involved in the relationship as it goes forward.

Unfortunately, nobody actually used the system. Everyone went back home and kept doing what they were doing. When some of the salespeople resisted doing work in the new system, the VP of sales didn't press them. When others saw what was happening, they reverted back to their old ways. And the VP of sales let them keep the status quo. He didn't want to rock the boat. Ultimately, the system never got used and our relationship was terminated.

The lesson: the success of your outsourcing project will depend on management's commitment to it.

Lesson 2: Someone Needs to Be the "Go-To" Person

Another client hired us to put in a software system for their service desk. The system was intended to track calls and help them automate the way they assign problems to technicians. Again, the client outsourced training and technical services to us.

This project was a failure, too. We installed the software and set it up. We trained the service desk. We customized the screens to be user friendly. We imported information from another system. But the application just sat there.

Why? No one knew who to go to for help. The moment we left the scene, everyone went back to doing things the way they did them before. When someone tried using the system and had a question, they didn't have anyone on the inside to talk to. People got frustrated and blamed the software. In reality, the company never designated a single point of contact responsible for the success of the system. When problems arose, everyone ran for cover. They pointed fingers at each other.

The lesson: every outsourcing project needs an owner who's responsible for the project's success.

Outsourcing Insights

Your "go-to" person doesn't need to be a technical genius and shouldn't be a senior manager. You want someone who is assertive, has the authority of management, and isn't afraid to make mistakes. Given the nature of this job, mistakes will happen—you don't want someone who's overly worried about making errors. These personality characteristics will help get the job done.

Knowledge Is Power

Various studies show that 20 to 35 percent of IT outsourcing contracts are not revived after they expire. Hopefully some of the lessons in this chapter can help you beat the averages!

Lesson 3: Agree Upon Deliverables and Goals Before Beginning

Customer relationship management systems are supposed to help companies nurture their rapport with customers from prospect to cash receipt to lifetime customer management. Unfortunately, many of these outsourced projects fail. But we had a great success with one client of ours, Richdale Chemical.

Why? Richdale wouldn't do the project without agreeing right up front how we'd be paid. The owners of the company had only one specific requirement—a weekly report showing which customers called in to their help desk and why. If we produced that report, we got paid; if we didn't, we failed. The mission was clear. We succeeded.

The lesson: make sure you have crystal clear deliverables when you start your outsourcing relationship.

Lesson 4: Don't Be Afraid to Outsource

In the health-care industry, giving up some level of control over functions that could affect the health and welfare of a patient is not a decision taken lightly. Many health-care providers resist outsourcing because they're afraid to take that risk.

Outsourcing Insights

When outsourcing in the health-care industry, you must be aware of significant legal implications and liability issues. Read up on the new medical privacy laws at www.hhs.gov/ocr/hipaa, for example.

After careful consideration, El Camino Hospital in California decided that the benefits of outsourcing certain functions far outweighed the risks. They've been outsourcing their information technology requirements for more than 20 years. They realized early the importance of using outside experts to handle this essential need.

El Camino Hospital outsources patient medical history, billing data, and care information to third parties. They understand the risks of using an outside service, but they believe the benefits, such as cost savings and better protection of the data by an experienced firm, outweighs these concerns. In recent years, the hospital has even been able to significantly cut medication errors by working with an outside service provider.

The lesson: don't be afraid to outsource. You could even save a life!

Lesson 5: Think Like an Outsider

A few years ago, the city of Minneapolis hired a new chief information officer (CIO). What he found when he arrived disturbed him. More than half of his budget and resources were spent on fixing computer problems. The city had no strategic direction for its information technology; instead, putting out fires was the name of the game. So the new CIO decided to make some changes. He talked to a few outsourcing firms and asked them what they would do as an outsider. The answers were obvious.

The CIO turned the IT department upside down. He outsourced most of the technical work. He argued that freeing up his technical staff from the day-to-day glitches would enable them to focus more on serving the overall technology needs of their users and customers. He was right. Key services are now being handled more effectively by their outside service provider. The staff has more time to analyze the best use of the city's technology.

The lesson: outsourced vendors can bring in a fresh perspective and significantly change the way you do things.

Lesson 6: Listen to Your Gut

Bob Mcloskey, the general manager of Tannenbaum Financial Services, knew that something was wrong. His company was awash in paper. As an insurance broker, Tannenbaum kept track of thousands of agreements and hundreds of thousands of pages of claim forms, applications, and other correspondence. Bob had no way to prove it, but his gut was telling him that all this paperwork was dragging down profits.

And he was right. Acting on his own instincts, Bob brought on an outsourced document management firm. Within a few months, the firm was scanning all their paper documents and filing them online. Employees were able to find documents much more quickly than before everything was put online. Clients could even view their own contracts over the Internet. Tannenbaum Financial experienced dramatic improvements in productivity as well as customer service. Bob listened to his gut, and his gut told him to outsource.

The lesson: sometimes the decision to outsource can be something other than analytical. Trust your gut.

CAUTION

Stay Alert!

Don't ignore your instincts. Combine gut feelings with facts. Just because your friend tells you you're crazy if you don't outsource something doesn't mean you should jump right into it! Always do a quantitative analysis (see Chapter 13) before making the decision to outsource.

Lesson 7: Don't "Dabble" in Outsourcing

A few years ago the Detroit public school system assessed their IT systems. They found that one good service provider serviced a portion of their network, but the rest of the servicing was done by a hodge-podge of part-timers and other employees on an as-needed basis. The school system relied too heavily on temporary workers to keep their systems operational.

The CEO of the school system decided that if they were going to get their network running as efficiently as possible, the school district would need to jump into outsourcing with both feet. Farming out only a portion of the services could be a recipe for disaster. He selected a single sourced network services provider to support the infrastructure throughout the school system.

The benefits were significant. Within a year, the school district had realized a savings in excess of $5 million by going full-board into outsourcing. These savings could be plowed right back into things such as textbooks and teacher salaries.

The lesson: don't outsource half-heartedly.

Lesson 8: Time Is Money

Remember the guy on *Saturday Night Live* who sat by the copy machine and talked to everyone who came in to use the machine? "Making copies," he said. "Making copies." Well, he wasn't the only guy wasting his time making copies. The director of facilities management at the Apollo Group had a similar problem. Responsible for the care and maintenance of the company's copiers at locations around the country, she found that the whole process of copying wasted a significant amount of employee time. People were standing around just "making copies." Even more time was wasted whenever a copy machine broke down or needed to be refilled with paper or toner.

She decided to outsource her copy problems to Ikon Office Solutions. Ikon took responsibility for the care and feeding of all copy equipment and provided a quick, internal copy service to the company. Employees could drop off materials to be copied, and then come back to get their completed jobs at a specified hour. Less time was wasted. More work could get done.

The lesson: outsourcing can make sense in a lot of ways, including saving time.

Lesson 9: Outsourcing Can Fuel Growth

Ever heard of Keller Williams Realty? It's a pretty amazing company, having tripled in size in just a few years. They've gone from 100 offices across the United States and Canada to more than 300 in this short period of time. They couldn't have done it without outsourcing. The company's intranet system played a key role in its extraordinary growth. An intranet is a private piece of the Internet that's used by select people (in this case, the employees of Keller Williams). Through its intranet system, the company communicated and shared information about new offerings, sales agreements, policies, announcements, and other correspondence. Without the intranet in place, the company would have had no other way to communicate this information so quickly. Keller Williams outsourced the entire intranet system to a company that provides intranets to customers—at a whopping 90 percent savings over doing it themselves. And the system was up and running 24/7.

The lesson: by focusing on what you do best and outsourcing the rest, your company can really take off.

Lesson 10: Great Outsourcing Comes from Great Partnerships

Owens & Minor is a huge company with equally huge outsourcing needs. As one of the leading distributors of medical and surgical supplies, the company inventories and ships products throughout the world. For the past decade, the company has had a close relationship with its primary outsourcing partner, Perot Systems. Perot handles much of the company's information technology, logistics, and supply-chain management.

The two companies have a great partnership. Perot Systems people involve themselves in strategic planning and management meetings held around the organization. They have taken responsibility for Owens's internal systems so that Owens employees can concentrate on new initiatives. They have access to the top executives of Owens and are well integrated into the company's culture. As a result of this open and

Stay Alert!

Be careful about getting too close to your service provider. The government may start thinking they're really your employee, and then you could have a problem. See Chapter 20 to find out what I mean!

honest relationship, both companies are able to work together like true partners. Recently, they were awarded honors by the outsourcing industry, highlighting their strong bond.

The lesson: a great outsourcing partnership can lead to great things.

Lesson 11: Share a Common Goal with Your Service Provider

Michelin Tires once had 18 distribution centers, with 700 employees working on more than 125,000 transactions each year using old and outdated computer equipment. Each month the costs of maintaining these centers rose, and they were really beginning to eat into the company's bottom line. Customer service and quick delivery are among the highest priorities for Michelin, so when they decided to outsource their distribution centers to TNG Logistics they wanted to make sure that TNG and Michelin shared the same goals.

They did. TNG not only managed some of these centers for Michelin, but also purchased a few as well. Michelin management was happy to see that TNG took on their old employees and treated them with the same amount of respect as Michelin had. TNG used the same type of professional development techniques. TNG even came up with better ways to move slow-selling products and to handle product returns.

The lesson: choosing a service provider that shares many of the same goals and culture will help make the transition a lot easier.

Lesson 12: Outsourcing Can Add Revenues

Everybody talks about outsourcing to reduce costs, but the University of Florida realized something else: outsourcing can also boost revenues.

The university outsourced the operations of its new bookstore and welcome center facility to Follett Higher Education Group. Although they were worried that having another company manage these areas would hurt their customer service, they soon found the opposite to be true. Follett helped design, build, and construct the new facility. And after the store was open, they took over the day-to-day management.

The results have been phenomenal. Customer service has improved. Existing bookstore employees happily moved to Follett, enjoying the same benefits as they did when working for the university. The bookstore now grosses more than $12 million annually, a significant increase over prior years. Additional revenue streams come from a parking garage, business services, and a dining facility. Follett's bookstore manager is considered part of the university. And the welcome center is a source of pride.

The lesson: with a little innovation, outsourcing can boost your revenue streams in ways you may not have thought of before.

Lesson 13: Not Outsourcing Can Be Costlier Than Outsourcing

E&J Gallo Winery makes fine wines that are enjoyed by many people around the world. But for a while, they just weren't getting the whole outsourcing "thing." And it was costing them money.

When Gallo hired a new director of IT operations, he was shocked by what he found. (In fact, he referred to it as the "Wild West!") It took an average of 20 days for an internal computer problem to be fixed. Employees who didn't "know someone" in the IT department found themselves taking their malfunctioning computers to local repair shops for service, or just buying a new one.

The 3,500-person company's entire help desk department consisted of four brave souls sitting in a closet-size office, with only an antiquated voicemail and database system as their tools. The new director realized that the costs of not outsourcing this stuff would bust his budget. He soon arranged to have help desk services outsourced to CompuCom Systems.

Within months, the results were apparent. All problem calls went to CompuCom's service center. Problems were fixed quicker. Potential trouble spots were identified earlier. Repetitive problems were tracked and resolved. Employee productivity increased. Employee morale improved.

The lesson: understand how outsourcing can impact your business. If you don't, you could be wasting valuable resources.

Lesson 14: Outsourcing Can Improve Your Customer Service

Why did you join the AAA (American Automobile Association)? If you're like me, it was probably so that you have someone to call if you ever break down in the middle of nowhere. The AAA knows this, and their ability to be "just a phone call away" underscores the reason why they exist. Many businesses, with fleets around the country, use the AAA in the same manner.

So if responding to their business customers in need of road assistance is one of the most important things about the AAA, what do they do? They outsource their call center! Even though the company is based in Florida, all calls go through an Electronic Data Systems call center in Detroit, Michigan. Both companies work closely to manage calls from commercial accounts. But even the AAA knows when to turn to the experts for such a vital service. Why try to build a first-class customer service organization when you can hire someone who already knows how to be one?

The lesson: some service providers know how to do a better job than you with your own customers.

Lesson 15: Offshore Outsourcing Oftentimes Doesn't Make Sense

Why does Toyota make its Corollas in Silicon Valley, California, probably one of the most expensive places on Earth? Why don't they just outsource the work to some third-world country where the labor is a few dollars per day and costs to operate are lower?

One of the reasons is that Toyota understands that it's less expensive to ship something 100 miles than 10,000 miles. Outsourcing this work to some distant part of the planet just wouldn't make sense. Many manufacturers agree. Even though wages and operating costs are higher, the time and expense required to move critical goods to places around the world can far exceed the savings. Therefore, many companies, such as Toyota, decide to keep their operations right where they are. It's just math. Geography means a lot. Time to market is important. Being near your customers is critical.

The lesson: outsourcing overseas may be good for some, but it is not that great of an idea for others. Which one are you?

Lesson 16: It's Easy for an Outsourcing Project to Go Awry

Poor Monty—he got in over his head. He had a dream of building a great order entry and processing system. His business, a purveyor of antique carpets, was unique—he needed to track thousands of designs, consigned inventory, and photos. He wanted prospective customers to be able to search for what they wanted on the web, place their order, and have their carpet in days. He hoped the system would tell him when inventories were low, or which carpet line was the best seller and the worst.

Monty's 40-person company couldn't afford its own development staff, so he outsourced the writing of this program to an outside software firm. Things took longer than expected. Costs spiraled out of control. Monty didn't keep a close eye on what the software firm was doing and rejected a lot of their work. Computer glitches slowed them down. Miscommunications resulted in lost hours.

Outsourcing Insights

Outsourcing is a relationship and a project. Outsourcing successes are due to strong project management by the team members involved. The larger the project, the greater need for internal project management skills.

Monty was busy running his business. He didn't have the time to be a project manager. The end result of his system came in below his hopes and above what he intended to pay.

The lesson: an outsourcing project needs good up-front due diligence, and then a lot of ongoing supervision or it can quickly go bad.

Lesson 17: Outsourcing May Get Your Job Done More Quickly

We did two projects last month. Both companies bought the same product from us. But one company decided to get it up and running on their own. The other company outsourced the installation and training to us. Guess what happened?

Well, to give you a hint, our first client is still trying to get up and running. It's not that they don't have good people or even the resources in-house to get the job done internally. They really don't need to outsource at all. But the problem is that they have a lot of other things going on. People are busy. They have other priorities, and they keep pushing their software project aside. The company that outsourced the work has the job done already. Sure, they paid more up front, but they're getting results right away.

The lesson: even if you have the right people in-house, you might get the job done more quickly by farming it out.

Lesson 18: Keep Realistic Timetables

How about this for a disaster: in 1997, Siemens Business Systems had a contract with the United Kingdom Passport Agency to issue their passports. Unfortunately, the contract went about $30 million over budget.

What happened? Siemens introduced a new IT system and, unfortunately, didn't allot enough time to properly test the new software. The resulting delays caused the budget overage.

The lesson: give your people and the outside service provider enough time to get the job done.

The Least You Need to Know

- Real-life outsourcing experiences tell us that management must be significantly involved, one internal employee needs to be the "go-to" person, and deliverables must be agreed upon before starting.

- Companies have succeeded in their outsourcing projects by not being afraid, thinking like an outsider, and listening to their gut before pressing forward.

- Outsourcing can add revenues, improve customer service, and get a job done more quickly.

- Offshore outsourcing sometimes doesn't make sense; and an outsourcing project can go over budget quickly without sensible timetables and good project management.

Part 2

Do You Need to Outsource?

Outsourcing isn't always the right decision for your business. It might make more financial and overall business sense to hire an employee for a task rather than to farm out the work. Then again, employees can be more expensive and require more of your resources. These are among the pros and cons to outsourcing you'll learn about in this section.

After you've been informed of the potential risks and rewards involved in outsourcing, I walk you through a step-by-step approach for making any outsourcing decision and help you establish your outsourcing goals. Do you want to create more revenue through outsourcing? Reduce your overhead and expenses? Both? I tell you what your options are and how to go about pursuing them.

If you decide to work with an outside service provider, I recommend resources for finding the right provider and point out some mistakes to avoid when selecting one.

Chapter 5

The Pros and Cons of Employees

In This Chapter

◆ How employees bring loyalty, availability, and more control to the job

◆ Why employing people is less risky, less time-consuming, and can add more value to your company than subcontracting

◆ What additional tax and filing costs you'll incur with an employee

◆ Why employees increase your compensation and overhead costs

Terry Williams, a product manager at Cennarex Corporation, had a decision to make concerning the company's latest product, C555. Should he hire a team of people internally to conduct the necessary three phases of clinical trials or should he outsource the work?

He consulted with Jim, another product manager at Cennarex, to find out the difference between hiring a group of people to do the testing or farming it out to a firm specializing in clinical trials. After all, he wondered, aren't employees better than contractors?

Jim disagreed. He had learned that there are some things that are best left to employees, and other tasks that are better suited for outsourcing.

Jim told Terry about his experience in a clinical trial where he outsourced the entire project to a third party testing firm. He found that the service provider got the job done faster and more professionally than he had experienced with employees.

Whether you're running a project like Terry's, or maybe just looking for someone to prepare your payroll, you'll eventually face the decision of whether to employ or outsource.

Before you make your outsourcing decision, it's important to know the good and the bad parts about employing people. This chapter will help you understand the pros and cons of hiring employees. First, let's look at the upsides.

The Benefits of Having Employees

Of course, if outsourcing everything was always the solution, no one would have employees! Obviously, this isn't the case. The billions of dollars that firms spend on outsourcing every year are dwarfed by the trillions they spend on payroll. There are just too many reasons why hiring employees is more beneficial than outsourcing.

Outsourcing Insights

According to a recent survey by PriceWaterhouseCoopers, more than 80 percent of companies outsource some type of task or project each year. The survey concludes that "by farming out management of operations that are not mission-critical, [these companies] are better able to concentrate on growth, competitors, and profitability." If you're not doing any outsourcing, you might be hurting your business.

The Loyalty Factor

Employment involves commitment. When an owner or manager sticks out his hand to you and says "Welcome aboard," you're not just being offered a job, you're being offered a commitment. The manager is hiring you as a permanent part of the family, so to speak. You're not being brought on to perform a task and then be let go. You are entering an ages-old relationship between employer and employee. Even in the world of "at will" employment, both parties hope to be working with each other for a long time.

Many of us desire job security. We want to be part of something. We want to succeed with a team. Working at a successful company makes us feel successful, too. Many people enjoy this security and don't want to lose it. There's a level of trust and dedication in employer-employee relationships that you'll probably never find in an outsourced arrangement.

Availability

If you outsource a project to an independent firm, there's no guarantee that your project will always be the firm's top priority. The firm will be servicing other clients. They may have different priorities from yours. You might have to navigate through an extra layer of management to get to the person you need to talk to.

Your employee isn't working for other clients. There are no professional demands for their time other than the demands your company makes. You can tell your employees how they should prioritize their work. A committed and loyal employee will usually be more accessible than the typical independent contractor.

> **CAUTION**
>
> **Stay Alert!**
>
> Don't work with any outsourcer who doesn't provide you and your staff with complete access to their people and resources. If you're denied mobile phone access, e-mail addresses, or pager numbers, and you're not convinced it's for the right reasons, your outsourcer may not be thinking of your best interests.

The Control Factor

You're not the outsourcer's boss. You're the client. There's a difference. A service provider doesn't want to lose clients. But someone working for the service provider is more concerned with making his or her boss happy. And as a client, you're going to have to take your place in line with all the other clients served by the firm you've outsourced. In essence, you're going to be competing against other clients at the service provider's firm.

Outsourcing may force you to give up some control. If you want complete authority over your task or project, you probably shouldn't relinquish it to an outside firm.

Keeping Up with the Joneses

Maybe outsourcing isn't the right decision because it's generally not done in your industry.

Would you be comfortable to learn that the pilot flying your plane isn't an employee of the airline, but rather an independent contractor? Or that your airline is the only airline in the industry that has independent contractors flying their planes? Maybe you care, maybe you don't. But a clever competitor could certainly exploit this fact to its advantage. They could accuse their rival of sacrificing safety for cost and question the company's dedication to their employees and customers.

Sometimes employing people is the safest route, rather than outsourcing, if only to keep up with the Joneses. Nothing against innovating, but going against the industry tide may present challenges that you don't want to face.

Playing by the (Tax) Rules

Hiring an independent contractor may also raise an eyebrow with the Internal Revenue Service (IRS). In fact, as I discuss in detail in Chapter 20, the IRS takes the difference between independent contractors and employees so seriously that they've established specific guidelines for determining whether someone is an employee or a contractor. A classical employee-employer relationship may keep you off the IRS's radar screen. (Remember, this applies to individuals, not outsourcing firms.) Tax exposures do worry owners and managers who hire independent contractors, so if you're the worrying kind, you're best off employing.

Putting someone on your payroll and paying required taxes and other benefits will eliminate any tax risks that outside contractors pose.

Show Me the Money?

Believe it or not, employees don't always need to be paid for all the work that they do. At the accounting firm where I used to work, everything was about making partner.

By dangling the carrot of partnership in front of their employees, the firm (and so many other accounting, law, and professional firms like them) extracted many hours of work well and beyond a typical employment arrangement. Try getting that much unpaid work from an outsourced firm or independent contractor.

Outsourcers are mostly motivated by cash. They work, they send you their bill, and you pay them. But with employees, the motivation can be a lot of things other than cash. The prospect of a new title, a corner office, or a key to the executive washroom are all little perks that can will an employee into many more hours of submission than someone from the outside.

The Value Add

For the most part, employees represent infrastructure. Having employees on your payroll tells the world that you've got enough work to employ all those people full time. You're a real company. People's livelihoods depend on your company's success. And this does a lot for your market value.

If you're thinking of getting a bank loan, or going public, what do you think helps say "invest in me": 50 employees on staff or 50 subcontractors? And if you're planning on one day selling your business, you'll be very interested in the value of *goodwill* that a potential buyer will want to pay for over and above tangible assets. Goodwill includes customer lists, established processes, and, very important, your employees who will carry on the work for the new owner!

Business Buzzwords

Goodwill is the excess that someone is willing to pay for a company over and above the market value of assets minus net liabilities.

Pennies from Heaven

Governments believe that hiring people is good for society. Some types of outsourcing, such as outsourcing offshore, is not encouraged by our elected officials. To them, outsourcing means "taking jobs away from Americans"—no matter that it might be the best choice for a business, enabling them to reinvest profits and expand. Since the days of Caesar throwing grain to the mob, politics are all about creating and holding onto jobs. People have to put food on the table and expect their government to help them if things get tough. The government wants people to have jobs.

Many government agencies offer low-cost financing or debt guarantees to companies in return for their commitment to hire more people. More people means more payroll taxes, which means more taxable revenues and … well, you get the point. So bear in mind your government may prefer a business that hires employees as opposed to those that outsource.

The Downsides of Employing People

Plain and simple, hiring an employee for a task costs more money than outsourcing the same job. That doesn't mean hiring is a bad decision and won't pay off in the long run. But making the wrong hiring decision can be a killer to a small company. I recently spoke to a sales manager at one company who went through an elaborate process of searching, interviewing, evaluating, and then hiring a senior salesperson, only to have to let him go three weeks later. The cost and time involved was devastating … and they never really got a chance to work with him!

Whatever you're going to pay a new employee, bump that up about 30 to 40 percent. That will be the real cost. After you've finished coughing up money for payroll taxes, health insurance, retirement plans, vacation time, sick days, and other overhead, you'll see what I mean. Putting people on the payroll definitely has its downsides.

Outsourcing Insights

Everything that an employer needs to know about the tax burden of his or her employees can be found in the IRS Publication 15, Circular E, "Employer's Tax Guide." There's also Publication 15A, "Employer's Supplemental Tax Guide," and Publication 15B, "Employer's Tax Guide to Fringe Benefits." After one look at these documents, you may want to outsource everything!

Uncle Sam Takes His Cut

First of all, you've got taxes to worry about. Forget about the withholding taxes, because that's just a wash—you're taking in the money and giving it right back to the government. The real expenses are employer's taxes, the largest being FICA and Medicare. Whatever you're paying someone, multiply that by approximately 17 percent. That's the additional cost you'll have to pay into the system. Now add on to that federal unemployment taxes and then state/local employer taxes and you're getting there. All told, you're probably going to pay close to 20 percent of a person's salary to the government right out of your pocket.

One of the biggest reasons why many business owners and managers try to subcontract is to avoid the employment tax bite. The IRS knows this and fights back. The IRS is very aware of the temptation to call someone a subcontractor when that person should really be an employee, and they come down hard on businesses, big and small, if they catch them. For more on this issue, see Chapter 20.

Uncle Sam Also Wants More Information

As if it's not bad enough spending all this extra money on taxes for your employees, you're going to have to incur even more costs to handle the necessary paperwork and administration. Each quarter, you have to fill out required federal and state (and sometimes local) payroll tax returns. Some taxing authorities require businesses to file additional monthly returns as well.

And heaven forbid you make a mistake on the return. You'll drown in computer-generated nasty-grams from the IRS (or municipality) before begging for mercy.

Oops, did I forget to mention all the year-end reporting requirements, too? As if the monthly and quarterly reports weren't enough, almost all taxing authorities want you to complete year-end reconciliations. One of the biggest hassles is generating all those W-2s for the IRS, which report the wages and withholdings of every employee who received more than a dollar from your company during the past calendar year.

Go ahead, do it all yourself. Or outsource it to a payroll company. Either way, you'll be spending more money for the pleasure of having your new employee on board.

A Few Days of R&R

In this country, a typical employee expects, at a minimum, two weeks vacation as well as time off for sick days. The Family Medical Leave Act requires employers to give an employee unpaid leave for certain medical issues. "Unpaid" means that the employer still has to fund their health insurance and other benefits, while leaving their job open. Never mind the cost of hiring a temp to get the work done in your employee's absence.

Independent contractors do not get vacation. They do not get sick days. If they don't work, they don't get paid. And if there's not enough work, they may not get paid either! For some managers, this arrangement, as compared to hiring full-time employees, is much more attractive.

To Your Health!

Employees expect health insurance from their employers—it's one of the primary benefits provided to a work force. Some companies have been asking their employees to help cover this expense, but even so, getting health insurance through one's employer is always less expensive than getting it on your own. Most employers contribute something to their employees' health insurance and find themselves struggling to control these costs. These same companies don't expect to pay the health insurance costs of outsourced contractors or individuals.

Saving for a Rainy Day

When you hire an employee, you've got to think about retirement … the employee's retirement. There's no law that says you have to put money away for them. But consider the reality: if Joe the warehouse manager starts slowing down after working his can off for your company over the past 30 years, what are you going to do … let him live off of welfare? There's an unspoken rule that employers look after their own. This is why so many managers and company owners implement retirement savings plans and encourage their employees to contribute to them.

These retirement plans almost always include contributions made by the employer. So expect that you will be paying in some percentage of your employees' salaries into this plan. Obviously, you don't need to do this for outsourced help. You don't have to feel any kind of obligation for someone who's not on your payroll.

Getting Personal

When you hire an employee, you're not just hiring a person. You're hiring that person's family, too. If the employee's son has a drug problem, it could soon become your problem. If the employee has a disability, you're required by law to provide an acceptable working environment for him or her. If the employee is going through lifestyle changes, maybe a divorce or a family illness, it's expected that your company will do its part to help them get through it. This may mean giving paid time off or some other form of compensation.

Of course, if your independent contractor faces the same challenges, you would be no less sympathetic. But the rules are different. You're not financially or morally obligated to do anything. An employer relationship carries with it a lot more responsibility than an arms-length relationship with a contractor.

Big Brother

Employees enjoy many protections under the law that don't apply to outsourced contractors. Employees are protected by the Department of Labor. There are Employer Retirement Income Security Act (ERISA) laws that govern how their retirement plans are managed and to make sure that employers don't discriminate in their favor with these plans. There's a federal minimum wage law. Contracts must be in compliance with the Fair Labor Standards Act. Safety and workplace rules, as required by the Occupational Safety and Health Administration, must be in place.

Outsourcing Insights

To find out whether you're in compliance with the employee laws that may affect your business, go to the Department of Labor's website at www.dol. gov/compliance. Here you can review applicable laws and regulations, use some of their compliance tools, get help from an employment advisor, and even submit confidential inquiries.

And that's not all! There are laws protecting employees against age, racial, and sexual discrimination. Hiring and terminating an employee is subject to strict guidelines that put employers into legal peril if violated. The Equal Employment Opportunity Commission oversees that employees get to play ball on a level field. And if you employ union workers, you have even more hoops to jump through!

Few of these laws protect outsourcers. An outsourcer is just a vendor, a third party.

Training

It is extremely important for employees to stay up-to-date professionally and technically. Each year companies spend millions of dollars training their employees on how to better use their computer software, administer personnel plans, and implement better safety procedures, as well as perform soft skills such as negotiating and public speaking.

An outsourced contractor, though, is on his or her own for training. A company expects that the outsourcer has done whatever he or she needs to do to be qualified for the task at hand.

Outsourcing Insights

Some companies pay for their employees to go back to school at night. This isn't cheap, but it could make for a loyal employee.

A Place to Work

And we haven't even begun to cover all the overhead costs involved with employing people. Your staff needs voicemail, e-mail, cubicles, office supplies, and other tools for their jobs. And they need extra administrative support to oversee payroll, benefits, problems, correspondence, and scheduling. Outsourced contractors, on the other hand, require very little investment in overhead.

The Least You Need to Know

- ◆ When it comes to deciding whether to hire an employee or outsource a job, there is no right or wrong answer. Each decision must be evaluated on its own business merits.

- ◆ The benefits of hiring employees include a more committed work force, more control of your project, and less tax exposure.

- ◆ Other benefits of hiring employees include more compensation choices, a higher perceived value of your company, and the opportunity of government assistance.

- ◆ The benefits of outsourcing your work include reduced payroll tax and filing costs, the avoidance of employee benefits and retirement plans, less regulatory red tape, and lower overhead expenditures.

Chapter 6

Why Outsource?

In This Chapter

- ◆ Showing your better side through outsourcing
- ◆ Reaping the financial benefits of outsourcing
- ◆ Improving your management through outsourcing
- ◆ Getting expertise through outsourcing

A health insurance company was struggling for a way to treat a unique case of hemophilia in the most cost efficient method possible. Rather than rely on their internal team of physicians, none of whom had much experience treating hemophilia and who kept recommending less-than-successful procedures, the company decided to outsource the recommendations to a third party team of physicians.

The results were astounding. In just a few months, the patient's hemophilia was under control and the cost of treatment fell by 75 percent.

This company certainly had some of the telltale signs of an organization that needed to outsource. They didn't have the experts they needed in-house. They were being financially pressed to come up with an answer to a very expensive problem. They were racing against time. And, most important, they wanted to make sure the very best care was provided to the patient.

Is outsourcing right for you? This chapter discusses the most popular reasons why managers turn to outside service providers and the benefits they receive by doing so.

Showing Your Better Side Through Outsourcing

You might decide to outsource to improve your image. Outsourcing your work can make you look like a larger enterprise, help you to make better use of the space you're in, help you find a potential partner, and even give your company the opportunity to provide more services to your customers.

There are many ways that outsourcing can help you show your better side. Here are a few important ones.

Outsourcing Insights

It's never a good idea to hide from your customers the fact that you're outsourcing work. Make sure you explain why you're using outside help instead of employees and tell your customers that you're ultimately responsible for the end work product. It shouldn't make a difference to the customer as long as the result is the same.

You Need to Look "Bigger"

Maybe you're making a proposal on a large project and competing against more established companies. Or perhaps you find that your company needs to provide certain services, such as technical support or quality assurance, which you currently don't offer. You won't be able to build this kind of infrastructure overnight, yet your customers expect you to have it. You need to "build a virtual company" by outsourcing these services if you want to stay competitive.

If you're trying to look bigger than you are, you don't want to do so in a way that misleads the people you do business with. But outsourcing certain services can give a little company the ability to play ball with the big boys.

You Require More Space and Don't Have It

Your space limitations may drive your need to outsource.

Feeling a little claustrophobic? Not sure where to put that new shipment of labels? Tripping over stacks of papers on the floor? Reaching over someone's desk to get to something? Many companies that need something done may not have the room to do it. And they're not prepared to rent or buy more property. So they decide to outsource the task. By outsourcing the work, you leave it to the independent contractor to find the necessary work space.

If you outsource a task because there's not enough room to do it at your location, you're still going to have some "space" issues to contend with. If the task is subject to regulation (such as food preparation), you must make sure that the outsourcer is in compliance; otherwise, you will be held accountable. If an outsourcer is doing a task for you off-site, you will probably need to make occasional visits to the other location to make sure things are in order.

Finding a Potential Partner

Outsourcing gives you the opportunity to find and work with a potential business *partner* before getting all formal about it.

By outsourcing an important task in your company, from bookkeeping to warehouse management to the design of your promotional materials, you are "partnering" with your outsourcer. In other words, you're sharing some percentage of revenues or profits. In some cases, the relationship actually evolves to something even more substantial. One IT company that outsourced development work to a programming firm eventually found themselves merging with the other firm. They turned their outsourcing arrangement into a legally binding partnership!

Your Customers Are Demanding More from You

You may turn to outsourcing because a customer has requested work from you that you don't normally do. You don't want to lose your customer's business if you can help it, so you outsource the work instead.

Business Buzzwords

Partners are defined as two or more persons associated as joint principals in carrying on a business for the purpose of enjoying a joint profit. A partnership can be a legal arrangement involving equity, or merely a sharing of revenues or profits from providing an end product to a customer. Many outsourcing arrangements are of the latter variety.

Stay Alert!

Although it's tempting to outsource work to help a valuable customer, don't spread yourself too thin. Your customer will blame you if an outsourcer does shoddy work. Sometimes it's better to just say no or to help your customer find another solution that doesn't involve you being in the middle.

Your biggest risk when outsourcing new work for a customer is making sure you're not taking responsibility for a job that you don't understand or haven't fully researched. Your customer is relying on you, and if you're the one billing for the outsourcer's time, you're responsible for the results of that work.

The Financial Benefits of Outsourcing

A primary reason to outsource is to save money. You can realize operational and administrative cost reductions through outsourcing. But that's not all. You can limit your capital investment, too, and preserve your cash flow for other, more important, investments. Also, outsourcing can help you generate more revenue from your customers as well as help reduce employee turnover expenses that plague many businesses.

Here are some ways that outsourcing can add dollars right to the bottom line.

You Need to Conserve Your Capital

Another sign that outsourcing may be the solution for you: your cash flow, or should I say ... lack of it!

If you're a manufacturer, you don't want to let that part out the door without quality control. If you're in the publishing business, you have to have your new manuscript edited before you can print it. If you're running a drywall business, you need someone to remove all of the construction debris.

Outsourcing Insights

The decision to outsource to save capital is very similar to buying or leasing a car. You can experience the benefits of ownership (or in our case, employing an individual) or decide just to rent (or outsource). You should look at other aspects of your personal and business life and decide what kind of person you are: an owner or a renter. This will help you decide whether outsourcing to save capital is the right choice for you.

In a perfect world, you'd have people on the payroll to do all these functions. But in reality, you can't afford to hire someone full-time just to perform one specific task.

You might not have enough work to keep him or her busy all day. You don't want to invest in someone unless you're sure that person is going to generate enough revenue to support his or her payroll.

Be aware, though, that although outsourcing might ease your cash flow in the short term, it might not always be the best long-term solution. And if you choose to outsource a critical function, such as your company's quality control, be sure that you're not sacrificing substance for cost.

Outsourcing Insights

If you're running your business or department on a shoestring, you might be a very strong candidate for outsourcing. You don't want to add more fixed costs to your overhead by hiring employees. Instead, you want to pay someone to get a specific job—and only that job—done. Tight cash flow and lack of capital are good reasons to seek outside help.

You Can Create Additional Revenue from Outsourcing

Do your customers ask you to provide services that you don't specialize in? Do you offer a service that can be safely handled by someone else not in your office? If so, you might be able to take advantage of farming out some work. Chapter 9 covers different ways of outsourcing to create revenue.

Outsourcing Insights

By outsourcing a service you perform, you're providing the outsourcer with a steady stream of income. Depending on the amount of dollars at stake, you might be able to negotiate a steep discount on the price the outsourcer would normally charge if they had to find the work themselves. Remember that the cost of sales and marketing can be between 30 and 40 percent of a company's revenues, so this should be the kind of discount you're looking for from an outsourcer.

You Want to Reduce Your Operating Costs

Often the cost of outsourcing something is less expensive than doing it in-house.

Many people decide to outsource to reduce their operational costs of doing business. Taking an operation that would normally be a department within the company (such as marketing, fulfillment, and quality control) and outsourcing it often can be much less expensive than doing it in-house.

You Want to Reduce Your Administrative Costs

A big reason why people outsource is to try to lower their administrative burden.

As noted previously, many companies outsource their payroll. You may find that going to the effort of generating payroll checks, administering the payroll system, and then completing the required tax returns is too time-consuming. You're probably right. By outsourcing this administrative task, you can probably get it done faster and cheaper. Companies outsource many similar administrative tasks to decrease the administrative expense associated with them. Chapter 10 discusses both operating and administrative costs that businesses often outsource.

CAUTION

Stay Alert!

A case of high turnover might indicate other problems that outsourcing can't solve. Before outsourcing a job, you may want to first look at factors such as pay, work environment, stress level, and complexity. Changing one of these factors may significantly impact how long an employee remains in a position.

Your Employee Turnover Is Too High

Is there a position in your company that always seems to need filling?

You might be a good candidate for outsourcing if you have an employee turnover problem. If you assign a specific job to an outsourcer, you can eliminate the need to hire and train new employees for the task each time someone leaves. The service provider not only takes responsibility for finding a replacement but also provides a trained person in the interim.

How Outsourcing Helps You Manage Better

A good outsourcing solution will help managers better manage their time, allowing them to focus on more important issues and delegate nonessential tasks.

Saving money doesn't necessarily mean spending less. It could mean spending more, but more effectively. Outsourcing can help you increase productivity and get things done more quickly. Here are a few ways how.

You Need Something Done Quickly

Sometimes you need to get things done fast and on a tight deadline. This may be the time for outsourcing.

Outsourcing to save time can be a good thing, but be prepared to pay a lot more for this luxury. The more advance planning you do, the more affordable the job will be. And remember, outsourcing companies that operate under the gun (such as shippers, diagnostic labs, attorneys) are human, too, and can make mistakes. Sending something to an outsourcer doesn't guarantee that you'll get the job done right, so take precautions!

You Want to Avoid Headaches

Are you the type of manager who wants to avoid as many headaches as possible? Do you prefer to pay the price and let someone else deal with those matters that are only a distraction from your main business focus? If so, you'll benefit from outsourcing.

Before you start using outsourcers to avoid dealing with every problem that comes up, ask yourself some questions. Is this headache indicative of a larger problem? Are you really doing what's best for your company by choosing the convenience of outsourcing? Are you becoming reliant on a luxury? Are you spending too much money on something unnecessary?

Outsourcing Insights

An outsourced solution may be more expensive than hiring someone full-time. But you can justify this cost if your existing people can get more work done in less time, or if the outsourced solution makes it easier for you to generate revenue. Think of it as buying "instant expertise."

You Need Better Time Management

You might find you need to delegate a task that is taking up too much time. You might also need to bring on someone with more expertise in a very important area, so a job can get done faster and more efficiently. If you find yourself consumed by repetitive and time-consuming tasks, you may be ready to outsource. Are you ready to start delegating to an outsider? Are you comfortable letting someone else take over control of an important function in your company?

You Have to Remove Stumbling Blocks

Sometimes to get a job back on track the project needs to be outsourced. I see this all the time with software implementations. The customer gets stalled on a certain technical issue and everything kind of sputters. They outsource the issue to an expert, who immediately solves the problem and gets the project on course again.

Companies also choose to outsource projects when they become bottlenecked. One client of mine used to come back from tradeshows with hundreds of leads, only to find these leads growing stale while someone found the time to enter them into their system, distribute them, and follow up. They hired us to perform these functions. By outsourcing certain sales functions, the good leads got into the salespersons' hands while they were still relatively new.

When outsourcing a stalled process, decide whether you're making a short- or long-term decision. An outsourcer can get a stalled process kicked into high gear, but will there be someone in-house to carry the momentum?

> **Outsourcing Insights**
>
> If you're bringing in someone from the outside to relieve a bottleneck or take charge of a stalled project, make sure you're giving him or her the proper authority. Your employees must know that he or she has your full confidence and represents you in action.

When Bringing in Experts Is Just What You Need

A very popular reason to outsource is to get access to experts and tools that aren't readily available internally. When you bring in an expert, you're also sharing the risk of a project or task with people who (hopefully) have more experience than you do.

How do you know that you might need an expert? Here are a few hints.

> **Stay Alert!**
>
> Outsourcing certain types of expertise can be pretty expensive. Qualified engineers, attorneys, or consultants often charge several hundred dollars an hour. If you find yourself outsourcing an expert, determine whether you can pass the cost directly on to your customer. Otherwise, you may want to work out a plan where you pay only when something is delivered.

You Don't Have the Expertise In-House

The story of our health insurer's problem at the beginning of this chapter is not uncommon for many businesses. Often a situation comes up that requires the expertise of someone who's not in-house. In that case, they needed an expert to figure out the best way to treat a unique situation so that the patient could receive the best care for the most affordable cost. Other companies face complex legal issues, quality control certifications, and government regulations that require expert help.

You Get Better Tools

If your outsourcer is worth their weight, they'll be using the best tools (such as specialized software, equipment, or proprietary knowledge) possible to get the job done for their customers. And you will benefit, too. The contractor may be using specialized and expensive technology that you would probably not buy yourself. When you interview a potential outsourcer, make sure to ask about the kinds of tools they use to do their job.

Outsourcing Insights

When you bring in an outsourcer to do a job for you, make sure you know what tools they will be using. The best outsourcers will invest in the best tools for their customers. An outsourced telemarketing company should be using the latest phone technology. Your outsourced call center ought to be using the best-of-breed service desk application.

You Can Share Resources and Reduce Your Risk

Investing a lot of money in a phone system is risky. So would be a similar investment in a new computer network or software to run your warehouses. There's no guarantee that any technology will work as well as you hope. Taking these financial leaps of faith without any safety net is a scary endeavor. To decrease the risks involved, many people decide to outsource.

Going into a project, such as managing your warehouse or doing laboratory testing, it's good to know that you've got another company involved with a lot at stake in the project. If your outsourced partner fails, they know they'll be losing a good customer and lots of potential future revenues, as well as risking a potential lawsuit.

Do you think you're a good candidate for outsourcing? Are all these benefits attractive to you? Before you jump into outsourcing head first, read our next chapter, and consider some of the challenges you'll face!

The Least You Need to Know

◆ Outsourcing your work can make you look like a larger enterprise, help you better utilize the space you're in, help you find a potential partner, and even give your company the opportunity to provide more services to your customers.

◆ You can realize operational and administrative cost reductions through outsourcing.

◆ A good outsourcing solution will help managers better manage their time by focusing on more important issues and delegating nonessential tasks.

◆ A very popular reason to outsource is to provide experts and tools that aren't readily available internally.

7

When You Shouldn't Outsource

In This Chapter

◆ Why your personality may not be right for an outsourced relationship

◆ Recognizing when the job functions are not outsource-able

◆ Why some traits of the outside service firm may drive you away from outsourcing

◆ Getting input from your customers and employees on outsourcing decisions

Gail was upset. More than 150 company reps had flown in from all over the world to meet for three days, and the feedback wasn't good. Complaints ranged from the temperature of the meeting rooms to the disappointing keynote address made by the outside speaker.

"What a mess!" Gail wailed to her colleague in the marketing department. "I should have never farmed out this event to an outsider."

"I thought Sullivan Meetings and Events is one of the best meeting planners around," her colleague said.

"So did I," Gail answered. "But they really dropped the ball on this one."

"What did they do wrong?" asked her friend.

"Oh, everything! There was always some sort of problem," Gail cried. "They complained that I wasn't giving them enough information about the attendees. I mean, some of this stuff was confidential! Then they complained that I was 'too' involved and making things worse. We also got confused who was responsible for what."

"Sounds like a real nightmare," Her colleague said sympathetically.

"Totally," said Gail. "I'll never outsource this event again."

Gail is right. She probably shouldn't outsource next year's sales meeting. And from the sounds of it, Sullivan Meetings wouldn't take on the job again even if it were offered to them.

Gail discovered that even outsourcing something can lead to problems. Maybe this event would have been much better organized if they just done it internally. Or maybe another event planning firm would have done a better job.

Outsourcing Isn't Always the Solution

Outsourcing isn't always the way to solve a problem; as a matter of fact, sometimes it can create more problems than it solves. Among the many reasons why you may want to avoid outsourcing a project or process, the following fall near the top of the list:

- ◆ You're not the type of person suitable for outsourcing.
- ◆ The job itself isn't outsource-able.
- ◆ There's a problem with the service provider.
- ◆ Your customers and/or employees aren't open to the idea.

In this chapter, we explore these factors further.

You and Outsourcing Don't Mix

The problem could be you! Sometimes your personality isn't suited for outsourcing. You might have certain traits that make it difficult for you to manage a third party.

If you have any of the character traits described in the following section, it might be a sign that outsourcing isn't right for you.

You Are a Micromanager

You like to know the details of everything going on. It's hard for you to relinquish control of a task. You want to see your people working right in front of you. You're uncomfortable with someone you don't know very well all of the sudden doing a task for which you're ultimately responsible. You want to know what's been done and what's still left to do at every moment.

Outsourcing means giving up control. You won't be able to manage every detail of a project when you're farming the job to someone else who may not even be working on your premises. You're going to have to let go a little bit when you employ a third party. If this concept gives you the shivers, you're probably not ready for this type of arrangement.

Outsourcing Insights

Outsourcing can help the micromanager, too! If you're the type of person who really likes to stay very close to the action, you probably get frustrated because you can't spend as much time supervising as you'd like. If you outsource a mundane activity and put it out of your mind, you may find yourself with more time to micromanage more important functions.

You're Impatient

You don't like to wait for answers. You don't like the idea that the person doing a job for you isn't available all the time. You don't want to deal with a different person each time you have a question. You find it annoying that you have to call someone every time you want an answer, instead of just walking down the hall. You don't like any delays in fixing a problem. You can't bear inconveniences.

Although outsourcing can be a great thing, it will also come with its share of inconveniences that you're not used to. You're not going to have people at your beck and call every minute of the day. You may have to wait longer for an answer. You may experience some turnover with the outside firm. If these kinds of inconveniences are a big problem for you, think twice before farming the work out.

You Don't Like to Commit

You hate signing long-term agreements. You want the ability to move people around from job to job. You want the flexibility to hire and fire at will.

Many outsourcing arrangements require contractual obligations. If a company is going to go through the hassle of hosting your e-mail, they're probably going to require you to sign up for a one- or two-year deal with them.

As long as you stay within employment laws, you can hire and fire people as you like. But when dealing with another company, you won't be able to slip out of a signed agreement unless you're within the boundaries of what's allowed by that agreement. If you're unsure about making the commitment, outsourcing might not be right for you.

The Liabilities Scare You

You don't like to take any chances with the IRS and other regulatory agencies of the government. You're not comfortable with the subcontractor rules (discussed in Chapter 20). You are nervous that you'll be audited and the IRS will determine that your subcontractors should really be employees. You are concerned that you could be sued due to negligent work done by the outside service provider. You don't like the idea of someone who's not an employee representing themselves as part of your company. You're uncomfortable with the ethical ramifications of using outsourced help to do work for you on behalf of your customers or clients.

Stay Alert!

If you're considering entering a significant outsourcing arrangement, always discuss it with both your corporate attorney and tax advisors. They will help you structure the arrangement to protect you against lawsuits both from the outside service provider and from the government (like the IRS, SEC, or Department of Labor).

The government sometimes views questionable outsourcing arrangements as a way to evade taxes and employment laws. Done legally, you shouldn't have a problem; however, it's still a gray area and you might have to defend yourself, maybe even in a court of law. If you're not up to the fight, you might want to keep the work in-house.

You Have Data Privacy and Confidentiality Issues

You don't like the idea that someone from outside of your company has access to your internal information. You are concerned that a service provider with access to confidential data may use this information elsewhere, or give it to a competitor. You're not confident that your contracts can do much to stop the service provider from divulging sensitive data. You lose sleep at night worrying about the consequences of your provider using your confidential data against you in the future.

Outsourcing means bringing in outsiders who are not bound to you as an employee. They will be someone else's people, with allegiance to their own employer. You probably won't spend the same amount of time with them as you do your employees. You won't know whether you can trust the people who are sent in to do the work. You're relying on the service provider's own screening controls to find the right people. If you're uncomfortable letting nonemployees handle sensitive data, you might not want to outsource the job.

You Avoid Confrontation

You don't like to argue or negotiate with people who are working closely with you. You have trouble treating outsiders as vendors, rather than employees. You don't like to be the bad guy. You aren't happy about sharing your service provider's time with his or her other customers. You aren't comfortable negotiating contractual arrangements. You don't like to have to admonish someone if they're not performing like you'd expect.

> **Stay Alert!**
>
> Always treat your service provider professionally, but try not to make them too much a "part of the family." You are outsourcing work to a vendor, not an extended employee. The vendor should receive no additional benefits or favored treatment that would be different from any other vendor. Keeping the appropriate level of distance between you and your vendors will make it easier for you to negotiate and resolve problems when they occur.

A supplier-customer relationship is different from an employer-employee relationship. It's less "touchy-feely." You will have conflicts. There will be scheduling mishaps.

You might be more apt to give an employee some slack while they ease into their job. But with an outside provider, you're paying what you may consider a steep rate per hour and you expect them to hit the ground running. Anything less than that could be a problem. Are you ready to stand up for yourself?

You Think Outsourcing Will Solve All of Your Problems

You're under the impression that sending out a job to someone else will let you wipe your hands clean of it. You believe that just because someone says they're an expert they really are. You think that people who work for an outside company won't make the same mistakes that people make when working for you. You think that because a firm does a lot more of something they've necessarily figured out how to do it right.

Outsourcers are people, too. They have their own strengths and weaknesses. They will make mistakes. By outsourcing certain work, old problems may disappear, but new ones will pop up! For example, your payroll service may do a great job with the weekly paychecks but might be slower than you hoped in responding to requests from the IRS. Nothing will be perfect.

If you expect all of your problems to go away, you're not entering the outsourcing arrangement with the right expectations.

You're Not Flexible

Your schedule is rigid. Your days are well planned out. You cannot tolerate things being out of your control. You don't like changing your schedule. You're not good at handling surprises. You're not open to change. You want things done only your way. You are set in your ways.

Outsourcing Insights

By outsourcing you're giving up some control. You're relying on others who are not in your employment to get a job done. You are going to have to be flexible with their schedule and with their own demands.

Remember that the telemarketer who's making phone calls for you from her house in Virginia is working for 10 other clients and has small children. She may need to change her schedule on you. She may have better ways of making calls or a different approach to the phone script you've given her. You're going to need to show some flexibility to make your outsourcing relationships work.

You Want Someone Else to Take Responsibility for Your Project

You like to make people accountable for their work. You shift ownership to others. You tend to lay the blame for problems elsewhere. You want your outside service provider to be ultimately responsible for the task they're given. You think that the outside service provider will stand up and accept this responsibility, even if things turn south.

If you think you're going to be able to wash your hands of the job by outsourcing it, you've got another thing coming. You may have all the confidence in the world that they'll take your headaches away. But if they don't, it's going to be your baby to fix. Outsourcing is another form of delegating. It's not going to make any problems disappear. You're the one who's ultimately responsible. You're going to have to stay involved.

The Job Isn't Right

Certain tasks should never be outsourced. Some jobs are best left to employees, even if outsourcing them might at first appear to be the cheaper way to go.

The Complexities Can't Be Delegated

A job, or parts of a job, might just be too complicated to outsource. For example, if your company designs custom labeling systems or constructs amusement park rides, you probably need to retain control over the entire process. Similarly, if a job involves purchasing highly specialized materials or requires very detailed quality testing, you may feel you need to keep it in-house.

Don't make the mistake of outsourcing something that's too complex to be outsourced. A full-time or permanent part-time employee may be required to handle specific, complicated, unique, and problematic tasks.

You're Stretching the ROI

Even after running the numbers, you conclude that the return on investment (ROI) for outsourcing something isn't that significant. You find yourself stretching some of your assumptions or accepting a return that's less than hoped for. You come up with values for intangible factors that you had previously dismissed as irrelevant. You begin to make up reasons why the ROI is acceptable. (See Chapter 8 for a discussion of ROIs.)

Given your risks and lack of guaranteed results, the ROI for any outsourcing decision should be substantial. You should be showing a significant return. If you're stretching the case for outsourcing, you might be fooling yourself.

> **Outsourcing Insights**
>
> The return on investment on your outsourcing decision should be well above the amount of interest you would receive if you invested that same amount of capital in the market. The return is oftentimes calculated over a period of time, usually two to four years.

Outsourcing Insights

A client of mine has excess cash. Instead of hiring an outside investment manager, they delegated the task to a trusted partner who enjoys managing money and has experience with investments. The extra time it took was minimal, the fee savings was substantial, and everyone felt better with one of the partners in charge rather than someone from outside the company.

You Already Have the Resources

Some people make the mistake of outsourcing a job when they've already got people in-house to do the work. Maybe an outside answering service isn't necessary—instead you could use someone in the office who doesn't have enough work to keep busy. Or maybe your partner's wife (who has a degree in accounting) could work part time and do the books instead of bringing in an unknown bookkeeping service. Rather than hiring an expensive company to host your company's e-mail, you find that you've got plenty of space on your server to do this.

If you've got the resources to do it yourself, it might make more sense to keep it in-house.

There's a Public Perception Problem

When the Philadelphia School District decided to outsource the management of some of its schools to an independent, for-profit company, there was an outcry. "You can't do this," shouted the teacher's union. "This is bad for our children," yelled activists. The media coverage was so intense that the project was almost scrapped. Luckily, the school board stuck to their plan and the project has been successful (so far). The public perception problem, though, was a big issue that had to be resolved.

If you think your decision to outsource is going to damage your company's reputation in the public eye, you might want to reconsider.

You Haven't Established a Business Case

Outsourcing for the sake of outsourcing isn't a good idea. In Chapter 8, you'll learn about the steps involved in making the outsourcing decision. For now, all you need to know is that the decision must make financial sense.

Every decision to outsource needs a business case. Whether it's a solid return on investment, an improvement in customer service, an increase in leads, or a reduction in cost … all of these are business cases for outsourcing.

The Service Provider Isn't Making the Grade

Sometimes the reasons for not outsourcing have nothing to do with you or the job itself. You may decide not to outsource because you can't find the right service provider to do the work.

Those High Fees Eat You Up

You might not be a good candidate for outsourcing if you can't afford—or simply don't want—to pay the fees that some service providers charge. Business process consultants typically charge you hundreds of dollars per hour. Attorneys charge a flat retainer each month to be available on call. Accountants who prepare your taxes may charge you, in your opinion, an arm and a leg. It's not unusual for people to decide to keep the work in-house because they can't bear to pay what they consider to be exorbitant rates to an outside service provider.

Outside service providers aren't nonprofit organizations. They have their overhead and expenses and they must pay high salaries to maintain good people. You're benefiting from their expertise and their convenience, but it won't come cheap.

> **CAUTION**
>
> **Stay Alert!**
>
> The lowest-price outside solution may not be the best. Sometimes there is good reason why a firm charges more than the market average. Good people cost money, and outsourcing firms are going to pass those higher costs along to their clients.

You're Not Comfortable with the Service Provider

Would you farm out your bookkeeping work to someone you don't trust? Would you rely on an outside answering service to handle all of your company's phone calls when they're unresponsive to your own requests? Would you hire a food service to provide your staff hot lunches when you notice that none of their people wear gloves when handling the food?

If you're not comfortable with the idea of working with an outside contractor, you should look elsewhere for a solution to your problem.

You're Not Mutually Benefiting Each Other

Relationships need to be beneficial to both parties if they're going to be successful over the long haul. I've made the mistake of entering into an outsourced controller service relationship where I've agreed on a much lower fee than was necessary to make enough money. Sure, the client got a great deal and was probably slapping himself on the back. But after just three months, I had to back out of the relationship. I couldn't sustain it. The relationship wasn't profitable enough for me. In the end, the client who thought he was getting a great deal wound up starting at square one with a new service provider.

> **Outsourcing Insights**
>
> Always strike a fair deal with your outside service provider. Don't get greedy and don't take advantage of them. You're relying on your outsourcers to handle important tasks for you. You don't want them to get annoyed and frustrated because they're not being paid what they think they deserve.

If both parties aren't benefiting from the outsourcing arrangement, it's destined to fail.

You Can't Agree on Deliverables and Measurements

What are your goals? Is the telemarketing firm tasked with providing you more leads or more "qualified" leads? Is your outsourced call center supposed to reduce the time it takes to get a call resolved or increase customer satisfaction? If the business process consulting firm is proposing to outsource your order entry process, what's the ultimate cost savings to you, after their fees?

All outsourcing relationships must have clearly defined deliverables and measurements to evaluate those deliverables. If you can't come to an agreement at the outset, it's probably a sign that you should start looking somewhere else.

You Don't Give Yourself Time to Properly Choose

Many outsourcing decisions are significant. In some cases, you're replacing employees. In other cases you may be turning the way you do things completely upside down. It's not the kind of decision you should take lightly.

Hiring a firm to do your payroll, provide human resources functions, or even to clean up your facility every night involves entrusting people outside your company with important and oftentimes sensitive tasks. Don't rush into these sorts of decisions.

Your Customers and Employees Are Telling You Something

Outsourcing may not be the right thing to do if your customers and employees aren't on board with the decision. These are the people who will most be affected by this choice. Be on the look out for the following warning signs.

Your Customers Demand *You*

There are just some jobs that your customer expects *you* to do, not an outside service provider. Imagine if you hired an attorney to litigate an important lawsuit for you and another attorney showed up. "Sorry," he says to you. "Andy farmed this work out to me. I'm John."

You're probably not going to care if your phone company sends out an outsourced specialist to fix your lines, as long as they get the job done. However, the phone company may care if the specialist they've chosen to service their customers is also outsourcing to someone else!

In certain lines of work, the customer doesn't want to see anyone else but you getting the job done. You could lose credibility if you use someone else.

> **Knowledge Is Power**
>
> In the past few years, companies such as Dell Computer and IBM pulled their outsourced call centers out of foreign locations and brought them back in-house because customers were complaining that the outsourced help wasn't adequate. The financial and public relations costs of these moves were significant.

You Don't Have Management or Employee Buy-In

Farming out a job will impact your employees. It will affect how things are done in-house. It may have consequences for your customer service. Both management and employees will be working with the outsourcer. If they're not onboard from the very beginning, they may be looking for reasons for the relationship not to succeed.

Don't make large outsourcing decisions unilaterally. Outsourcing projects are doomed to fail if your management team and employees don't buy in to the idea.

Corporate Culture Says No

Unfortunately, outsourcing implies the loss of jobs internally. It involves paying someone outside of the company to do a task. Some companies revolt at the idea of outsiders coming in to do the work employees used to do. Outsourcing copying work to FedEx Kinkos probably wouldn't raise any eyebrows, but outsourcing a critical task to an untested vendor might raise concerns for both employees and customers. Just the mention of outsourcing can damage employee morale.

Some companies can't outsource because the concept of outsourcing doesn't fit into the culture of the organization. If your company has this kind of culture, you may not be right for outsourcing.

The Least You Need to Know

◆ If you are a micromanager, impatient, averse to risk, or inflexible, you should think twice before you enter into an outsourcing arrangement.

◆ Certain types of jobs should never be outsourced.

◆ When you're dealing with service providers that charge too much, make you uncomfortable, and can't agree with you on deliverables, it might be best not to outsource.

◆ When your customers expect your company to do the work, outsourcing isn't right for you.

Chapter 8

The Seven-Step Decision-Making Process

In This Chapter

- ◆ Determining the financial justification for your outsourcing decision
- ◆ Coming up with objectives, metrics, and timeframes for your financial analysis
- ◆ Calculating direct and indirect expenses as well as revenue
- ◆ Analyzing the results of your analysis

You're the marketing manager for a health and fitness club. You're responsible for creating and maintaining the company's image and brand. You're also responsible for generating new membership leads for the sales staff. You have six full-time employees in your department. Four of them do telemarketing.

You're not satisfied with this effort. You're pretty sure a more experienced team would generate more leads. You also think it could be done for less money. One day you receive a direct mail piece from a telemarketing firm.

"Hmm," you think to yourself. "I think it's time to consider outsourcing."

You research the pros and cons of the outsourcing decision. You talk to a few people and interview potential telemarketing firms. You narrow the field to a few good choices. As you learn more about the process, you begin to feel comfortable with the idea of outsourcing. But you also know that your boss is going to want to see proof, and that proof is going to have to come in the form of an ROI analysis.

Business Buzzwords

Return on investment (ROI) is a measure of how effectively you can use your capital to generate income. Keeping $1,000 under your bed doesn't result in any return. Investing the same $1,000 in a money-market account might bring you an ROI of about 5 percent a year. The higher the return, the better.

Oh no! The dreaded, yet necessary, *ROI (return on investment)* analysis. You're now forced to put aside all opinions, emotions, and gut feelings. None of this matters unless you can justify the ROI. So pull out the calculator and put the visor on. It's time to crunch the numbers.

In this chapter, we go through the steps to figure out whether the dollars and cents of your outsourcing decision add up.

Step 1: Determine Your Objectives

Before you rev up the spreadsheet, you need to determine your objectives. By now you should have a good idea of the kind of results outsourcing can help you achieve:

◆ **You want to increase your revenues.** You want your outsourcing decision to result in increased sales for your organization.

◆ **You want to decrease your costs.** It may be cheaper to farm out work than to do it in-house.

◆ **You want more productivity.** An outside service provider may be able to complete a task much more quickly and efficiently than you can.

◆ **You're looking to create long-term value.** Outsourcing a specific process can make a company significantly better at what it does. This may translate into an increase in the company's overall market value.

◆ **You want the company to focus on what it does best.** By outsourcing secondary tasks, your company will be able to focus on your company's key value propositions.

Every outsourcing decision must have an objective. For example, the objective of outsourcing a call center offshore is usually to reduce costs. Outsourcing technical services may be a revenue creator. Farming out your inventory to an outside warehouser might get products in and out faster. Bringing in an outside chief financial officer is intended to improve your company's credibility and give a boost to shareholder value.

Sometimes an outsourcing decision has more than one objective. The independent contractor that is doing your outsourced service work not only generates revenue for your company, but is also getting jobs done faster than ever. Substantially decreasing your call center costs results in higher profits and higher company value.

If the objective for outsourcing your telemarketing operations is to increase revenue, then your analysis will need to show how an outside telemarketing firm will create more revenue for the same dollars invested.

Step 2: Determine the Timeframe

Are you aiming to see results within a few days? Months? Years? You need to come up with a timeframe for measuring the effects of your outsourcing decision. I've found that smaller companies expect to see a substantial return on their investment in a much shorter timeframe (like 30 to 90 days). Larger companies have the resources to stick it out longer, even years if necessary.

Going back to our example in the beginning of this chapter, your boss has asked you to prepare an ROI analysis. You've arbitrarily picked 18 months as the timeframe to see some results from the outsourced telemarketing company. Not a bad idea, because these things take time.

Step 3: Determine the Metrics

Your *metrics* are an extremely important part of the outsourcing decision. You need to evaluate the success or failure of the project on quantitative information. It can't just "feel good."

Business Buzzwords

A **metric** is a value that's part of a system used to measure the results of a process or calculation. Using metrics usually involves the employment of mathematical and statistical analysis.

Metrics can come in many different flavors, including the following:

◆ **Ratios.** A ratio represents the relationship between two financial values. For example, an outsourced collection agency might be tasked with increasing your accounts receivable turnover ratio (sales divided by accounts receivable). The higher the turnover, the shorter the time between selling and collecting cash.

◆ **Benchmarks.** A benchmark is a standard against which something can be measured. You may decide to outsource certain research and development expenditures in order to bring your overall research costs in line with industry averages, or benchmarks.

◆ **Fixed amounts.** Your metric might represent a fixed dollar or unit amount. You may determine that your outsourced payroll company will decrease your payroll administration costs by exactly $1,000 dollars each quarter. In our ROI analysis, we want to receive 500 qualified leads a month from our outsourced telemarketing firm.

◆ **Relative amounts.** A metric may be an amount that's relative to another amount, usually expressed in the form of a percentage. For example, to keep your freight costs steady at 2 percent of revenue, you decide to outsource delivery to a trucking company.

◆ **Comparatives.** Your metric may be a unit or number that you compare to another unit or number. You farm out all printing operations to another company to reduce your printing costs, compared to the same costs from last year.

For our analysis of whether to outsource telemarketing operations, we're using the number of qualified leads as our metric. Your outside telemarketing firm will be judged on one thing and one thing only: the number of qualified leads they can produce for you on a monthly basis. Based on past history, you know that your salespeople can convert approximately 25 percent of those leads to sales. Your telemarketing company will need to provide more qualified leads than do the internal people you're using now in order to meet your revenue objectives.

Step 4: Detail All Direct and Indirect Costs

What *direct costs* will you save by outsourcing your telemarketing department? For one thing, you will lose people. This means you'll no longer have to pay their salaries. You'll also avoid paying employer's payroll taxes, your share of their health insurance, and your contribution to their pension plan. Other expenses that will immediately fall away will be telephone costs and office supplies. All of these direct costs should be reflected on your analysis.

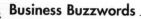

Business Buzzwords

Direct costs are those expenditures that can be absolutely linked to a task or activity. For example, the direct cost of mailing a letter includes the price of the stamp.

Indirect costs should be considered, too. The most substantial indirect cost is management and supervisory time. For your analysis, you've determined that you spent about 5 percent of your time supervising the telemarketing group. You have to train new people, deal with personnel issues, and help others when a problem occurs. There's a strong case to be made that your outsourced firm will take care of these things for you.

Business Buzzwords

Indirect costs are those expenditures that are related to an activity, but are not directly attributable to the activity. For example, when you mail a letter you've got the direct cost of postage, paper, and envelopes. But to write the letter you may have made use of a computer, which also used up electric power. And you also probably used a word processing program, too. The electricity and cost of the word processing program are indirect costs of producing the letter.

But let's not ignore reality. Even though you'll be outsourcing this work, you'll still want to stay involved. You'll still be getting updates from the service provider and providing some oversight. Not as much time as if you were doing this in-house, but you will be spending time on the project. For this analysis you're going to show both a reduction and addition of management time, so it's a wash.

Step 5: Determine Your Outsourcing Costs

Now that you've looked at the savings from outsourcing the work, it's time to see what the outsourcer is going to cost you in new expenses. The telemarketing firm you want to hire is asking for a flat $15,000 per month, plus reimbursement of any out-of-pocket expenses, including phone service.

When determining outside costs, make sure you've really uncovered everything your service provider is going to charge you for. If your service provider charges by the hour, do your best to nail down a good estimate of the hours that it will take to do the job. If it's a fixed-cost arrangement, agree on whether any increases are allowed and how much.

And don't forget indirect costs. We mentioned management time in the previous section. We're including that in our calculation. There could be other indirect costs, such as additional time needed by your employees on the project, or the contribution of office space, vehicles, tools, and so on by your company.

Step 6: Determine Revenue Increases (If Any)

Will outsourcing your payroll to a third party increase your revenues? (See Chapter 9 for examples of the many ways that you can create revenue opportunities through outsourcing.) If you're the one doing the work, and by farming it out you have additional time to work with prospective customers, maybe so. If you decide to set up an offshore call center, will your new and improved customer service people generate more add-on sales from your existing customer base?

The telemarketing firm that we want to hire is not any less expensive than our internal staff. What you're betting on is that their expertise will result in more leads for the sales group and therefore more sales. In many cases, outsourcing may produce more revenues as an ancillary benefit. In your case, the whole decision to outsource will depend on this revenue increase for its justification.

Step 7: Adding It All Up

The moment of truth. You've considered all the costs you'll be saving, the additional costs you'll be incurring, and any new revenue you'll be adding. Now it's time to do the math.

Is the Benefit Substantial?

As you'll see later in this chapter, our analysis shows a $39,000 benefit to the company by outsourcing telemarketing. If your company does $20 million a year in sales, perhaps the total return isn't substantial enough to go through the effort. For a much smaller organization, this amount might represent a significant chunk of your operating costs, thereby justifying outsourcing the work.

How Long Will It Take for the Benefit to Be Achieved?

The analysis we prepared assumes it will take 18 months to save $39,000 (or about $2,200 per month). Can you wait that long?

How Probable Is the End Result?

Just because we say we're going to save $39,000 doesn't mean we will. We're basing our entire decision on the telemarketer's promise that they'll increase your leads by 25 percent, but they're not guaranteeing this. If leads don't increase by 25 percent, your net benefit will fall. And heaven forbid they do even worse than your own staff. Your calculation hinges on the reliability of these assumptions. It may be a good idea to leave some cushion in your analysis to cover yourself!

Is the ROI Enough?

In this scenario, we're investing $298,000 and eliminating $292,000 of expenses, so our net cash outlay is $6,000. Over the next 18 months we're estimating a return of $39,000. I can't think of any mutual fund that would provide that kind of return in so short a timeframe.

But what if your net cash outlay were $30,000 with an expected return of $39,000 over 18 months? That's still more than a 20 percent return on your money. But it's pretty risky. Maybe you're better off sticking that same amount in a Fortune 500 stock fund with a

Stay Alert!

Stay diligent. Keep your spreadsheets updated. Don't fall behind. Keeping tabs on the financial benefits of an outsourced project is more difficult the longer it's spread out. Decisions made a year or two before can sometimes seem like a lifetime ago!

Outsourcing Insights

Try to structure your outsourcing agreements so that your outside service provider shares some risk. If he's promising an extra 100 leads per month, hold back half of his payment until he delivers what he's committed. Otherwise, pay him something relatively less.

Outsourcing Insights

Some top mutual funds have returned as much as 30 to 40 percent to investors over certain periods. Most average anywhere from 5 to 15 percent. Before you sink funds into any project, try to evaluate your return on investment versus what you could achieve if you took the same amount of money and invested it in marketable securities (assuming you have the knowledge to do this).

track record of 12 percent returns instead. At least this way you're less likely to lose everything.

Are There Intangibles?

The opportunity to take $6,000 net cash and turn it into $39,000 of income is certainly appealing. However, as you learned in Chapter 7, it might not be the right kind of investment for your company. We're not going to rehash these reasons here, but bear in mind that these intangibles should be considered before making any decision.

And now it's time to put the numbers to paper. What follows is a step-by-step analysis for evaluating our telemarketing outsourcing decision. Your own analysis may be different, depending on your decision and the facts. But what you'll find here is a great blueprint for helping your thought process.

ROI Analysis for Outsourced Telemarketing

Proposal

To replace our internal marketing department with an outsourced marketing firm.

Step 1: Objective

To increase new revenues by 5 percent by increasing qualified telemarketing leads by 10 percent.

Step 2: Timeframe

18 months, with monthly evaluations.

Step 3: Metric

Number of qualified telemarketing leads given to salespeople (these are leads that have been interviewed by the telemarketing firm and who satisfy certain conditions as determined by the sales team).

Step 4: Direct and Indirect Costs Saved

Salaries

4 employees @ $2,500 per month/employee	$180,000
Taxes (15% of salaries)	$27,000

Employee Benefits

      Health insurance, pension $30,000

Office Expenses

    Phones $36,000

    Supplies $9,000

Management/Supervisory Allocation

    5% of marketing manager time/expenses $10,000

    Total Costs Saved by Outsourcing $292,000

Step 5: Direct Outsourcing Costs/Benefits Incurred

Telemarketing Firm Monthly Fee

    $15,000/month $270,000

Reimbursement of Expenses

    $1,000/month $18,000

Management/Supervisory Allocation

    5% of marketing manager time/expenses $10,000

    Total Costs Incurred by Outsourcing   **$298,000**

    Net Cost for Outsourcing   **$6,000**

Step 6: Benefits Incurred

    Monthly leads generated now   400

    Monthly leads estimated   500

    Increase in leads   100

    Close ratio   25%

    Increase in closed sales   25%

    Average monthly sales/revenue value $100

continues

continued

Increase in monthly sales	$2,500
Increase in sales over 18 months	$45,000
Net Revenue Increase by Outsourcing	**$45,000**

Step 7: Net ROI

Net Outlay per above	($6,000)
Net Revenue Increase per above	$45,000
NET Return on Investment (18 Months)	**$39,000**

The Least You Need to Know

◆ There are seven steps for calculating your outsourcing decision's financial benefits/costs.

◆ Before you begin to add up the numbers, you must first determine your objectives, timeframe, and metrics.

◆ Make sure you consider all direct and indirect costs you'll be saving and the new costs you'll be incurring under the arrangement.

◆ If appropriate, don't forget to consider the additional source of revenue that your outsourcing project could provide.

◆ Even after adding up the final result, you should still consider the significance of the savings, whether you could get a better return elsewhere, and other intangible factors.

Chapter 9

Creating New Revenue Opportunities by Outsourcing

In This Chapter

- How outsourcing marketing tasks generates leads
- The different ways you can outsource your sales activities
- Billing for your service
- Making money from other people's creativity

James runs a very successful engineering firm. His billings are more than $5 million a year, yet he employs fewer than 10 people. How can he do so well with so few people?

He makes money through outsourcing.

James outsources all of his marketing to a marketing company. They get him leads and pass them on to his two independent sales reps. Then he hands the work over to an internal project manager, who farms out the work to one of the independent engineers his firm works with.

None of his sales or service people are actually employees. James bills for the work done by other people.

James figured out that there's a lot of money to be made by outsourcing sales, marketing, customer support, and even creative services to his own clients.

In the next two chapters, we're going to look much deeper into all of the activities and tasks that people outsource for profit. These activities contribute to the bottom line not only by reducing expenses but by increasing revenues. Let's first consider ways you can boost your sales through outsourcing.

Outsourcing Your Sales and Marketing Functions

Coca-Cola Corporation, which has one of the most recognizable brand names in the world, spends up to 20 percent of its annual revenue on marketing. You might think that a company of this size can afford to do much of this in-house. But they don't. The marketing machine that backs the brands of Coke, Sprite, and Dr. Pepper relies on many hired guns for help, located all over the world. They get more bang for the buck by outsourcing this work. If Coca-Cola sees the need for outside help to generate interest in its products, why shouldn't you?

The following sections outline the various types of marketing tasks companies frequently outsource.

Stay Alert!

Be careful about the recently enacted "do not call" legislation. Your outside telemarketing company should be in compliance with these laws or you might be held liable. For that matter, any telemarketing service provider you hire should offer to educate *you* on this matter, too! More information on the National Do Not Call Registry can be found at www.donotcall.gov.

Telemarketing

Doing telemarketing in-house is expensive and time-consuming. You'll have to hire (and fire) employees, teach them what you want to say, and supervise their work. And there's no guarantee of success, even though you're paying out salaries. Some managers don't want to put up with these headaches. They'd rather let a professional telemarketing firm or individual do the work and pay them by the leads they generate.

It's not all easy, though. Outsourcing telemarketing comes with its challenges. For example, how many times have you received a marketing call from someone who doesn't speak very well, with dogs barking in the background, or who has little knowledge of the product being pitched? Some people prefer to keep their telemarketing in-house for closer supervision.

Even with these challenges, many people like to outsource their telemarketing to professionals or firms who specialize in generating leads.

Overall Marketing

An independent marketing firm can help you create a detailed marketing plan, identify target markets, establish brand identification, assist your company with a print or e-mail advertising campaign, or create metrics to analyze the results of your activities. The firm can also oversee the implementation of a plan.

You can hire independent marketing firms on a fixed-price basis, for monthly fees, and by the hour, depending on the task.

Public Relations

If you're trying to make a big splash, you're going to need some help with public relations. Public relations firms help build brands by getting the word out to the media. But these kinds of firms do a lot more than make a few phone calls and send out press releases. They help shape a company or product's image. They help with damage control if disaster strikes. These firms also can help you manage your relationship with shareholders, employees, customers, and vendors.

Good PR is an expertise. And it's usually not a full-time job. There are thousands of individual public relations consultants and hundreds of established public relations firms.

> **CAUTION**
>
> **Stay Alert!**
>
> Public relations firms can get pretty expensive. Many charge monthly fees and make you commit to minimum contractual periods. Because of the nature of their work, it's difficult to relate these fees directly to specific deliverables. Make sure to clearly define what your expectations are.

Research and Analysis

Market research and analysis firms can investigate market trends, new opportunities, potential demand, and how well you're doing against your competitors. The results of this work can turn into additional or new sources of revenue for you. Sure, you can do market research in-house, but many people prefer to delegate these sorts of tasks to a person or firm who specializes in this kind of thing.

Outsourced market research firms generally charge flat fees for the reports they produce. If you decide to outsource your research, you can purchase already prepared reports or hire these firms to conduct specialized research on your behalf.

Direct Marketing

Outsourced direct marketing firms can send out letters, postcards, e-mails, brochures, and any other promotional item you can think of. For extra fees, they will help you design a strong direct marketing campaign from the ground up. Outsourcing this function can generate lots of leads for your company.

> **Outsourcing Insights**
>
> Direct marketing isn't limited to mail campaigns. Many companies provide direct marketing e-mail services, too. They might enable you to send hundreds or thousands of e-mails to prospects that have "opted-in" to your campaign.
>
> However, watch out for unscrupulous marketing firms that sell your information to companies that may use your name for marketing purposes. Your reputation could suffer if you end up on the wrong list.

Event Marketing

Maybe your company is planning a product launch. Or attending a trade show. Or setting up an open house for a new office. Perhaps you've decided to throw a whiz-bang Christmas party or corporate picnic. Suppose you have an annual conference for your partners, or a shareholders meeting after you release your financial statements. Maybe you intend to conduct quarterly sales meetings with sales representatives around the country. All such corporate events take a lot of effort to succeed.

You can have one of your employees organize the entire affair, or you can outsource it to an event marketing firm.

An event marketing firm will take responsibility for making sure your event is planned, promoted, and handled properly. They won't be responsible for your shipping manager's behavior or the long-winded speech delivered by the president, but they will make sure the location is booked, the food is delivered, and the activities are organized.

Advertising

Let's say you want to create an advertising campaign for one of your products.

It's a little intimidating, isn't it? You would need to come up with an idea and then design and place the ads. You would need to decide which media outlets would be the best for your ad. (For example, you probably won't do too well if you advertise your nail polish in *Sports Illustrated*.) You would need to figure out how often the ad should run and in which parts of the country. Good marketing managers understand their limitations. Most outsource advertising work to an advertising firm.

Outsourced advertising firms add their own expertise to your marketing. Most firms bill a percentage of the dollars you're spending. If you're looking for a firm to help you design the campaign, you can hire a good advertising company at additional fixed or per diem rates.

Getting Help to Close the Deal

Do you have your own internal sales force that sells direct, or do you outsource your sales force to an independent company? One answer might make more sense for you—let's take a closer look.

Independent Sales Reps

An outsourced sales force can be pretty darn profitable—just ask Mary Kay Ash. Back in 1963, and with her life savings of $5,000, she started a little cosmetics company with the dream of "offering women unprecedented opportunities for financial independence, career advancement and personal fulfillment."

Mary Kay's model was to outsource her sales force. This way she could avoid the costs and challenges of employing and motivating internal sales people and instead focus on helping independent women succeed on their own.

And boy, has she succeeded. Today Mary Kay Cosmetics is a billion-dollar company with more than a million independent salespeople hawking their products in more than 30 countries around the world.

Mary Kay Cosmetics isn't the only company that has recognized the power of outsourcing their sales force. Fortune 500 companies from Dupont to General Electric use independent sales agents to move at least some of their products. It's not an easy road to travel, though. By outsourcing your sales force, you'll be exposed to issues of loyalty, consistency, and liability. But a well-run outsourced sales program could reap huge benefits for your company while minimizing the cost of carrying employees.

Building a Channel of Partners

Rather than signing up independent agents, you might decide to outsource your sales process to a partner *channel*. Microsoft Corporation successfully uses this approach.

There are thousands of "Microsoft Partners" throughout the world. These companies range from individual computer shops to multi-hundred-employee organizations. They go through a certification process to sell, implement, and support Microsoft products, and they pay annual fees for the privilege of selling them. Microsoft supports these products and provides the retailers with leads in their areas of expertise. Microsoft's internal sales group is compensated on the performance of their outside partners.

> **Business Buzzwords**
>
> A **channel** is a means for distributing your products through a network of experienced and trained service providers.

Even a goliath such as Microsoft could never maintain the level of sales that it does now without its partner channel. Outsourcing their product sales is a critical part of their business model.

The Middleman

The middleman may be a *distributor*, a *wholesaler*, or a *retailer*. A distributor is nothing more than an outsourced sales force for the manufacturers it represents. Distributors are especially useful as the middleman between a manufacturer and the thousands of customers who use its products. These manufacturers do not have the infrastructure to market and sell to their customer base. Middlemen oftentimes hold inventory in a large warehouse and handle all of the headaches that come with shipping and then servicing the products they represent.

A distribution channel is a classic way to outsource sales. In the technology industry, for instance, the big players are Merisel and Tech Data. Both companies catalog thousands of software applications, get volume discounts from the software manufacturers, and sell these products to tens of thousands of businesses around the world. The software manufacturers, meanwhile, focus on making software products and providing support to the end users.

> **Business Buzzwords**
>
> A **distributor** is an individual or a company that markets merchandise to retail stores or acts as an intermediary between a store and a manufacturer. Distributors generally maintain inventory. A **wholesaler** buys larger quantities of goods than a distributor and gets the goods at a lower price. Wholesalers then sell their goods to distributors, other wholesalers, and to retail outlets. A **retailer** sells goods to the ultimate end-user.

Making Money by Outsourcing Services

My company makes money from outsourced services. It's not our only revenue stream, but it's our most significant. Of course, we earn a margin on the software we sell. We also have a few employees who provide certain support services. But our biggest revenue stream is from our team of independent contractors who consult, implement, train, and support our clients. I pay them by the hour, and then I turn around and bill their time at a value-added rate to my clients. There are many ways to make money from your outsourced help. Here are just a few.

Customer Support

Large technology companies such as Dell and IBM have outsourced their call centers to facilities in India. Other technology companies, including Microsoft and Oracle, outsource their support centers to third-party companies located elsewhere in the United States.

But you don't have to be a technology goliath to outsource your customer service. If your company sells products that require ongoing telephone support, you have options other than hiring employees or starting up a service center. Titan Corporation is a small company that sells phone systems to large- and medium-size customers. After a phone system is installed it's pretty common for the customer to have follow-up questions, oftentimes months after the initial sale. Titan outsources this customer service responsibility to a third party service center.

On-Site Services

Do you need to go on-site to service your customer? For specialized tasks, you might not need to hire someone full-time. Instead, you can call on other contractors with the requisite skills when required. And you may be able to bill these costs at a value-added rate to your customers.

Programming Services

Another revenue-generating activity that businesses often outsource is application programming. Many software programmers prefer to work on their own terms—they're independent by nature, don't like to be tied down by work rules, and sometimes consider themselves to be mavericks. They work crazy hours and like their freedom. As a result, many of them turn down employment jobs for the chance to work as independent contractors, or they work for software firms that understand their personality types.

In addition, many software companies have outsourced programming operations to lower-cost countries or cheaper areas of the United States.

If your firm creates solutions that involve writing computer software, it's very likely that you will subcontract out some or all of this development to a software firm or outside programming team to do the work, and then build in this cost when you invoice your customer.

Professional Services

Many professional service firms have discovered the revenue-generating potential of outsourcing their own work. It's very possible that the services you're paying your accountant or lawyer to perform have been outsourced to someone else. Do you care?

Some professional service firms (such as accountants, engineers, and lawyers) have seasonal or unreliable revenue streams. For example, many accountants are busy during tax season, but experience a significant slowdown during the rest of the year.

Rather than paying the wages of a full-time employee, accountants have discovered that contracting out services to independent people working from home solves a problem for the firm, its clients, and its people. The firm pays for qualified services only when needed. The contractors get to do work on their schedule and make extra money (and keep their skills sharp). The clients pay these bills to get their tax return done on time.

Stay Alert!

When outsourcing professional services, especially legal services, consider ethical ramifications. These are more fully discussed in Chapter 23.

How Creative Minds Can Turn a Profit for You

If you're like me and don't have an artistic bone in your body, there are lots of ways to mutually profit with our artistic friends.

Graphic Design

Stephanie, the marketing manager at a large children's clothing company, was tasked with an overhaul of the company's corporate image. Everything from their website to their stationary and the corporate logo would be redone to reflect the brighter colors and different tastes of kids today. She hired a consulting firm to help her shape this image, and the consulting firm turned around and contracted out the design of the new image to an independent graphic artist. Stephanie never met the artist. She worked entirely through the consultants she hired. But the consultants would have never passed first base without being able to provide Stephanie with the sample designs and drawings created by their contractor.

Graphic design work is an art form much in demand. Printers, publishers, technical writers, and marketing departments frequently seek out independent artists to help them express on paper the images they have in their minds. These artisans combine technical skills with their creativity, relying on complex software on high-powered computers to generate their artwork.

Art

Many artists are not so starving. They're part of corporate America. Casey Chapman Corporation sells thousands of empty containers and tins to companies who then fill them with cookies, candies, and other goodies to be sold during the holidays. The appeal of these items is in their beautiful artwork: scenes of eighteenth-century sleds, laughing children, snowfall over small villages, and old St. Nick delivering his gifts.

Yet the people at Casey Chapman could barely finger paint, let alone create the beautiful artwork they put on their tins every year. They outsource this work to artists, paying them a nominal fee and then a percentage of the sales on their tin design. With-out these artists there would be no Casey Chapman Corporation.

Many companies make money from the efforts of subcontracted artists. Greeting cards, website designers, magazine and book publishers, and coffee mug manufacturers are but a few. Many painters and sculptors would never dream of working full-time for a company. They do a lot of this corporate work on the side, as a means of making a living while they create their next masterpiece. They're a great revenue source for a lot of us who flunked art in high school, but got our Bachelor's degrees in business.

Photography

The outsourced creative world doesn't stop with painting and sculpting. Photographers are in on the action, too.

Mulligan Brothers, a family-owned publisher based on Long Island, specializes in printing annual reports for public companies. Whenever they need to include photographs in the reports, they've got a list of independent photographers available to do the job.

> **Knowledge Is Power**
>
> Freelance photographers generally get paid for each photo accepted; others get paid a project fee, no matter what photos are ultimately used in the finished product.

It's rare to find photographers on-staff, unless your company is in the media business. Even if you're in the media business, such as newspaper publishing, businesses often purchase photos from freelancers rather than hire photographers—just ask Spider-Man, I mean Peter Parker!

Writing

Former President Clinton's autobiography was big business for his publisher. At $21 a copy for the hardback edition, book sales grossed more than $20 million, with paperback, audio, and international sales adding to the pot. It's no secret that Mr. Clinton didn't write the book by himself—he had an independent writer help him.

Politicians hire speechwriters all the time. Magazines pay freelance writers for their content. Book publishers cut checks to writers to write a book on specifications they provide with no future royalties or ownership rights. These same publishers farm out editing to independent contractors, too. And their readers pay for the services.

The Least You Need to Know

- Outsourcing marketing tasks can help your sales team with lead generation and marketing awareness.

- A well-run outsourced sales program can include independent reps, resellers, or distributors.

- IT outsourcing is one of the most popular ways technical firms generate service revenue.

- Many professional service firms have realized the potential of outsourcing some of their work and then billing for the time.

- Artists don't need to starve, especially considering the many opportunities to outsource their creativity to corporations that need the help.

Reducing Costs by Outsourcing

In This Chapter

◆ The kinds of administrative expenses that are outsourced

◆ Examples of outsourced professional services

◆ Using non-employees to help run your business

◆ Options for contracting out your manufacturing and operations

◆ Making use of outside business consultants

Tony, the chief financial officer at the Friendly Community Credit Union, was getting a little antsy. The credit union provided their members with low-cost loans, inexpensive credit cards, and other incentives. Unfortunately, there was a problem. Some of the members weren't paying their bills on time, especially their credit card bills.

"I have to do something to reduce this delinquency rate, and fast." Tony thought to himself. "I could add someone to do collection work, but my budget won't allow a full-time person."

It was about that time that Tony received a letter from CAA Collection Services offering their services on a contract basis. After only a few meetings, he decided to outsource his collection process.

Within six months, CAA had succeeded in bringing Friendly's delinquency ratio down to below the industry average. And it did so without upsetting its members or costing the organization an excessive amount. He reduced his collection costs and increased cash flow.

Tony was extremely pleased with the results.

The previous chapter discussed the many ways you can increase your revenue and make more money from outsourced help. Now we're going to turn to the other side of the income statement. In this chapter, we explore the various ways that outsourcing can help you reduce your expenses.

Outsourcing Your Administrative Overhead

Take a look around your office and you will be hard pressed to find something that can't be outsourced. Office tasks are generally repetitive, mundane, and a nuisance. Yet ironically, this work can be the most critical to any organization. Let's face it, you've got a major headache if an invoice doesn't get sent to a customer or if employees don't get paid on time. Lost revenues and unproductive employees will result in lost productivity.

Let's look at some of the more common administrative tasks that you can outsource.

Payroll

You're spending too much time calculating weekly pay. You can't keep up with the changes in payroll tax rates. Your withholding payment to the IRS was accidentally made a day late, generating an avalanche of notices that required responses. You're not comfortable filling out those monthly and quarterly payroll tax returns. Your employees' health insurance premiums aren't properly deducted. Your software program crashes, losing a month of data. You can solve all of these problems by contracting with an outside payroll company.

After you hire an outside payroll company, you, too, will experience the joys of placing a single phone call (some companies let you do this online), reading out the hours, and any changes in deductions and, like magic, receiving your completed payroll at your doorstep the very next day. And it will be accurate, too! You'll be paying a flat fee, even if the company makes mistakes or takes longer than usual to finish the task, so that should keep your costs under control. Best yet: you can forward any of those nasty little letters from the IRS (usually *their* miscues) to the payroll company to deal with.

Stay Alert!

Privacy and security issues abound when outsourcing payroll services. Make sure that your employee data cannot be taken by other employees. Make sure that your payroll service company is bonded for their own employees' mistakes. If you give permission for the service company to automatically withdraw money from your account, set up a separate payroll account and only fund it with the exact amount required.

Bookkeeping

Someone's got to do the books. Many small businesses, and even divisions of larger companies, rely on outsourced bookkeepers and bookkeeping firms to keep their ledgers in shape. Most get paid by the hour or by monthly fee and do not incur enough time in the month to be considered anything near a full-time employee.

With the technology available today, an outside bookkeeping firm can remotely connect to your computer and print out checks, invoices, and even update your general ledger. The advantages are large: someone to accomplish this necessary evil without incurring payroll and other employee benefits costs.

A full-time bookkeeper may cost you $25,000 per year plus benefits. But an outsourced bookkeeping firm, with a trained staff and process in place, may be able to perform the same tasks for you for $1,000 per month.

Office Space

Can't afford a high lease payment, or a full-time receptionist, copy machine, conference facilities, cleaning services, or a kitchen for your employees? Outsource it!

If you don't mind sharing certain basic office features with other companies, outsourcing your office might be right for you. Sometimes known as *incubators*, common office facilities

Business Buzzwords

An **incubator** is an organization designed to assist start-up companies, generally with respect to providing shared office space, office services, knowledge, and technical assistance.

have become extremely popular around the country, especially for start-up companies and those of us who want to keep our overhead as low as possible. Because so many expenses are outsourced and shared, the overall cost of renting office space from an incubator is lower than the typical lease.

Human Resources/Benefits

I dare you to take a basic human resources training course and not walk away feeling intimidated. In the regulatory world in which we live, you may not be surprised to find out that even a simple little employee savings plan requires periodic discrimination tests, tax filings, and communications with participants. Failure to fulfill any of these requirements could put you in a heap of trouble.

You could hire someone to do this. But thank goodness, this stuff can be outsourced. As with most things, when there's a demand, there's a solution. And over the past 10 years there's been a proliferation of firms that will assume responsibility for administering everything from your employees' long-term disability payments to vacation plans. Outside benefits administrators will even track sick days, employee performances, and safety procedures in your factory for you.

Answering Services

Is it really necessary to have a full-time receptionist just to answer the phone? It's so easy nowadays to outsource this function, merely by rerouting phone calls to an independent answering service. Quite a few professional service firms, particularly in health care, take advantage of these services.

Many managers agree that outsourcing the receptionist duties to an answering service is a good way to reduce administrative costs and improve customer services. No matter when a customer calls, they'll get a live person on the other line. If your company provides round-the-clock service, outsourcing your receptionist duties may be a no-brainer.

Outsourcing Insights

Instead of outsourcing your answering service, you can outsource your voicemail so that any calls are answered automatically and forwarded to a number you provide. Many voicemail service providers can either notify you of a new call or route the call your way.

Data Entry

My sister, a doctor, has a small family medical practice in town. Depending on the workload, her little practice might generate a few hundred invoices a week. She could hire someone internally to do data entry, but it's not an easy job. So she decided to outsource this work to a data entry firm specializing in medical billing.

Every day she overnights her paperwork to her data entry firm and, within 24 hours, the bills have been entered accurately and sent on to the insurers for payment. Outsourcing her data entry allows her to focus more time on helping her patients and less time on administration.

By outsourcing, my sister avoids the costs of employee turnover plus additional training costs she would incur to get new employees up to speed on the system.

Temporary Firms

Temporary firms provide workers who can perform tasks such as filing, answering the phones, preparing bank reconciliations, or helping with a big direct mail campaign. Sometimes you have enough of this work to keep employees busy full-time. But often such work is sporadic enough that many companies farm it out to temporary office firms.

Some companies use temp firms in a pinch, others consider temp staffing a part of their organization. Expect to pay $10 to $30 dollars an hour, depending on where you live and what kind of work you need. In return, you'll save on employee costs and have extra hands available when you need them.

Collections

Need help getting paid? You can always outsource to a credit and collection company, which will gladly call your delinquent customers and keep 25 to 40 percent of what they collect.

Another type of outsourced collection service is called *factoring*. When you factor a receivable, the collection service pays you for it immediately, less a discount (their commission). The

Business Buzzwords

Factoring is the purchasing of accounts receivable from a business by a person or company who assumes the risk of loss in return for an agreed-upon discount.

factoring company then takes on all of the collection headaches. Factoring is a great way to outsource your cash collection process and get paid right up front. Depending on your volume and your internal resources, you might want to consider outsourcing this part of your sales process.

Word Processing

Not a great typist, but have a lot of typing to do? You don't have to hire someone. You can outsource this chore, too.

Companies that need lots of typing done quickly and don't have anyone in-house for the job rely on contracted word processors. Even if they have people in-house, it could be costly to take them off of other tasks to devote time to typing; plus, customer service or other support could falter.

One independent word processor I know does work for a manufacturer that needs to create product documentation, a pharmaceutical company that prepares huge regulatory filings, and a website designer who needs help typing up content, among others.

Drivers

When you're an executive, you get the perks. Like someone to drive you places.

Maybe you're running a company located in the middle of a big city and have to attend meetings and conferences all over town. Your company may decide to contract with a driving service to shuttle you and other execs around so you don't have to worry about catching taxis or dealing with public transportation.

Of course, your company could just hire someone full-time to do this, but you would then have to incur the expense of maintaining an automobile, as well as insurance and other costs. A limo firm distributes these costs among all of its customers, so you're only paying a portion of what you would have to pay if you owned your own limo.

Food

Many larger companies have employee dining facilities. The justification for this expense is to provide its employees with great meals at a subsidized cost and to keep them on the premises so they can get back to the grindstone as soon as possible. Rarely does a company run this kind of operation itself. Instead, they contract out the entire food service to a catering company that specializes in feeding large groups of people on a recurring basis.

Even if you run a small company, you may want to consider contracting out some type of food service. Many companies provide their employees with free gourmet coffee from a weekly service that stocks an automatic coffee-making machine, which makes delicious individual cups. This avoids those "who drank the last cup" arguments over the old coffee maker, as well as the not-so-enticing chore of scraping off the black bits inside the burned coffeepot.

Stay Alert! _____

Preparing and selling food on a recurring basis to your employees may subject you to state and federal regulations. It's best to hire a service firm that has fulfilled these requirements.

This way the job gets done the right way, by people who know what they're doing. Plus, a lot of catering companies can purchase food and other supplies at a discounted rate, and may pass the savings along to you. And just think of what you'll save by not having to rush your employees to the hospital because of a bad cup of coffee!

The Right Professionals for the Job

The largest companies in the world sometimes perform their own legal work, prepare and sign their own tax returns, negotiate insurance coverage directly with underwriters, and have in-house technical and creative staffs to test and document products and processes. Then there are the rest of us, who need to outsource all of these professional functions.

The following sections outline typical professional services that most companies outsource.

Legal

Outsourcing general legal work is very commonplace. Even larger companies find themselves turning to external law firms to handle matters such as immigration, employment law, and intellectual property matters, and to defend themselves against high-profile cases and class-action lawsuits.

Outsourcing legal counsel makes sense for the business owner or manager who wants a legal advisor on call for issues that come up but who doesn't need to hire a full-time attorney. Even a lower-level attorney on-staff could cost more than $150,000 per year. Retaining a legal firm enables you to make use of a highly experienced attorney's services for a fraction of the cost.

Tax Preparation and Accounting

No one can be an expert at taxes unless they devote themselves full-time to the practice. Most of us would rather let the experts deal with this necessity. Plus we may get some good tax savings advice from someone with experience.

Writing and Editing

Did you know that the book you're reading right now has been reviewed by an outsourced editor? Found any glitches yet? You probably won't! Outsourcing the editing process has become a standard publishing industry practice that helps keep costs low.

Outsourced writers make their mark everywhere. For example, the owner's manual of that new car you just bought was probably written by an outsourced technical writing firm. The instructions for that washer you bought a couple of years ago was probably delegated to an independent writer to prepare.

If you need to create manuals, brochures, technical materials, presentations, or other written correspondence, and you don't have the expertise in-house to do this, you'll want to outsource this work to someone capable. By hiring writers on a freelance basis, you'll avoid having to pay to keep a writer on-staff.

> **Outsourcing Insights**
>
> A great place to find a freelance writer is the National Writers Union (www.nwu.org). The NWU is a trade union that not only serves the freelance writer community but also maintains a great job site for contracted projects.

Engineering

If you're building a new office building and you hire a general contractor to oversee the project, don't be surprised to find yourself working with their outsourced mechanical and electrical engineers during the process. Or if you're in the oil business you're probably used to working with many chemical engineers, both companies and independents who contract themselves out to larger firms.

Businesses also hire independent engineers to produce architectural plans, computer-aided design drawings, operations research, and integrated circuit designs. Some larger companies may employ these kinds of professionals, but because the subject matter can be so complex (and sometimes overwhelming), outsourcing some or all of this knowledge can save costs by getting the right experts for exactly the right job.

Hiring Non-Employees to Help Run the Business

The trend toward outsourcing has affected management itself. If you're a venture capital firm or an investment company, do you want to shell out hundreds of thousands of dollars (or the equivalent in stock) to fund a management team for a risky venture? Maybe it's more cost effective to bring in people as needed, and only fill the job with full-time people after you're assured of a revenue stream.

It's as if everything is potentially outsourceable, including company management! Although some people joke that one day the president of the United States will outsource his own job, there are many valid reasons for outsourcing certain senior management jobs, at least for the short term. Here are a few typical management responsibilities that companies sometimes choose to farm out.

> **Outsourcing Insights**
>
> Many start-ups can't afford to put a full management team in place. They look to outsourcing firms to provide them with financial managers and other specialists on an interim basis. If you're in a similar situation, ask your venture capitalists or outside investors for recommendations. Anyone with investing experience has probably worked with outsourced management firms before.

Chief Financial Officer/Controller

It's very common for companies, particularly start-up firms, to hire chief financial officers (CFO) and controllers on an outsourced basis. That's because investors may be reluctant to spend the extra money on full-time financial management when they aren't even turning a profit yet. Plus, many outsourced CFOs and controllers specialize in start-up work. Their job would be through once the firm grows to the point of hiring someone full-time.

You don't have to be a start-up firm to enjoy the benefits of an outsourced CFO or controller, however. It might be less expensive to pay for the service on an as-needed basis.

So if you start thinking that bringing on a CFO or controller might help your business, you may want to consider first outsourcing the job and seeing what kind of benefit you receive!

CIO

Most larger enterprises have a chief information office (CIO)—someone who sets and implements the technology direction of the firm. Many other companies have also tried to bring CIOs into their organization. Except they really don't perform the function of a CIO. Instead they are relegated to fixing computers and dealing with network problems instead of providing strategic technical direction.

> **Stay Alert!**
>
> When considering hiring or contracting with a chief information officer, make sure you understand the differences between a technology executive, who charts the course of a company's technology, and a technology manager, who implements and supports chosen technology.

A real CIO shouldn't do this. Often an offshoot consulting service provided by technology companies, the outsourced CIO won't fix your mouse, isn't going to call up technical support for you, and may not even know how to set up a simple Microsoft network. But he or she will be well versed in the technology to help you make sure you're spending the least amount of money on the most productive tools. You'll be kept current on major trends in technology and up to date on what applications and hardware others in the industry might be using to their advantage.

Other Management Responsibilities

You may already have a full-time financial or technical person, but you might still have gaps in other management areas. Here are a few tasks that are typically performed by a company's management, which you might contract out when resources are tight:

♦ **Recruiting.** A good search firm acts as your agent in the recruiting process. The firm will prepare the right solicitations, do all of the prescreening and prequalification that you don't have the time (or the experience) to do, and present to you a handful of the best candidates. In return, they'll ask for about a third of the candidate's first year salary if you hire their candidate. Many of these firms work on a contingency basis only, so if they don't find the right person for the job, they don't get paid.

♦ **Project management.** An outsourced project manager can take ownership of a project and ensure that everything gets set up, people are trained, and questions are answered. Their fees can be tied to accomplishing certain agreed-upon deliverables. Outsourcing project management when you don't have the internal people to do the work may help you get the project done on time and within budget.

◆ **Technical and regulatory affairs.**
Larger companies maintain internal regulatory staff to deal with the forms, questions, filings, and documentation that federal, state, and local government, or businesses that work with those governments, require. Smaller companies often outsource this job to consulting firms, lobbyists, and technical independents to help them.

Stay Alert!

One of the biggest mistakes managers make when outsourcing project management is not giving their project managers the authority they need to succeed. Make sure this doesn't happen on your project.

Contracting Out Your Manufacturing and Operations

Many companies are learning that just because they can come up with a good product idea doesn't mean that they can actually produce the product. Or at least make it efficiently. They look to the outside for people to take care of certain operational tasks.

Contract Manufacturing

If you dig a bit, you'll find instances of outsourced manufacturing just about everywhere. IBM has its Thinkpad computers made by another company overseas and then puts the IBM label on it. The Gap employs many dozens of other companies to make its garments and then sells them as Gap items. Random House contracts with outside printers to produce its latest bestseller. Companies that produce goods for other companies are called *original equipment manufacturers (OEM)*, and the process is quite commonplace.

How does outsourcing your manufacturing save costs? How about avoiding the purchase of expensive and specialized equipment, renting space, and maintaining a manufacturing facility complete with laborers, systems, and overheads!

Business Buzzwords

An **original equipment manufacturer (OEM)** is a company that purchases equipment or products from other manufacturers, adds something of value (it can be as simple as their own label), and then resells the items under their own name.

Contracting out one's manufacturing comes with significant risk. A souring of relationships, mismanagement at the manufacturer, noncompliance with existing or new regulations—all of these factors could bring your operations to an unexpected halt, or even put your company out of business. OEM is a good model for certain types of business, but it's also a perilous one, so be careful!

QA/QC

Do you manufacture products that require quality assurance and control (QA/QC) before shipping out to customers? You can hire the appropriate people to do this work for you. Or you can send these products out to an independent firm that will do quality testing before sending the products to your customers. Just like contracting out manufacturing, you'll save the costs of building a QA/QC facility, plus you'll be using firms with more expertise at doing this kind of work.

Inventory

Many companies choose to outsource their inventory management. Firms that import wine, cheese, food products, controlled substances, or live animals have very specialized warehousing needs that they can't afford to build and maintain. Many more companies just simply don't have the space to store their products or the people and systems required to manage the ins and outs. This is where outsourced warehouses come in. Rather than buying more space or renting another warehouse, you can arrange for your product to be sent to a warehousing company that will track everything for you, from receipt to shipment.

A good example is the relationship between Wal-Mart and some of its largest suppliers, including Proctor and Gamble. Using technology called RFID (Radio Frequency ID), P&G can manage its own inventory on Wal-Mart's shelves remotely, notifying its customer when product is needed or should be returned. By outsourcing this inventory management, Wal-Mart is saving its own internal supervision costs.

> **CAUTION**
>
> **Stay Alert!**
>
> Just because an outsourcer has inventory space available doesn't mean they're good at inventory management. Look for companies that specialize in inventory management, and make sure they have the right systems for accurately tracking your products.

Laboratory and Outside Testing

Have your blood drawn at the local hospital and there's a good chance that it will be sent to an outside firm for diagnostic work. Return a malfunctioning computer component to the manufacturer and it'll probably be sent out to someone else for repair. Software companies such as Microsoft employ thousands of independents to try and "break" their code. Outsourced testing facilities is a big business because the work is specialized, repetitive, and can be done independent of most operations.

Shipping and Transport

You're going to need to get your products to your customers somehow. But it's pretty expensive to buy and maintain trucks, let alone employ your own drivers to do this work.

Because of this, many companies have found it cheaper to outsource shipping and transport. These companies are also oftentimes reluctant to take on the administrative and regulatory burdens of maintaining their own transportation fleet and instead find it more effective to outsource this job to someone more experienced in the field.

Outside shipping companies keep specialized refrigerated rigs for food, caged facilities for livestock, and specialized containers for hazardous materials. They employ drivers experienced in handling these types of items. They're familiar with the challenges of negotiating high-traffic areas, fuel usage, and customers' changing demands.

Trash Removal and Cleaning

Waste material is typically a byproduct of manufacturing processes. Because this material may be slightly more hazardous than most common household items, it may need to be disposed of in a specially assigned landfill. The cost of transport, the regulatory paperwork, and the potential liability of incorrect disposal may be enough to convince you to outsource this job to a waste-management firm.

Most of us outsource our trash removal. Be it the contracted person who empties the trash at

Stay Alert!

Even if you outsource trash removal to a waste-management firm, you are still liable for hazardous materials in your waste. Take the extra steps to make sure your outsourced waste-removal company is disposing of your waste in approved locations.

night to the large-scale scrap removal of an imploded building, we realize that some things, especially trash, are best left to someone else!

Security

Does your company need security? You could hire someone to provide the services. But you don't know the first thing to look for in a security guard. And even if you did manage to find the right person, what kind of pay would be needed? And what happens if he calls in sick for the night—who takes his place?

It could be much more cost effective to outsource security to a company that knows what they're doing. In addition to providing the necessary off-hours manpower, their consultants can also advise you as to what additional actions are needed to really lock up your place. Outside security experts can help you choose a good alarm system and tell you where you might need extra locks on doors and windows, and where to install video surveillance of your more exposed areas.

Facilities Management and Repairs

A client of mine recently purchased their first building, a 50,000-square-foot structure in excellent condition and located near the highway. My client didn't budget to hire a facilities manager, but they needed one badly. Luckily, they outsourced this work to a small contractor who specialized in daily repairs for commercial enterprises. He came to fix problems when called at his hourly rate of $50 and saved them from bringing on someone full-time (at an annual salary of $50,000) for work that only occurred sporadically.

Another company I know had a different story to tell. A large conglomerate, the company owned dozens of manufacturing, administrative, and warehousing facilities around the country. Instead of hiring, training, and supervising facilities people at each location, the company outsourced their facilities management to a third party who provided the monitoring and manpower needed.

Using the Best Business Consultants

Let's face it: you're not an expert at everything and never will be. No matter how many people you manage, or how large your company is, you're going to encounter issues so specialized that you're going to need to employ an outside consultant to help. What an independent consultant brings to the table, hopefully, is years of experience with a varied list of other companies who have tread the same path that you're about to tread. Plus, that same consultant may help you operate more profitably by offering advice and guidance on a number of business issues.

Here are a few areas where you may find yourself outsourcing this kind of expertise.

Stay Alert!

Many consultants are hired for one-off projects, whereas many others stay on for long-term engagements. Make sure your contracts spell out the term of your project and specifically address how your consulting arrangement will end.

Planning

Writing a business plan isn't something you do every day. Coming up with a detailed map to launch a new product line may only happen a couple of times during your career. Fitting out a manufacturing facility to be able to handle production at different volumes takes a considerable amount of foresight. Many managers don't feel comfortable tackling these responsibilities alone, so they bring in outsiders to help. These outsiders help them make the best profit-making decisions possible.

Business planning experts will assume responsibility for thinking through and coming up with solutions to planning-related problems. By outsourcing the writing of a business, product, or technical plan, a manager can spend time hiring others to perform additional functions or negotiating office space for the new venture. A product manager may be comfortable implementing a launch plan as long as the nuts and bolts of the plan are outsourced to someone else.

Business-Process and Management Consulting

A *business-process* consultant can make a major impact on the way an organization does business.

Not all of us can afford to keep business-process specialists on the payroll full-time. Yet I can't name a single customer who wouldn't love for an experienced outsider to come in and make solid recommendations for improving their operations. Companies that realize they need this kind of help usually agree

Business Buzzwords

A **business process** is a collection of related structural activities that produce a specific outcome for a particular customer.

that it's best to outsource this role to someone without any relationship to the company. A business-process consultant is then retained perhaps on a short-term basis to look at a specific sore spot, or for the long term to review, recommend, and (most important) implement changes across the company.

Special Projects

Special outsourcing projects that come up periodically require outside consultants. Three of these types of projects are Sarbanes-Oxley, ISO 9000/9001, and Six Sigma:

- **Sarbanes-Oxley**—In the wake of the Enron and WorldCom scandals, Congress enacted the Sarbanes-Oxley legislation. This law requires public companies, and people doing certain types of business with public companies, to document the flow of transactions, both financial and nonfinancial, with their customers, suppliers, and employees. The legislation is thick with requirements and, as you can imagine, there's a significant amount of complexity. Just about every public company that needed to be in compliance with these rules had to outsource this compliance work with independent consultants.

- **ISO certifications**—ISO 9000/9001 is a series of standards developed by the International Organization for Standardization, or ISO. These standards define quality for manufacturing and service industries and cover everything from management to systems to resource requirements within an organization. Typical issues that must be addressed include defining your organization's quality processes, controlling your company's quality documents, and providing the needed infrastructure of satisfactory quality control.

Outsourcing Insights

You don't necessarily need to hire a consultant to get a Six Sigma or other certifications. There is an industry of training companies, books, and other resources to help you do it yourself if you choose.

- **Six Sigma**—Six Sigma is an American-based quality concept. Although I've rarely seen businesses requiring that their customers or vendors be Six Sigma–certified, like ISO, I often run into this type of quality culture at larger organizations that constantly try to improve themselves. If you're interested in implement-ing the Six Sigma concepts into your quality process, you're probably going to need to outsource some of these tasks to someone with experience.

The Least You Need to Know

- Administrative costs are one of the first things managers look to reduce.

- Commonly outsourced administrative processes include office space, human resources administration, answering services, data entry and word processing, temp workers, collection work, transportation, and food.

- Although large corporations can typically handle most legal, accounting, insurance, writing, and engineering responsibilities in-house, most companies need to outsource this expertise.

- There's been a significant trend toward outsourcing many management responsibilities.

- To cut costs, many companies find themselves contracting out such key operating processes as manufacturing, quality control, shipping, and testing.

- No matter the size of your company, you're most likely going to need to outsource special projects to independent consultants at some time.

Avoiding Common Outsourcing Mistakes

In This Chapter

◆ Errors to watch out for early on in the outsourcing relationship

◆ Problems that can occur in the midst of an outsourcing project

◆ How lack of measurements can turn a good relationship sour

◆ Tips for avoiding some of the more common outsourcing mistakes

Bill received a call from Gary, his company's corporate controller. Gary had some questions about a recent project where Bill had outsourced some legal work.

"Bill," Gary began, "I've got a purchase order here for $5,000 in legal work, but I've got over $20,000 in invoices from this firm. What's up?"

"Well," Bill said, clearing his throat. "Things got a little out of hand."

"Out of hand?" Gary inquired, his voice rising.

"The attorneys had to do more filings than planned. I wasn't thrilled with the competence of some of their work and made them do it over."

"So you outsourced this work to a legal firm and they took four times as many hours as estimated?" Gary asked incredulously. "Why didn't you stop them earlier?"

"Well," said Bill sheepishly. "By the time I saw the hours running up we were too far into the project, so I had no choice but to let them finish."

"Geez, Bill," Gary whistled. "This is a problem. A big problem."

Bill clearly made a few mistakes on this outsourcing project. But sometimes only a few mistakes spell big financial trouble for a company. In this chapter, I discuss some of the more common mistakes people make when outsourcing work and suggest some ways you can avoid those mistakes.

Mistakes Before the Project

Before you begin an outsourcing project, you need to think about a lot of potential issues. Without the right planning or a clear definition of the task, you could be heading for trouble.

You Do Not Clearly Define the Problem

Many people make the mistake of outsourcing work to a service provider without clearly describing the project. Defining the problem to be resolved or the task to be accomplished is the first step toward finding the right solution. If the service provider doesn't know what they are being hired to do, how can you expect them to do it?

If you're going to hire a developer to create a computer application for you, you must clearly state what you want the program to do. If you decide to farm out the writing of a sales brochure to a marketing firm, make sure both parties agree on what the final document's message and target audience will be. Creating an outsourced service desk in another country? Make sure everyone agrees on the unit's responsibilities before heading down that road.

It's critical to create a bulleted list of "deliverables" you expect from the project. Keep them short, simple, and reasonable. Review this list face to face with your outside service provider, and have them sign off on this list. Make sure to refer back to this list frequently during the course of the project.

You Fail to Plan

I've seen clients outsource entire processes to outside firms without spending more than a few minutes planning out how it's all going to work. These projects usually end in failure. If you don't spend the necessary time planning your outsourcing projects, you're destined to fail, too.

Outsourcing Insights

When entering into an outsourcing relationship, don't forget about the hidden costs. Expenses such as travel, tools, supplies, and even insurance can unexpectedly add to your estimates.

Suppose you decide to outsource your inventory management to another warehouse. Among the many questions you need to consider are the following:

- How will this transition occur?

- How will you notify your shippers?

- Will the shippers have to change their procedures?

- Is the warehouse organized to handle requests directly from your customers as well as your own customer service department?

Whether you're outsourcing your inventory management, payroll, or an internal quality control process, take the time to make a plan. Consider all people who will be affected and what their needs will be. Look at the calendar and make sure the right people will be around when the project occurs. Write out a step-by-step checklist for implementing the plan. Have others involved review it, and then get key management's sign-off. Finally, make sure your service provider agrees to the plan.

You Don't Check Out the Service Provider

When you're having a problem, it's easy to contract with the first person who appears with a solution. Unfortunately, if you don't do your due diligence (see Chapter 13) when choosing an outsourcer, you could wind up getting burned.

Among the questions you should ask are the following:

- Is the provider financially stable?

- Is he or she competent?

- Do they have sound internal systems themselves?

Outsourcing Insights

Web-based services such as Knowx.com and Intelius.com perform "background checks" of individuals and companies by searching public records. You might consider using them to check out people and companies you're considering doing business with. A typical search costs between $50 and $100 and can provide you with information about any liens, lawsuits, and other public filings.

◆ How deep are their resources (their staff, administrative support, technical knowledge, etc)?

◆ Do they have good clients who will attest to the quality of their work?

◆ Do they have an acceptable credit rating?

◆ Are they involved in any litigation?

How do you find out this information? Start with the contractor's references. Review examples of work they've done for other companies. Ask a lot of questions. You're probably going to be relying pretty heavily on this person or firm, so it's worth spending a little time, money, and effort investigating them. (I suggest more ways to check out a potential outsourcing provider in Chapter 13.)

You Wrongly Estimate the Cost and Complexity

Another mistake people make is to think that an outsourced project will be quick and easy. I don't think I've ever been involved in an outsourced project that was ever quick or easy! There always seem to be complicating factors. It always takes longer than you think it will.

New software applications have bugs and errors and need to be properly tested. The office refurbishment will be disruptive and may uncover structural problems. Your trucking company will run into traffic issues and problems locating drivers. Have you prepared yourself for these kinds of headaches?

Think of as many worst-case scenarios as you can. Ask others to think of things that could go wrong. Build in cushions for time and expense.

You Don't Identify All the Risks

An outside bookkeeper could potentially steal your money. An outsourced regulatory affairs consultant could ruin the chances of your new product being approved by forgetting to fill out a key form. The hired driver who is driving your execs around town may have had a few too many drinks at lunch.

These are all risks that you take when you farm out a responsibility to someone outside your direct control. Your failure to identify and plan your response to these risks in advance could leave your outsourcing arrangement—and your project—in shambles. If you're not sure of all the risks, talk to someone who's outsourced a similar job before. Look on the Internet. Ask the service provider's references directly. When you think you've identified all the risks, make sure you're prepared to address each one.

You Don't Have a Backup Plan

After you've identified all of the things that could go wrong in an outsourcing project, make sure you've got a Plan B ready to go … just in case.

If your payroll service isn't working out, make sure you've got another payroll service in the wings. If your outsourced human resources firm isn't performing up to your satisfaction, be ready to switch these services to another firm. If you're generating revenues from billing out independent contractors and one contractor does less-than-satisfactory work, be prepared to replace him.

> **Outsourcing Insights**
>
> Always interview more than one potential service provider, and then save the information about the providers you don't hire. You may need to call on them if your first choice doesn't work out.

Your outsourcing arrangements can fail if you don't prepare for contingencies. Ask yourself, "If this goes wrong, what's my alternative?" Have this second solution in place and you'll sleep better.

You Didn't Get It in Writing

Don't make the mistake of not having a contract with your service provider. A good outsourcing contract will not only protect both parties legally, it will also spell out exactly what's expected from both of you. Negotiating a contract also gives you a chance to iron out all details before leaping in.

Chapter 21 discusses contract issues in greater detail.

Mistakes During the Project

You've thought out your relationship, even done the necessary planning and due diligence. But even the best-laid plans can go haywire. Here are a few mistakes you'll want to be sure to avoid when your project is in the hands of your outsourcer.

Not Investing Enough Resources

Don't make the mistake of thinking that just because you outsourced a job it will require no additional commitment of your resources or time.

> **CAUTION**
> **Stay Alert!**
> It's never easy to bring an outsider into your company, especially if they have to work with sensitive information to get their job done. You should always have outside help sign a nondisclosure agreement, commonly referred to as an NDA. An NDA will legally protect you if you suspect a contractor is stealing sensitive information.

Someone's going to have to be the main contact with the service provider. The service provider may need special access, security codes, and authority to complete their task. They might need to consult with other people in your company or even need some of your employees to pitch in and help on the project. Service providers must be given access to anyone who can help them with their tasks. They need to be able to operate as freely as you can allow.

Not giving your service provider enough resources to get the job done is a recipe for failure.

Paying for Nothing

Many people make the mistake of entering into outsourcing relationships that pay by the hour, without any ties to performance. Without checks in place, it's all too easy for a contractor to accumulate a couple of hundred hours of work, with nothing to show for it.

Do your customers pay you if you never shipped them their order? Do you get paid if you haven't done the job you were hired to do? Probably not. The same principal should apply to your outside service provider.

Arrange for your service provider to be compensated on the completion of agreed-on deliverables. Make him or her take responsibility for the end result. Don't make the mistake of just writing checks without any guarantee of getting the job done. Payment for services is usually understood to be acceptance of those services.

Failing to Factor in Productivity Losses

Sure, it may be attractive to move that call center out of your office to a low-cost part of the country or even overseas. Wages can be significantly lower. So are rents and other operating expenses. On paper, it seems like a no-brainer: the costs savings could be substantial.

But don't forget that when outsourcing, just looking at cost savings can be a mistake. That low-cost part of the world may also come with an uneducated work force, or people who speak a different language, or with a noticeable accent that makes communication difficult. Basic service calls that took 5 minutes to answer might now take 25 minutes. This can not only upset the customers who need things done quickly but also other customers in the queue.

Never outsource on just cost savings alone. Make sure you consider productivity factors, too. Compare the people at the proposed location to the people at your current location. Determine whether your outsourced solution will impact your current productivity levels.

> **Outsourcing Insights**
>
> According to a recent survey, language barriers are one of the biggest impediments to outsourcing overseas. Customers have shown themselves to be very sensitive to service reps whose speech is noticeably accented. Some firms invest heavily in language and diction training to make their workers more "Americanized."

Not Respecting the Service Provider

Unfortunately, many businesses make the mistake of treating their outsourced help as second-class citizens. Blaming the consultant when things go wrong is the easy way out.

But treating the service provider with little or no respect during the course of your relationship will only breed resentment and disloyalty. Abusing the "computer guy" for the latest glitch every time he walks in the door will cause him to avoid you when you need him the most. Sticking your telemarketers in an unheated back room won't motivate them to do their best work, either; neither will delaying payment to them just because you can.

Treat your service providers as well as you would treat your employees. Make sure they have the right working conditions, are paid on time, and are looked on as equals among the rest of your company. Show you're grateful every once in a while. Everyone likes to know they're appreciated. Mutual respect will go a long way.

Overlooking Cultural Differences

People in different parts of the country and from other parts of the world may not work in the same manner as you do.

There are the obvious cultural differences you'll encounter by opening up that call center in India (see Chapter 19). But outsourcing your technical support to a firm located in a small Louisiana town has its own cultural issues, too. You need to account for local holidays, a less-frenetic pace than in the Northeast, and a lot more Southern geniality. Some parts of this country have more immigrants or minorities than others, which may pose some language, cultural, and religious challenges. Other parts of the country have a more educated populace than others.

When contracting out work to a person or firm outside of your local area, don't make the mistake of thinking that they're going to be the same as the local work force. Investigate the area beforehand. Find out whether there are any cultural or educational differences that could impact the way business is done. Structure your relationship to deal with these differences. Prepare yourself to adapt how you do business.

Having Too Many Overlapping Responsibilities

Without a clear understanding of who is responsible for what, some tasks may fall through the cracks.

Who's responsible for backing up that server—the IT staff or the outside IT company? Where do responses to that direct-mail campaign go—to the inside marketing group or the marketing firm who did the campaign? Who's updating the vendor records when contact information changes—the purchasing department or the outside bookkeeper?

When duties overlap there's room for error because someone else thinks that the other guy is getting the task done. You can avoid this mistake if you get everyone together to hash out each person's responsibility. And don't forget to put everything in writing.

Lacking Management Commitment

The tone must be set from the top. So if management isn't involved in the outsourcing relationship, you're probably going to have a problem.

CAUTION **Stay Alert!**

Depending on the size of your outsourcing project, it may be necessary to have more than one manager involved. In addition to spreading the workload and responsibility, an extra manager will prove invaluable in case one of the managers leaves the company. Outsourced projects can wither without management support, especially if the original champion of the project is no longer with the company.

If management doesn't get behind an internal initiative, the initiative usually doesn't sprout wings.

Make sure that, as management, you support your outsourcing relationships. Communicate the importance of the relationship to your employees and show your involvement. Be as directly involved as you can in the project …

Too Much Micromanagement

… but don't go overboard! Too much micromanagement has also proven to be a problem in outsourcing relationships. Remember that you're hiring the outside firm to take care of a problem or job that you can't or don't want to manage in-house. You're relying on their expertise and their ability to get the job done. Micromanaging every step they take may inhibit their progress, and even ruin your relationship.

Too Little Management

Some managers make the mistake of giving too much responsibility to the outside service provider. They get romanced by their experience and knowledge and leave too much of the decision making to them. If you do this, be prepared to see the project go in an entirely different, and unwanted, direction. The service provider will still want to get paid for their efforts, and you'll have a mess to clean up.

The outside experts may talk a great game. They may really seem to know what they're doing, too. But don't make the mistake of turning over the entire project to them. It's your project, and you're responsible for its success or failure. Never forget that.

Not Enough Communications

Don't make the mistake of not communicating with your outside service provider on a regular basis. By checking in regularly, you can avoid problems before they happen, or prevent small problems from turning into big ones.

Never assume that no news is good news. Make sure you're in constant touch with your service providers as if they were your own employees. Ultimately, you're responsible for the outcome.

How should you communicate with your outsourcers? Schedule weekly meetings—either face to face or by conference call. Agree on acceptable communication methods before the relationship begins and use them. In addition, make sure your service providers can be accessed whenever or wherever you want.

Mistakes After the Project

Outsourcing relationships can turn south at their completion, too.

Lack of Measurement

If you haven't figured out how to quantify success or failure, you'll never really know how well the outsourcing relationship went. Did overdue accounts decrease by 10 percent after hiring the outside collection agency, as the outsourcer promised they would? Did payroll administration costs go down after outsourcing this function? How about your intention to generate an extra $500,000 of revenue by outsourcing an on-site service staff? Do you now have one report showing sales activities from your outsourced sales management system, or are you still wading through those 20 reports like before?

Before starting your project, you should have agreed on specific and measurable deliverables. When your project is near completion, do the numbers and see whether your outsourced service provider met those deliverables. If you plan on employing this service provider again, you can use these metrics to determine the deliverables of your next project together.

No End Game

Some managers make the mistake of never planning for the end of a larger scale project, or even life after the project. Perhaps you've become a victim of *scope creep*. When this happens, your costs continue to go up with only diminishing returns.

How will the subcontractor's knowledge be "transferred" to you? Was the project documented so that you can go back and reference technical items? Were your people given adequate training so they can run with the ball now that the project is over? What kind of relationship will you have with the service provider going forward? Who's going to be around to answer questions or provide ongoing service as needed? If you're considering outsourcing another project, when does the old one end and the new one begin?

Business Buzzwords

Scope creep is when additional changes are made to an existing project that adds to the cost and time of the project. Project managers hate scope creep because it adds to the original requirements and causes some projects to carry on without resolution.

Don't make the mistake of involving yourself in the never-ending project. Decide early on what defines the end of the project, set your dates together, and work toward that end.

The Least You Need to Know

- Common outsourcing mistakes before a project even gets underway include not defining the problem or planning out the project and underestimating costs, complexity, and risks.

- Make sure you have a good backup plan and a thorough contract in case things go awry.

- Many outsourcing projects fail because customers fail to respect the outside service provider or fail to account for regional cultural differences.

- During the project, don't skimp on resources, communicating, or management involvement.

- When your project is wrapping up, be sure to measure its success and agree on post-relationship services.

Where to Look for Outsourced Help

In This Chapter

- ◆ Planning your search
- ◆ Preparing a Request for Proposal (RFP)
- ◆ Tricks for getting outsourced help on the Internet
- ◆ Finding your solution the old-fashioned way
- ◆ Using your contacts to locate your contractor

After much thought, Melissa decided to outsource her software project instead of having the work done in-house. Now it was time to find the right person to do the job.

"This should be a snap," thought Melissa. "I need a few programmers, so I'll just jump on the web, do a few searches on Google, and get this going."

It didn't take long for Melissa to realize that finding the right software development firm wasn't going to be as easy as she thought. Typing in "software development" or "programmer" in various search engines returned hundreds of thousands of hits.

And even after identifying some viable candidates, Melissa still wasn't convinced that she was selecting the right firms. Should she send out a Request for Proposal? How do those work? And who else can she talk to?

People find their service providers from all sorts of different places. The process isn't all that different from looking for an employee, but instead of reviewing resumés, you're probably going to be reading through proposals.

No matter where you look, your first step is to make a plan.

Planning Your Search

Before you jump into your search, take the time to prepare for the next few stages of the hiring process. After you're inundated with responses, you'll be glad you planned ahead.

Prepare a Job Description or Request for Proposal (RFP)

Before you start, you should write out a complete and detailed job description or RFP (to be discussed in the next section) and have it reviewed by anyone else involved in the decision.

Consider How You Will Manage the Responses

Make sure you decide in advance how your office will handle responses to the RFP. Put someone in charge of organizing all the phone calls, resumés, crank calls, proposals, and e-mails that you will get in response to the posting.

Outsourcing Insights

Keep all resumés and proposals on file for at least one year. You may find yourself referring back to this file for help on another project.

Create a Database for Tracking Responses

Use a database to track the contact information, background experience, and qualifications of each potential service provider. Others in your company can add data as they interview the applicant or find out more information. This way you can call up information that you need quickly and even analyze the information better.

Schedule Time to Evaluate and Respond

Searching for the right outsourced solution is going to take a lot of time. Make sure you set aside enough time for doing a thorough job.

Preparing the Request for Proposal (RFP)

A critical part of looking for the right outsourced solution is preparing a Request for Proposal (RFP). RFPs are not needed in many outsourcing situations (for example, I doubt that you'll need to send an RFP to Kinko's). But depending on the project and whether you're looking for a long-term solution or help on a short-term project, a good RFP will help you and your prospective service provider nail down the project details.

Take a look at some of the ways preparing an RFP can help you:

◆ An RFP gets your thoughts in order.

◆ An RFP ensures that the proposal process is fair for all companies involved.

◆ The RFP enables both the company and the proposed outsourcer to qualify each other. If you're not a good match with your service provider, you may find yourself suffering from communication problems that result in missed deadlines, cost overruns, and inferior results.

◆ The RFP process gives everyone a chance to work together before actually committing to a project.

Outsourcing Insights

Some people think that RFPs are only for big business and government. Not true. Many smaller firms are learning that the benefits of preparing an RFP, even a simplified one, far exceed the time and effort involved.

Stay Alert!

Small outsourcers may not be familiar with the RFP process. Before sending out your RFPs, you should first contact the prospective outsourcer(s) and make sure they're ready to receive and respond to your request within your timeline.

Requesting Information Before Requesting a Proposal

Depending on the scope of your project, you may want to send out a *Request for Information (RFI)* before you send out the formal RFP. You would use an RFI if you're considering a lot of prospective service providers and you want to narrow the field.

Business Buzzwords

An **RFI (Request for Information)** is a document that is sent out in advance of an RFP. It asks for data from prospective outsourcers so that the requestor can determine if the outsourcer is qualified to receive a formal RFP.

RFIs are intended to gather data from prospective outsourcers that will help the requestor determine whether the outsourcer is qualified to receive a formal RFP. Using an RFI helps you narrow down the list of prospective outsourcing solutions for your project or task. It's a waste of everyone's time to send out RFPs to companies or individuals that are unqualified to do the work.

What Should You Include in Your RFP?

A good RFP should give the prospective service provider everything he or she needs to know to prepare their proposal. Depending on the particular task, you might need only a single page or several hundred pages to convey the information.

Obviously, the RFP needs to look professional. It should also be in a format that can be delivered via mail, fax, or e-mail. A typical RFP should include the following information:

- ◆ Your company's background
- ◆ Contact information of key management personnel at your company
- ◆ A description of the problem you need solved
- ◆ A description of deliverables you expect
- ◆ Any relevant technical information
- ◆ A clear deadline for submission
- ◆ A proposed timeline of the project
- ◆ The location of the project
- ◆ Any assumptions you're making
- ◆ Contact information for submitting proposals
- ◆ A budget for the project
- ◆ Instructions for how the service provider should organize their proposal

RFP Best Practices

An RFP is a great way to sort out the best candidates for the outsourcing job you have in mind. But just sending out an RFP isn't going to do the entire job for you. You need to put some thought into your RFP in order to get the best results.

Here are some specific best practices when sending out RFPs:

◆ **Send out RFPs well in advance of your deadline.** Many companies like to send out RFPs about six to eight weeks in advance of the submission deadline, but this may vary depending on the project. You want to give these solution providers a reasonable timeframe in which to come up with the right answers for you.

> **Outsourcing Insights**
>
> If you're mailing the document, spend the extra postage for a return receipt or use a delivery service that tracks document delivery. Or have an assistant call or send an e-mail to confirm that it was received.

◆ **Confirm receipt.** Wouldn't it be a shame if the document never reached its intended recipient? Take the extra step of making sure the potential service provider received your RFP.

◆ **Send the RFP only to people you want to work with.** It takes a lot of time and effort to appropriately evaluate responses to your RFP, so you should be selective in sending them out. Rarely should you send out more than a dozen.

◆ **Always give feedback.** Whether or not you accept the proposal, always take the time to give feedback to the outsourcer.

> **Outsourcing Insights**
>
> A good book that can help you prepare your RFP is *Request For Proposal: A Guide To Effective RFP Development* by Bud Porter-Roth and Ralph Young (Addison-Wesley Professional, 2001).

◆ **Get other examples.** Before preparing your own RFP, check out RFPs for similar projects to get ideas for how to structure your own.

The Internet: A Good Place to Start Your Search

You've planned your attack. You've prepared your RFP. It's time to begin the search!

The web can be a great tool for finding outsourced help, as long you use it effectively. Among the most useful sources on the web for finding service providers are search engines, outsourcing websites, and employment websites. Let's consider each of these sources more closely.

Outsourcing Websites

Plenty of sites specialize in putting businesses in touch with independent contractors. Some of the most popular are …

- **Guru.** www.guru.com

- **Elance.** www.elanceonline.com

- **Freelance Work Exchange.** www.freelanceworkexchange.com

All of these sites link directly to independent contractors and outsourcing firms, broken down by areas of expertise. One of the major search engines (i.e., Google.com or Yahoo.com) can direct you to even more specific outsourcing websites.

Be careful though. Posting an RFP to some of these sites will guarantee receiving many e-mails from overseas candidates offering to do large, complex jobs for ridiculously low fees. Some of these sites are so overrun with foreign and other workers who are impossible to evaluate that it's a challenge to evaluate qualified alternatives.

Job Sites

The most popular job sites are Monster (www.monster.com), Career Builder (www.careerbuilder.com), and Yahoo! Jobs (formerly Hot Jobs—www.hotjobs.com). You don't have to limit yourself to the big boys, however—type in "job search engines" in Yahoo! or Google and you'll find lots of other good sites at which to start your search.

CAUTION

Stay Alert!

Although very user friendly, most job sites generally attract people with some knowledge of computers and the Internet. You may be limiting your search for outsourced help by relying solely on these websites.

If the big, general job sites don't generate the kinds of leads you're looking for, there's a good chance there's an employment site out there that's specific to your industry. For example, Dice (www.dice.com) offers job listings for technology professionals. Marketing Jobs (www.marketingjobs.com) does the same for the marketing world, and Robert Half (www.roberthalf.com) for finance and accounting. If you're in the pharmaceutical industry, check out

Pomasite (www.pomasite.com). If you're in the media industry, Media Bistro's Free-lance Marketplace (www.mediabistro.com/fm) is a good source. You'll find lots of hired guns by taking this approach.

If you're going to use a job search website, keep the following tips in mind:

◆ You'll find that most of these sites are outsource friendly. In fact, when you fill out an ad to place, you'll probably be asked what kind of job you're listing, specifically if it's on a "full-time" or "project" or "contract" basis. The latter two terms are used to describe all kinds of outsourced work.

◆ Use *both* employer and candidate tools. By all means, post your ad. But also search through the pool of available candidates.

◆ Make use of the various alert tools that these sites offer. With these tools, if someone posts a resumé with a certain type of experience or with specific key words that you define, the site will automatically inform you.

◆ Get ready for junk mail, such as advertisements and solicitations. You're going to get some unwanted responses to your ad no matter how hard you try to avoid it.

> **Outsourcing Insights**
>
> You'll bump into many out-placement firms on job sites. If you can't find that right con-tract worker on your own, an outplacement firm may be a great solution.

Outsourcing Associations

If you're not sure about finding the right outsourced solution on your own, outsourc-ing associations and groups will be more than happy to help you in your hunt. In addition to putting service providers in touch with clients, outsourcing organizations provide regulatory information and legal tips. You can also sign up for newsletters on outsourcing and find out about related seminars and conferences.

Start your travels at The Outsourcing Institute (www.outsourcing.com), a not-for-profit professional organization devoted solely to outsourcing. You might also check out the Outsourcing Directory (www.outsourcing.org), a compendium of resources for both sides of the outsourcing relationship. Outsourcing Pipeline (www.outsourcingpipeline.com) is a publication that focuses primarily on the legal, political, and technical issues surrounding outsourcing, and is a good source for finding people, too! The Outsourcing Benchmarking Association (www.obenchmarking.com) will not only give you lots of reading material on the pros and cons of outsourcing in your industry, it will also give you access to thousands of members—both providers and seekers of work.

Newsgroups and Chat Rooms

Posting a help-wanted message in an industry-specific newsgroup or chat room may elicit some responses, but I wouldn't rely on this method entirely.

Industry Associations

Another great source for finding outsourced help is your industry or trade group. Thousands of these groups represent millions of businesses throughout the world. And there are industry associations just for service providers, too, such as the aforementioned Pharmaceutical Outsourcing Management Association (www. pomasite.com), the IT Professionals Association of America (www.itpaa.org), and the Association of Support Professionals (www.asponline.com).

Most of these associations host conferences, forums, and other such gatherings on a periodic basis. This is a great place to network and reach out to people or member firms that may perform subcontracted work.

Advertising the Old-Fashioned Way

If you're looking for a person or company to perform some type of outsourced work, you've got plenty of options to choose from without even turning on your computer.

Outsourcing Insights

Many newspapers are owned by large media conglomerates that own several newspapers. You may be able to get incentive pricing by advertising in more than one of the company's publications. Also find out what days are big "job ad" days for your paper and advertise then. For many newspapers, it's Sunday and Wednesday.

Classified Ads

Just because you're not looking for an employee doesn't mean you can't take out an ad in the local papers. You just need to be clear that you're looking for subcontracted help instead of a full-time employee.

In addition, be sure to including the following information:

- ◆ Mention the timeframe. If you're looking for short-term help, then say it.

- Create a unique job description or title. Your advertisement is going to be competing against others, so try and make it stand out.

- Advertise your company. Your ad should include a line describing what your company does.

- Note the location of the work. Some independents may have chosen this lifestyle because they want to live in a certain location or they can only work from home.

- Specify required and preferred experience. For example, if you're looking to outsource a software project, your programmer may be required to have experience with a specific programming language or development environment (although skills with certain databases are only preferred).

- Indicate what kind of compensation you're offering. Don't shy away from the money, even at this early stage.

- Make it easy for people to respond to the ad. Include either a phone number, fax number, or e-mail address. Or include a short website address and let them come to your site and fill out a form that ensures you get key information you'll need.

Outsourcing Insights

Have a procedure for confirming receipt of every response you get so that applicants know they're in the running. In addition, sending a thank-you letter reflects highly on your company.

Outsourcing Insights

American City Business Journals (www.bizjournals.com) publishes weekly business newspapers in most of the larger cities in the country, from Memphis to Honolulu. These are good sources for finding out about consultants and contractors serving your area.

In addition, just about every major industry has its own trade magazine or publication. These industry journals publish advertisements, press releases, interviews, and articles about people and companies that may be perfect outsourcing candidates. Some of these publications even have their own help-wanted sections and many have great websites, too.

Additional Ways to Find Good People

Although using the Internet or traditional print advertising is the most popular method for finding the right service provider, there are many other tried-and-true ways, as well. Using the Yellow Pages and asking friends and family may also find you the person you're looking for.

Outsourcing Insights

Many established industries have their own "yellow pages," buyers guides, and product/service directories, such as the Thomson Directories (www.thomsondirectories. com).

Yellow Pages

If you've decided that you want to outsource a common task with another company, there may very well be an industry of outsourcing firms ready to vie for your business, and they'll be in the book!

Spreading the Word

Don't forget to ask your network of contacts whether they can recommend any contractors they've worked with in the past.

The Least You Need to Know

◆ Before starting your search, write a detailed task/project description and have other management review it.

◆ A good RFP should provide the outsourcer with everything he or she needs to know to prepare a detailed proposal.

◆ Make sure you have a plan for tracking and reviewing proposals and communicating with prospective outsourcers.

◆ You can find outsourcers in many of the same ways that you find traditional employees. In addition, many organizations and websites specialize in putting outsourced service providers in touch with potential clients.

13

Selecting the Best Service Provider

In This Chapter

- Understanding the differences between hiring a new employee and selecting an outsourced service provider
- The 12 steps for selecting your service provider
- Key questions to ask your service provider

David, a vice president at a large manufacturing company, decided that providing meals to their employees would improve morale and maybe even increase productivity. Clearly, he was not about to go into the self-catering business, so he decided to outsource.

Not a lot of companies do corporate catering in his area, but he found a few restaurants that were interested in the job.

But now what? What steps should he take? What questions should he ask? Maybe he should just hire an employee to do this ... who knows?

Picking a catering company, a telemarketing firm, an accounting service, or a call center is not a task to be taken lightly. You have to do a lot of research, planning, and number crunching before contracting with a service provider.

In this chapter, I discuss the things you need to consider, and the steps you need to take to help you select the right service provider for the mission.

Hiring the Service Provider vs. Hiring an Employee

I noted in Chapter 5 that the process for selecting your service provider isn't all that different from selecting a new employee. But because you aren't hiring an employee, there are some key differences. Let's consider what those differences are.

Employment Laws Do Not Apply

When you're selecting a new employee, you must conduct yourself in accordance with federal and state employment laws and regulations. You're not allowed to discriminate based on age, sex, religion, handicaps, and so on. You must offer a minimum wage. You need to document your actions thoroughly during this process in case your behavior is ever called into question.

Outsourcing Insights

To get an idea of all of the employment laws that the typical business is required to know, go to the Department of Labor's website at www.dol.gov.

Your service provider will not be an employee. Whether you're contracting out with a large firm or one person, your relationship is purely one between a vendor and a customer. Here you can offer the work based on what the market will bear, without being constrained by any additional regulations.

Great Expectations

When you hire an employee, your expectations are that he or she will work hard, show up on time, and do whatever they think is necessary to get their work done. You'll expect professional behavior. You'll expect them to work well with others and to represent your company in the most positive light possible.

In most cases, your expectations of your outsourced firm will be much, much higher. With a service provider, you expect every dollar you pay to be matched with results. You don't want to hear about vacations, personal issues, lack of resources, or the car accident on Route 29 that caused him to be late for an appointment. Service providers are expected to get their jobs done with as little hand holding as possible from you.

Paying to Play

Employees are generally all paid the same way: they get a weekly or hourly wage. They often get benefits such as health-care and pension plans. Sometimes they're eligible for bonuses and profit sharing.

So here's the difference: if you're an employee and you promise to get a job done in 8 hours and it takes you 12, your boss may be annoyed, but you're still getting your paycheck. If you're an outside service provider, then guess who eats the additional four hours? You! (Of course, this depends on the financial arrangements you make at the outset.)

Selecting the right service provider also means coming up with the right way to pay the provider. It's not a simple weekly paycheck. Compensation may be contingent on certain results, it may be based on time and materials, or it may be a flat fee. See Chapter 18 for more on paying your outside service provider.

It's in Writing

If you're a bigwig executive, you'll probably have your lawyer draw up a detailed employment agreement with your employer. If you're in the middle- to upper-management ranks, you might enter into a less-involved contract. Most other employees come onboard under *at-will* employment laws.

As you'll see in Chapter 21, the service provider's contract will be much different. And just about every third-party relationship will require a written agreement between the parties.

Business Buzzwords

At will employment is when an employee takes a job with a company with free choice and discretion, but without any contract. The company has no long-term obligation, however, to keep the employee on the payroll.

Skeletons in the Closet

When you're about to hire an employee, you'll probably want to look into their work history. You'll call their references and perhaps even request a background report on them. But short of hiring a private investigator, your choices are going to be somewhat limited.

Not so the case when you're selecting the service provider. As long as you're considering an established company to do the work for you, you've got several investigative resources at your disposal. Your typical employee may have worked a few other jobs before, but the potential firm you're evaluating probably has dozens, hundreds, or thousands of customers that you can speak to. If they're a public company, you have access to all sorts of financial information.

Are You Committed?

Ask any manager and they'll tell you that one of the toughest things they have to do is terminate people. When you hire an employee, you're making an implied (although not enforceable, depending on the "at will" laws in your state) commitment to them that, as long as they do a good job for you, you'll be doing your very best to keep them employed for as long as you can. The government even does its best to protect employees who are terminated by offering them unemployment benefits and extended health-benefits regulations.

Your outsourced arrangement is contractual and may require you to stick by the agreement for a certain period of time, but it's clear to both parties that there is no obligation beyond what's stated in the contract. In addition, because the service provider has other customers, their allegiance to you isn't 100 percent like an employee. Your level of commitment to them, although it may be strong, probably won't have the same intensity as yours to a good employee.

Seeing Is Believing

Your candidate for a job can tell you how great she is and even give you excellent references. But how about seeing her in action? If she's a writer, you can look at her material. But if she's a network administrator, it's going to be a lot tougher to verify that what she's telling you is true.

The outside service provider, however, can be checked. You can visit their offices and their customers' offices. You can watch their people do the work. You can talk to their customers to find out how satisfied they are with the service.

Steps for Selecting the Service Provider

Now that we've established that there are certainly differences when you're choosing a new employee for a job versus outsourcing, we can turn to the selection process.

I've come up with 12 steps to take from the time you've identified your list of outsourcing candidates to the point where you're ready to put a contract into the hands of one of them.

Step 1: Determine Objectives, Deliverables, Measurements

Hopefully you've done this even before you started searching for candidates or sending out your Requests for Proposals. But let's restate this step here just to make sure you fully appreciate its importance. You do *not* want to hire an outside service provider unless it's crystal clear what they're being hired to do and how they're going to be measured. This will help both you and the potential candidate qualify (and disqualify) each other for the job.

Step 2: Gather All the Data

As you're evaluating your potential service providers, you should be gathering as much information about them as possible. Set up a database or a file with the pertinent data. You're going to want one place to go to when it's time to review everything and make your decision. You'll be adding to this data as you do your due diligence.

Outsourcing Insights

Many people like to keep prospective employee data in a database, such as Microsoft Access, FileMaker, or FoxPro. This way you can query the data quickly and produce reports and output that may be more useful.

Step 3: Do the Research

Next you're going to want to do some initial research. Your goal here is to narrow the list down to something more manageable. You'll use whatever resources you can find on the Internet to find out more about the potential service providers. Maybe you'll call all of them with some basic questions about their services. You might talk to a few other people about those on your list to see if anyone should be eliminated right from the get-go.

Don't forget to document your findings.

Step 4: Eliminate/Disqualify/Narrow

The results of your research should help you narrow the field down to something less unwieldy. It's important that you make the short list as soon as possible so you can focus your energies on the remaining players. As I mentioned elsewhere, make sure you keep the data on those who don't make the cut just in case you need to go back to them at a later date.

Step 5: Interview by Phone

Your next step is to do a more detailed phone interview. The purpose of this step is to further narrow your field down to the final three. Later in this chapter, you'll find a series of questions that you'll want to ask. Keep the answers to your questions in your database or file, of course.

Outsourcing Insights

When conducting a phone interview, always make sure to have your key questions prepared in advance and in front of you. This will help you move the conversation along and stay focused.

Many firms may direct you to their website for information, which is fine. But always spend enough time talking to someone senior enough so they can give you specific answers as to how their company will accomplish the job for you.

Step 6: The Final Three

After your phone interviews are complete, it's time to narrow down your list to the final three candidates. These are the people you're going to really zoom in on.

Step 7: Meeting the Candidates in Person

Finally, meet the candidates. With only three choices, you'll want to bring them in individually and interview them. You may want to repeat some of the same questions that you asked on the phone again. You'll want them to meet with others in your company. You'll want to show them around and explain further what will be required.

You could also use the in-person interviews as a chance for the prospective contractor to give a formal presentation on their work.

Step 8: Site Visit

Return the favor and visit the service provider's facilities, too. Maybe you're hosting your website with an outsourced provider and want to check out their computing facilities. Or perhaps you're relying on an outsourced customer service operation and you'll feel much more comfortable examining the call center yourself. An on-site visit to the service provider's offices will tell you a lot about a company.

Step 9: Referrals and More Research

It's time to interview the outsourcers' other customers. Don't be afraid to ask the customers a lot of questions about the service provider. You may decide to further deepen your research based on the new information you've found. Maybe you can even arrange to visit some of the customers in person to see the service provider in action.

Outsourcing Insights

Great sites for investigative research include www.knowx. com, www.yahoo.com, www.google.com, www. privateeye.com, and www. backgroundsonline.com.

Step 10: Review Proposal/Contracts

At this point, you should be leaning toward your choice. Now is the time to request proposals from the final candidates and compare the proposals against each other. If you and your service provider have each done your respective jobs right, there really should be no surprises in the proposals you receive. Each proposal should really be a confirmation of what you've already discussed.

Step 11: Negotiate

The proposal is the service provider's initial offer. Most expect a counteroffer. Maybe you need more services added in. Prices may be too high or delivery times too long. It's okay to parry back and forth until you both finally agree on the terms of the proposed relationship. Undertake all of the important negotiations before you decide on a final choice. This way the service provider knows that they're being compared to their competition, giving you leverage.

Step 12: Choose, but Don't Burn Bridges

It's time to choose your service provider and prepare the contracts. But don't forget to take the time to contact those candidates that you didn't choose and explain to them the reasons behind your selection.

What Kind of Information Should You Seek?

During the selection process, you're going to be talking to multiple candidates and getting information over the phone, by e-mail, on the Internet, and in person. You're going to have to ask a lot of questions to get the information you need to make an informed decision. I've prepared the following lists of questions to help you get that information.

Information About the Company

You want to gather a lot of data about the company's history, stability, experience, and processes. The following questions will help you get that information:

- What qualifies the company to do the job? Do they hold certifications? Are they experienced in doing this kind of work?

- What is their availability? Will you be able to call them any time? Are they reachable by pager or e-mail? Are there time zone issues?

> **Business Buzzwords**
>
> A **named insured** is an individual or entity specifically named on an insurance contract as protected under the contract. Some customers require that their company is named under a vendor's general liability policy to reduce their risk.

- Is the company insured? Are they bonded? Do they have a sufficient amount of liability coverage? Can they produce evidence? Can your company be included as a *named insured?* (See Chapter 22 for more on liability issues.)

- Does the company offer service level agreements? Are these agreements standard? What type of service do they commit to? Do they have different levels of services? Are you going to be treated the same as a bigger customer?

- Are there any conflicts of interest? Does the company do work for one of your competitors? Maybe there are issues with proprietary data. Are there family members or other related parties that could cause some kind of a problem? Can your service provider treat you completely at arm's length?

◆ What action is the company willing to take if you're unsatisfied with their people? Do they have procedures in place to handle complaints?

◆ What percentage of business would you represent for the service provider? Would you be a significant client or barely a blip on their radar?

◆ Are there any past legal issues with customers or employees? Do they have a good credit history? What is their financial health? Has there been any evidence of wrongdoing or instability with this company?

Outsourcing Insights

Don't expect perfection. Some companies may have been sued by an irate employee. There may have been a time when bills were overdue because of an isolated cash-flow incident. When looking at a company's background, keep your eyes open for trends, not specific events.

◆ How long has the company been in business? Do they have a history of good business practices? Do they belong to industry or professional organizations? Are they a member of the Better Business Bureau?

◆ Are their customers satisfied with the quality of their work? Will the company put you in touch with their customers? Can you find customers independent of those that the company provides and contact them to get feedback?

◆ Does management of the service provider pay the appropriate level of attention to their customers? Have you met senior management? Are they involved in the selection process? Will you have an ongoing relationship with them once you hire their company? How accessible are they?

◆ What is the rate of turnover of the company's personnel? Is this rate consistent with their industry? This information may be available in published reports about the company. Is there any reason behind a higher-than-normal rate?

◆ What is the quality of the company's infrastructure? Do you need to see their "bricks and mortar"? Does the company seem established and stable?

◆ How responsive are they during the selection process? Are they quick to return your calls? Do they show a real desire to do work with you? Are they turning around your requests for information in a timely manner?

◆ What other resources will the provider need? Will they be outsourcing any work themselves? Do they have the necessary tools to do the job? Are you required to provide them with resources that they don't have?

◆ How creative are they? Are they capable of coming up with unique ideas? Or do they just seem to offer "boilerplate" solutions?

◆ Are there any clear areas where they exceed their competitors? Do they have significant strengths or weaknesses that set them apart?

◆ Is their culture a good match for you? Do they have the same level of work ethic, intensity, and attention to detail? Will they work well with your people?

◆ What is their ability to scale up? If you need more service from them, can they provide it? As you grow, can they grow with you? Or will you outpace them over time and need to select another service provider?

◆ What are their strategic direction and growth plans? Are they committed to continue to provide the kinds of services that you need from them? Are they looking to branch into other areas that are of no use to you?

Information About the People with Whom You'll Be Working

You may be comfortable with the firm, but are you comfortable with the people who will be doing the work for you? You need to ask more questions about the individuals whom you'll be working with:

◆ How are workers tested and screened for medical issues or dependency problems? Do they have to pass certification exams? Do they go through an interview process? Do they have to demonstrate their skills before being hired by the service provider?

◆ Are these people getting paid what they deserve? What kind of benefits do they get? Could they be potentially disgruntled? Speaking to their employees may get you some of these answers.

◆ How long will you need the people you'll be working with? Are there limitations to their time?

◆ What skills do the workers possess? Do the assigned individuals have the necessary qualifications to do your specific job? Are they inexperienced? Are you going to be paying to train one or more people?

Outsourcing Insights

The longer you commit to an outside service provider, the better deal you'll get. Many outsourcers focus on keeping their people billable, and will guarantee certain individuals or reduced rates for those customers that show a long-term potential.

◆ Do the workers have good communication skills? Will they be able to speak to both your employees and customers in a professional manner? Can you rely on them to say the right thing and ask the right questions?

◆ What responsibilities do you want the workers to assume? Have you agreed on the job descriptions? Are the workers fully aware of how they will be evaluated?

◆ Who will supervise the workers? Will this be the responsibility of the outside service firm or you?

Information About the Job

Even after you satisfy yourself with the company and the people they'll be providing, you'll still want to make sure that they're going to do your specific job as expected. Here are some job-related questions that you should pose to the potential service firm before selecting them:

◆ How are services priced? Have all hidden costs been disclosed? Are all prices, terms, and payment details documented in your contract?

◆ How will payment be made? Is this a fixed-fee project or by the hour? Is payment contingent on results? Have you agreed on the measurements that will be used to evaluate the service provider? Is the payment by check? Cash? Stock?

◆ How long will their quoted prices and rates remain in effect? Will there be increases? Do they have the ability to change their pricing without your approval? Are they willing to commit to a long-term price?

◆ What if the job becomes permanent? Are there procedures and payment terms in place if you want to stop outsourcing and actually hire the people doing the work? (This actually poses some ethical issues; see Chapter 23 for details.)

◆ What security measures does the company have in place? If they're dealing with confidential or private information, how will they make sure it doesn't get into the wrong hands? How can you make sure that they're following these rules?

◆ How will your account be managed? Will you be dealing with senior- or junior-level people? Will you have access to

CAUTION

Stay Alert!

Make sure you keep copies of contracts, paperwork, data files, and other critical information. This will be important in case you ever need to change service providers.

senior-level people when you need them? Who will be your point of contact? What happens if that person isn't available? Who do you go to for billing questions? Service questions?

◆ Are special tools needed for this job? Are these tools provided by the third party or do you need to provide them? Does the person doing the job know how to use these tools?

◆ Are there enough resources to get the job done? Are you being assigned enough people? Do they plan to allocate the appropriate amount of time and resources? Are they sympathetic to your deadlines?

The Least You Need to Know

◆ You have more flexibility when selecting a service provider because it's not necessary to adhere to various state and federal employment laws.

◆ When selecting a service provider, you need to gather the necessary data, meet the final candidates in person, and gather and review their proposals.

◆ When asking about the service provider's operations, be sure to inquire about their hiring practices, financial history, and insurance coverage.

◆ The people supplied by the service provider should be qualified, experienced, and have good communication skills.

◆ You must find out whether your potential service provider is prepared to do the job at hand with the right tools, resources, and support capabilities in place.

Part **3**

Outsourcing in Action

Now that you've taken the plunge, you're going to want to get the most out of your relationship with your outside service provider. In this section, I look more closely at two of the most popular forms of outsourcing: employee leasing and information technology outsourcing.

You will learn about the challenges of managing the relationship with your outside service provider and what you can do to overcome them. And because you need to know whether outsourcing is working for you, I explain the various ways for measuring the results of your outsourcing arrangement. Finally, I describe the benefits and pitfalls of global outsourcing.

Chapter 14

Outsourcing All Your Employees

In This Chapter

- ◆ What human resources outsourcing is and who does it
- ◆ The benefits of HR outsourcing
- ◆ The downsides of farming out your work force
- ◆ How to choose a good PEO
- ◆ The cost of HR outsourcing

When the letter came from the health-insurance company, Becky groaned loudly. "Great," she said aloud. "Another increase in my rates. This is killing me!"

Frances, walking by Becky's office, overheard her.

"You know, Becky," he said, popping his head in her door. "I've got a neighbor who told me he actually got his company's health-insurance rates reduced this past year."

"Oh, sure." Betty said sarcastically. "What did he do, fire all of his employees?"

"Well," said Frances. "In a way ... yes."

Now Becky was paying attention.

"You're kidding, right? He didn't just fire all of his employees, did he? Did he go out of business?"

"Just the opposite," Frances replied. "He just had his best year ever."

"What's the catch?" asked Betty.

"Well, he fired his employees, and then leased them back," Frances told her.

"Leased them back?" Betty repeated. "What do you mean?"

"It's becoming a really popular form of outsourcing," Frances continued. "You fire your employees, and then have them rehired by an HR outsourcing company that has much better benefit plans, and other services, too. Then you lease them back."

"Sounds kind of like a tax dodge to me." Betty said cautiously.

It's not. Human resources (HR) outsourcing is one of the most popular forms of outsourcing in the country today. According to the NAPEO (National Association of Professional Employer Organizations), approximately two to three million employees are leased. HR outsourcing firms account for more than $18 billion in employee wages and related benefits. In addition, such arrangements, if structured properly, are perfectly legal and are often a great way to reduce the costs of employee benefits and administration.

This chapter describes how leasing your employees can benefit you.

Outsourcing Insights

There are important differences between companies that offer HR outsourcing services and those that offer temporary workers. Certainly, both arrangements can involve short-term work done by non-employees, but HR outsourcing firms don't recruit employees for you, and they don't use their/your employees for work outside of what you require.

What Is HR Outsourcing?

When you "lease" your employees, you're actually terminating them so that an outside firm can hire them and then "rent" them back to you under specific contractual terms. The outsourcing company takes responsibility for certain tasks and costs related to your employees as well as providing other cost savings, which will be described shortly.

HR outsourcing is a radical idea for many managers and owners because when you outsource your employees from another company, the people who were once *your* employees are now *their* employees. You technically have no employees on staff.

Two type of firms specialize in HR outsourcing: HR outsourcing companies and professional employer organizations.

HR outsourcing companies were the first to come up with the concept of outsourcing employment. In the early days, it was just fire, hire, and lease. No other human resources or other services or benefits were considered. Leasing arrangements were for short-term arrangements or for special projects. Although still around, many HR outsourcing companies have generally been replaced by professional employer organizations.

Professional employer organizations (commonly referred to as PEOs) have sprung up from HR outsourcing companies to provide even more services for their customers. PEOs provide a much wider variety of services than traditional HR outsourcing companies.

Your contract with the PEO will spell out the relationship you'll have with your employees and the PEO. An employee will not notice any difference other than their paycheck coming from a different company (and hopefully lower benefits costs!). PEOs like to call themselves *co-employers.*

> **Business Buzzwords**
>
> A **co-employer** relationship involves sharing and allocating employer responsibilities between a third-party leasing firm and its customer.

Among the services a typical PEO provides are …

 ◆ **Payroll services.** A PEO will handle all of the tasks you would expect to be handled by an outsourced payroll service. The PEO generates a full payroll, including checks, withholdings, and tax payments.

 ◆ **Filings and record keeping.** Because the people working for you are no longer your employees, you no longer are required to maintain all of the required paperwork that comes along with employment. The PEO will handle tax filings and communications with the IRS. The PEO will also keep track of vacation days and sick days as you would normally be expected to do. Many PEOs do the accounting and keep the books and records for stock options and other compensation plans due to the employee, too.

 ◆ **Human resources.** Most PEO firms advertise themselves as outsourced human resources departments, too. They document disciplinary procedures, coordinate employee evaluations, develop systems for record keeping, conduct screening and exit interviews, recruit new employees, and write employee handbooks, manuals, and other documentation.

- ◆ **Benefits administration.** If you choose the PEO's offering of health insurance, pension plans, or other profit-sharing arrangements, the PEO can also then help you administer the plan. This means they'll be the main point of contact for questions, claims, paperwork, and reporting to the staff. The PEO will also liaise with insurance companies and other financial services firms on your behalf.

- ◆ **Consulting.** PEOs want to be your partner, not just a service provider. Many provide helpful consulting services. They leverage off the experience from their own client base and offer suggestions for compensating, managing, and getting the most productivity from your work force. A top-notch PEO firm will be up to date on all the most recent state and federal rules and regulations on labor and tax laws to help guide you through the red tape.

> **Stay Alert!**
>
> Many states regulate the licensing and registration of leased employees. These states usually recognize the PEO as the statutory employer. The Internal Revenue Service also has withholding rules specifically for PEOs and specific guidance about how PEOs may provide retirement benefits. Make sure your PEO is in compliance with these rules.

> **Knowledge Is Power**
>
> According to *CFO Magazine*, the most commonly outsourced human resources functions are (in order) payroll, health and benefits, long- and short-term disability insurance, COBRA administration, employee assistance programs, employee service call centers, information technology services, and retirement/savings plans.

The Upsides of HR Outsourcing

HR outsourcing can be a great thing for any size company, big or small. And it's really taken off over the past few years. Let's look at some of the more significant reasons why today's managers might want to consider outsourcing employees.

You Will Be Able to Provide More and Better Benefits

If your PEO is large enough, then they may be "employing" thousands, maybe even hundreds of thousands, of people. When it's time for the PEO to negotiate benefits for its employees, they're looked on as a large company, with lots of potential revenue for the benefits provider. This type of leverage usually results in plans that offer the best type of benefits available. Your people share in these benefits, too.

Your Compensation Costs May Decrease

Just as PEOs can use their leverage to negotiate better benefits for their employees, they can also negotiate better workmen's comp rates. Depending on the state you're in, you can save quite a bit on workmen's compensation insurance by leasing your employees.

You Can Enjoy Both Payroll Processing and Human Resources Services

Maybe you want to outsource your payroll processing. And maybe you could use some other personnel help, too. A PEO will allow you to outsource both your payroll functions and provide full-blown human resources management services, too. Outsourcing to a good PEO can give your employees the type of human resources services only found in much larger firms.

You Won't Have to Worry So Much About Regulatory Compliance

Most employers know of the hassles dealing with the regulatory agencies. There are IRS rules for withholding and paying in taxes. There are Department of Labor regulations concerning immigration, discrimination, and disability. But if you've outsourced your employees to a PEO, you can rely on them to stay on top of these rules. Remember, though, you're still ultimately responsible in the eyes of the government.

You Can Get Help with Safety and Loss-Control Issues

Outsourced HR outsourcing firms can help you minimize liabilities, too. Many provide services that help you evaluate (or even implement) employee safety programs. Others also look at your overall work force environment and help determine whether you face any undue risks of lawsuits or complaints by your people.

You Can Create the Right Documents for Your Staff

A PEO can assist you in revising your existing employee manuals and documentation or creating altogether new guidelines and procedures. In addition, a PEO worth its salt will help you implement these procedures and policies and communicate them to your staff.

Someone Else Will Do Your Claims Processing

An employee goes to the doctor and submits her invoice to her employer for reimbursement from the company's Health Savings Accounts Plan. Another wants to borrow money from his pension account. A warehouse person needs to create a separate withholding for a child-support payment. These are but a few of the claims the typical personnel department must contend with. By outsourcing your employees, you would no longer have to deal with the paperwork these claims create.

You Will Have to Write Just One Check

Whether you've got 50, 500, or 5,000 people in your company, you're only going to write 1 check. This will be to your PEO. As you've now outsourced your payroll, and all related deductions, payments, and withholdings, your service provider will be the one cutting all those checks and doing all the processing.

> **CAUTION**
>
> **Stay Alert!**
>
> Don't give in to the temptation of setting up an automatic bank transfer from your account to the PEO's to fund payroll. Instead, review the amounts required and either authorize a transfer or send them a check. No one should have the authority to transfer money out of your account without you reviewing it and approving first.

You'll Get Expert HR Advice

PEOs want to be your partners. They want to provide more than just a payroll service. They want to advise and be your human resources experts. This is a good thing. They don't manufacture tires or window shades. They're in the business of employment and employment services. Their expertise will be of high value to you, just like the expertise of any other professional your company employs. Keep in mind that these additional services and advice will cost extra!

You'll Reduce Your Overall Paperwork

Because the PEO handles all the bureaucracy of your personnel system, you will have less paperwork to deal with. The PEO will keep most of your people's records and other employee documents for you. Your filing costs will substantially decrease. And if you're worried about accessing your files, a good PEO may provide web-based retrieval on demand.

Your Employees Will Be Protected

Your employees will be relieved to hear that they lose no rights as an employee. Even though the PEO is technically their employer, federal and state laws recognize you as the person who's ultimately responsible under the legislation and will hold you accountable. Assuming you're out to do the right thing by your employees, while also achieving the other benefits of HR outsourcing, this should be a comfort to you and the people whose livelihood depends on you.

Stay Alert!

The IRS requires businesses to maintain certain employee documentation. A list of these documents can be found by searching at www.irs.gov/businesses/small/. Make sure that you have ready access to any of these files if you need them. Keep these records around even after transferring your people to the PEO, as you'll still be responsible for them up until that point.

The Downsides of HR Outsourcing

HR outsourcing arrangements have their cons, too. Here are a few that you should be aware of before entering into this kind of relationship.

You Could Be Liable for Even More Stuff

Even though you're outsourcing your payroll and human resources, most HR outsourcing agreements are pretty clear that you're liable for any employment-related issues. In other words, you're not going to escape responsibility just because you're outsourcing.

In some cases, and depending on the state you're in, you may actually be increasing your liability. For example, depending on your state's worker compensation laws, an employee who's hurt on your premises may be able to sue you as a third party, as opposed to an employer. Your worker compensation coverage may not cover this type of lawsuit and could leave you exposed to even more damages.

Employees with Pre-existing Medical Conditions Might Not Be Eligible for Benefits

As "new" employees of the PEO, your people will be subject to whatever requirements are set forth by the leasing company's health-insurance provider. If any employees have pre-existing medical conditions, the new insurance company usually has the right to refuse to cover them.

You Lose Control of "Your" People

Some employers (and their employees) don't like the idea of another company taking over their role as the employer. If the PEO fails to comply with the law or makes mistakes, you'll be the one who's ultimately responsible. Also, these companies have the right to hire and fire just like any other employer does. The employer of record is the leasing company, not you. This means that the leasing company can fire employees you perceive as valuable assets.

Employee Relations Could Suffer

Some employees think that HR outsourcing firms are one step away from being laid off. Others view this action as disrespectful to the work force. However, your outsourcing arrangement should have little, if any, effect on your employees' benefits or day-to-day work. Good communications throughout the process, combined with an education of what HR outsourcing really is, should temper any employee concerns.

"Your" People Might Have to Deal with More Red Tape

Suppose that you're an employee and have a question about your health insurance. You may be used to stopping by the human resource person's office or sending off a quick e-mail. Well, that's going to change if you decide to outsource. Now the employee will probably have to call a toll-free number, identify himself and the question, and then wait. Some PEOs have websites that provide answers to frequently asked questions; others have more elaborate service desks to respond to phone, e-mail, or web requests. In any event, there's a chance that what was once personal service becomes a little impersonal, and employees might have to go through an extra step or two to get an answer to their questions.

Unscrupulous Operators Could Leave You Liable

In 2002, an HR outsourcing company based in Long Island, New York, withheld taxes on thousands of their employees and, whoops, forgot to pay them—repeatedly. When they were finally caught, not only was the leasing company in trouble, their customers were ultimately liable for the tax payments. The situation is still being battled out in court. The lesson: when leasing employees, you are putting a lot of trust in your PEO, so do your due diligence before you hire!

Stay Alert! _____

Your PEO should be bonded and have the appropriate liability insurance to cover losses. Make sure to get proof of this insurance before entering into your relationship.

You'll Have to Contend with State Regulators

Rules and regulations regarding HR outsourcing vary from state to state. This is because HR outsourcing firms take responsibility for worker compensation insurance, a state-driven coverage, and the state wants these firms to comply with certain requirements. You should make sure your leasing company complies.

Labor Unions Don't Like It

As you consider HR outsourcing, keep in mind that some labor unions frown on such arrangements, viewing them as a way that employers may skirt responsibilities in labor-related cases.

Changing Your Mind Is a Pain

When you decide to lease your employees to a PEO, the decision doesn't have to be permanent. Subject to your leasing contract, you can always go back and bring your people back on to your payroll. But remember that this will incur a lot of paperwork and negotiations. It may also incur instability among your people.

You Have to Put Money in Escrow

Most HR outsourcing companies require you to keep at least one pay period's liability in escrow with them in advance. This is to protect them in case you don't make good on your commitments. Make sure your contracts protect you against unauthorized withdrawals of these amounts. Also make sure you agree in advance who gets the interest for the escrow funds.

How to Choose a Good HR Outsourcing Company

With approximately 2,000 PEO organizations in the United States, you'll have no problem finding one or more who'll be happy to work with you, but it might take some effort to find one that will work well for you. In addition to servicing you, this firm is going to service your work force. You must keep your employees' best interests in mind when shopping for PEOs.

How do you choose which one is right for you and your employees? Here are a few steps to take:

- **Check out the PEO's financial stability.** Research them on hoovers.com, dunandbradstreet.com, or other Internet-based credit services and make sure they've got a strong balance sheet and good credit history.

- **Find out if the PEO participates in any industry associations.** A good PEO will belong to trade groups such as NAPEO (National Association of PEOs) and participate in industry-wide conferences and events.

Outsourcing Insights

Already have a great health plan? Many PEOs can "unbundle" their services so that you can keep those benefits in place that you want to keep, while still taking advantage of the added benefits these firms offer. Make sure to ask your PEO about this.

- **Make sure the PEO has experience in your industry.** The roofing industry must contend with labor and insurance issues that differ from the retail services industry. For your PEO to truly be a partner, they should have experience in your industry so you're getting the best service possible.

- **Talk to the PEO's customers.** Never hire a PEO without getting some referrals and talking to their customers. When you speak to referrals, ask them whether they know any one else using the PEO so you can try and talk to customers that haven't been referred directly by them.

♦ **Match the PEO's benefit programs to your needs.** When you start an HR outsourcing program, your employees will likely be starting out with an entirely new health-insurance company or other benefit program. Try to ensure that the program is as good as, if not better than, the one they're leaving. Your employees take their family's medical care very seriously, so make sure you carefully consider all the options and consequences before making any drastic changes.

> ### Knowledge Is Power
>
> According to the U.S. Small Business Association, the average annual cost of regulation, paperwork, and tax compliance for firms with fewer than 500 employees is about $5,000 per employee, compared with $3,400 per employee for firms with more than 500 employees.

♦ **Verify that the PEO is in compliance with state regulations.** Many states require employee leasing firms to register as such and to demonstrate that they are in compliance with state regulations. Check with your state's labor or employment department to verify that your PEO is in compliance with all applicable laws.

♦ **Test the PEO's flexibility.** No company is completely the same. Perhaps you offer a special vacation package or stock options program. Make sure that your PEO will be flexible enough to handle your special needs so that you don't find out later that things have to be changed.

♦ **Make sure the PEO's support structure is reliable and available.** Your employees may need help over the weekend or you may have people working for you in different time zones. Make sure your PEO can handle questions wherever and whenever they come up.

How Much Does HR Outsourcing Cost?

Most PEOs charge between 2 and 10 percent of each employee's pretax salary. Others charge a fixed fee. Most have upfront setup fees ranging from $500 to $5,000, depending on the size of your company. Consulting services are oftentimes charged by the hour, and special charges can be negotiated as fixed prices.

Stay Alert!

Be aware of additional fees that are levied when services are changed. You should agree on all fees up front. Your PEO should provide a breakdown of all fees charged.

Remember that, like all other outsourcing arrangements, a good service level agreement will be crucial to the success of your PEO relationship. Make sure all terms and conditions are in writing and that you have an attorney review them.

Make sure to add up these charges beforehand and compare them to your current employee costs. Don't forget to factor in the intangible value of reduced administrative time and headaches.

The Least You Need to Know

- HR outsourcing arrangements will require you to "terminate" your employees so they can be rehired by an outsourced firm, and then leased back to you.

- Professional employer organizations (PEOs) provide a wide variety of HR outsourcing services including payroll processing, benefits administration, and consulting.

- The pros of HR outsourcing include less-costly but often high-quality employee benefits, reduced administration time, and a greater offering of human resources services for your employees.

- The downsides of HR outsourcing include loss of control, a potentially adverse public relations effect on your work force, and some upfront escrow payments.

- Consider references, experience, and flexibility when choosing your HR outsourcing firm.

- Typical HR outsourcing firms charge a percentage of payroll, but price structures vary depending on the service provided.

Outsourcing Information Technology

In This Chapter

◆ A look at the different types of IT outsourcing

◆ Why IT is the most popular form of outsourcing

◆ Deciding whether IT outsourcing is right for your business

◆ Tips for making the most of your IT outsourcing relationship

Say what you will about salespeople, but a lot of them are technologically challenged. So when Agekezy International purchased laptops for their 50-person worldwide sales force and told them to call Bonnie whenever they had any problems, Bonnie knew she had her work cut out for her.

And, of course, there were problems. As a matter of fact, poor Bonnie was inundated with calls.

One guy's laptop wouldn't turn on. (He didn't press the "power" button.) Another salesperson's laptop kept turning dark on him. (He had set the "sleep" function to every 20 seconds.) Another salesperson complained that his laptop keyboard acted funny. (He later admitted to spilling coffee on it the first day he had it.)

And these were the intelligent questions. After a few weeks of handling calls such as this, Bonnie was pulling out her hair. She went to her boss to plead for help.

"These people may be great sales reps," Bonnie told her supervisor, "but they can't tell a computer from a TV set! I'm getting calls from them day and night!"

Her supervisor calmed her down with a just a few magic words.

"I know." He agreed with her. "I've seen how much time this is eating up. I think we need to outsource this work."

Bonnie found a computer firm that serviced the types of units that her salespeople carried and struck an outsourcing arrangement with them.

The salespeople were given a toll-free number to call, and the computer firm took care of their problems. They connected through the Internet to fix errors. Sometimes the salespeople shipped their laptops to the firm for serious repair.

And so it was that Bonnie had her life back. With a little bit of IT outsourcing, a large administrative problem was solved.

Information technology (IT) is the most popular type of employee outsourcing. It has been estimated that IT outsourcing will grow to $1.2 trillion in 2007.

Firms such as IBM and Electronic Data Systems have provided outsourced data center operations for customers for decades. But the industry has exploded in the past decade due mostly to three words: World Wide Web.

> **Knowledge Is Power**
>
> According to *ComputerWeekly*, an industry trade magazine, IBM garnered about 11 percent of the global IT outsourcing market in 2004, making them the biggest IT service provider of them all. IBM says it seized a quarter of all U.S. outsourcing sales in the past year.

Twenty years ago it would be have been extremely difficult, and costly, to service a client's computer network in Nashville from the home office in Chicago. With today's Internet tools, such long-distance IT jobs have become routine. It's this ability to connect to systems throughout the world via the Internet that has fueled the growth of IT outsourcing.

This chapter examines all the different types of IT outsourcing available to you, why IT outsourcing is so popular, and how to make the best use of these services.

What Is IT Outsourcing?

Oh, the many things you can outsource! Technology firms can help you in almost limitless ways. But you'll want to take note of one underlying factor among these choices: almost all of them use the Internet heavily, probably more so than others. If the web goes down, your outsourcing provider's got a problem—and so do you. So with that in mind, let's look at just a few ways that you can use someone else to do the IT dirty work for you.

Application Service Providers

Why buy a software system and go through the trouble to run it in-house when you can just rent one and pay a monthly fee? Most of today's major software vendors offer "hosted" plans. They act as application service providers, or ASPs. You use their servers for all your needs. If you're running an application through your Internet browser without installing anything onto your computer, you're using an ASP.

Application service providers make available a wide variety of programs, including accounting, e-mail, customer relationship management, sales force management, and customer service software.

> **CAUTION**
>
> **Stay Alert!**
>
> Application service providers face two major challenges: data security and uptime. Data kept by a third party can end up in the wrong hands, or even get lost. If the Internet goes down or your connection is compromised, you will also be unable to access the program and your data. Make sure you consider these risks when considering an ASP.

Websites

The rise of the Internet has spawned thousands of "web-hosting" companies throughout the world. These companies rent out space on their computers to customers for the customers' websites. If you're using a web-hosting company, you're outsourcing information technology. It's very common to pay $50 a month to host your website with a company somewhere else in the country. They take care of the servers, the administration, the domain registration, and the security necessary to put a website out for public consumption. Imagine the cost if you had to set all this up and administer it yourself! Plus, that's one less thing you'll have to worry about!

E-Mail

Many larger companies purchase their own e-mail server software such as Microsoft Exchange or Lotus Domino. This keeps all the e-mail administration and processing in-house. Others elect to outsource. For example, the same company that hosts your website can probably also provide you with many e-mail boxes. You can point your e-mail "clients" (like Microsoft Outlook) to the boxes on your hosting firm's server and then you can retrieve and send out your e-mails through them. Remember that Google, Yahoo!, AOL, and MSN do e-mail hosting, too.

E-Commerce Services

In the business of selling over the web? Then check out Yahoo!'s Merchant Solutions, Microsoft's bCentral, or Paypal. In addition to these large players, hundreds of companies will host your e-commerce site for you. They provide all the tools you need for selling something online, including credit card authorization, inventory management, billing, and customer data tracking. Most charge a monthly rate and often take a percentage of the sale, too. Of course, you can avoid these costs by hosting your own e-commerce server. But that can get expensive and require a level of technical expertise you might not have.

Outsourcing Insights

Try to choose a local company when outsourcing your infrastructure management. Some things just can't be done remotely, and you'll want the company you're working with to be able to quickly send someone on-site to fix a problem.

Infrastructure Management

When you outsource IT infrastructure management services, you're putting another firm in charge of the operation, stability, and security of your network. Companies that outsource their infrastructure management have made a strategic decision to not invest in hiring and maintaining an internal IT staff. The outsourcer may service you remotely (using the Internet), provide on-site technicians, or a combination of the two.

Managed Service Providers

Why spend money on infrastructure if you can get away without it? Toss out all those servers, routers, and switches. You never knew what they did anyway, right? Just hook up everyone's desktop to the Internet and have a managed service provider host all of your applications! You'll pay per user per month, but this way you won't need to worry whether you're running the most current version of server software, have installed the latest security patches, or made a recent backup of your data. Your managed service provider will take care of all of your applications. The good ones will send you data backups whenever you want and do their best to make sure things are running around the clock.

Data Centers

Those giant reel-to-reel tapes and wall-to-wall UNIVAC mainframes from the old days may be gone, but data center outsourcing is alive and well. Underneath the side-walks of many major cities sit vast tunnels of underground secured computing facilities that house data from companies all over the world.

If your business stores a large volume of data, or even a lot of confidential data, then you may want to consider using a data center. This way you'll be sure that it's being stored in an offsite location that employs security and protection above and beyond what you may be capable of doing internally.

> ### Knowledge Is Power
>
> Outsourced data centers proved their value after the devastation of 9/11. Information stored outside of lower Manhattan was brought back online shortly after the attacks occurred, ensuring stability to our financial system.

Application Development

A computer is nice, but without software applications it's brain dead. Who writes all of this software? Some companies can buy their answers off the shelf, but many others must custom create their own programs. You can hire an internal software developer, or you can outsource the work to an application development firm. Application software outsourcing is most popular with companies that need their own custom applications but don't want to be in the software business.

> **CAUTION**
>
> ### Stay Alert!
>
> Outsourcing your application development doesn't end with the delivery of the finished software product. Things changes. Bugs may pop up. Maybe you need an upgrade. Perhaps something new you install two years from now causes the application to go awry. It's a good idea to maintain a good ongoing support contract with your outsourced application developer.

Help Desk

Once upon a time, a company grew and grew and kept adding employees. They all had computers. The computers all had little problems. The company had to hire more employees, just to help the other employees with their computer problems. They called this the help desk. It began to get expensive. What did they do? They outsourced!

Sure, you can hire those internal people who do nothing but fix the computer problems of the other internal people. You can even spend more money on software and tools to assist those people who are assisting the other people. Or you can wipe your hands of the whole annoyance and contract with an outside IT firm to troubleshoot these problems.

Asset Management

Companies like to know when someone does something to their computer that they shouldn't be doing (such as installing a game or potentially harmful application). You can buy software that will help scan, track, and manage your employees' computers. Or you could just outsource the job to an asset management firm. They'll do the scanning, keep track of the ownership, and report to you any changes in configurations.

The Phone System

As more companies are turning to web-based phone systems, IT departments are increasingly taking more responsibility for their company's telephone systems. The Voice over IP phone (VoIP) industry is booming. Forget the receptionist or the whole voicemail system. Instead, let it sit on an outsourcer's computer. You can send and retrieve your phone calls from there just like you can e-mail!

Is IT Outsourcing Right for You?

Are you ready to outsource some IT functions? No matter how big or small your business is, you can probably benefit from some aspects of IT outsourcing. Here are some reasons why.

You're Concerned About Security

You've got a lot of confidential data, and you're sick of getting viruses and worms. You're afraid some malicious person may attack your network. You're finding it difficult keeping up with the latest security trends and technology.

Maybe now it's time to hire an outside technology firm to manage your infrastructure and put the best security techniques into practice.

Outsourcing Insights

To keep taxes and liabilities under control, some firms choose to outsource the use of all their IT equipment with an outside firm. This way none of the equipment (such as fixed assets or furniture and fixtures) shows up on their balance sheet.

You're Spending Too Many Internal Resources on IT

You're paying a full-time IT staff to do nothing but fix computer problems. You're spending too much money every year upgrading computers and buying new servers. You're tired of employee downtime due to computer glitches.

Outsourcing your IT staff would relieve you of this internal overhead and (hopefully) bring in help only when you need it. This might be the time to consider what a PEO has to offer (see Chapter 14).

The Technology Is Getting Too Complex

You're finding it difficult to keep up with all the changes in technology. You're spending too much money training your internal people so that they can keep current. You would prefer to let a firm that's in the IT business manage your network and websites full-time.

You've Got Too Many Software Programs and Databases

Maybe you need to combine data from different sources into one definitive database, thereby reducing duplicate data and creating an environment that's more productive.

Knowledge Is Power

In the year 2000, the IT industry reached an important milestone. For the first time, more than half (54 percent) of IT services purchased in North America were outsourced.

Your Hardware Is All Over the Place

Still have those computers sitting around from the dark ages? Printing out letters on dot-matrix printers? A good IT outsourcer will evaluate your network and help you move into the twenty-first century. If you find yourself behind the times, and you need to get caught up, you may want to outsource your infrastructure management to someone else.

> ### Outsourcing Insights
>
> Companies that rely heavily on technology and companies that make very little use of technology both have good reasons for outsourcing their IT.
>
> Companies that are very technologically oriented often partner with an outside service provider to make sure their systems are running 24/7. For instance, large Internet firms often contract with IBM, Sun, and EDS for data processing. Companies often hire software development firms to fine-tune bugs on mission-critical applications.
>
> Small mom-and-pop business that rely very little on advanced technology but perhaps want a website, can benefit from outsourcing this service to a web-hosting service so they don't have to go through the bother of learning the technology and hosting the site themselves. Or maybe they have a simple set of books that they need to access both from home and work. They can pay a monthly free to Intuit, who makes an online version of their popular QuickBooks program, and are able to access the books wherever they have an Internet connection.
>
> Remember that you want to focus on what you do best and get someone else to do the IT stuff for you.

Cash Flow

Building a good IT infrastructure is expensive. Maybe you've got better places to spend your money. So instead you keep your overload low by outsourcing your help desk, asset management, or infrastructure management to someone else and pay a monthly fee.

You Don't Know Where or How to Get Good IT People

Finding good IT people isn't easy. Try placing an ad on an online employment service—you'll get resumés from all over the world. How can you tell who's better than the other? IT firms are in the business of deploying top notch IT people. They know what to look for and who to hire. By outsourcing an IT need to an outside provider, you're leaving it up to them to find the right people to do the work.

You Want to Stay on Top of New Technology Trends

Maybe you've got an IT staff, but all they do is put out fires. You need someone to take IT leadership. You'd like a good chief information officer, not just a "techie person." A good outsourced IT partner can serve as a consultant to your business and make sure you're pointed in the right direction, technology-wise. (See Chapter 10 for more on CIOs.)

Making the Most of Your IT Outsourcing Relationship

IT is a tricky area. There are a lot of people out there making a lot of promises. Because losing control of your IT infrastructure could be a business-breaking problem, keep the following points in mind as you pursue an outsourced IT relationship.

Emphasize Security

The last thing you want to happen when outsourcing any IT function is to compromise your network's security. Make sure that your IT outsourcer uses sound security practices. Never give away passwords. Do not allow the outside service provider to exclude you from any part of your system, even for so-called "security purposes."

Stay Alert!

Have your service provider sign confidentiality and nondisclosure agreements (see Chapter 21).

Research the Vendor's Financial Health

Take the time to check out your IT service provider's long-term financial health before establishing a relationship. You don't want to have the company who's hosting your website, your e-mail, or your accounting system to go belly up.

If the vendor shuts its doors and does a runner, how will you get your data? If you're relying on the service provider for strategic services, what happens to you if they suddenly stop answering the phones? Although you can never fully guarantee that such an event won't happen, you can reduce the risk by going with a business that's on sound financial ground.

Anticipate the Unanticipated

Technology sometimes fails us. The Internet goes down. Cell phone connections drop. Routers go bad. Computers crash.

What happens if your website is unreachable? Do you have a backup site? What if the power goes out? Can you still get your billing done?

For every IT process that you're outsourcing, think of the worst-case scenario and have a plan with your outsourcing partner for dealing with it.

Beware of Inflexibility

IT people can get very gun shy. Wouldn't you be if one little virus can bring down your entire network? But that shouldn't stop your service provider from being flexible enough to respond to your needs.

Don't enter into a relationship with an IT service provider who doesn't understand your business and isn't willing to adapt what they do to help you succeed. "That's not how we do it here" is not always an acceptable answer.

Outsourcing Insights

Margins on hardware and equipment are pretty tight. Software margins are a little better. But the biggest margins are in the services. When negotiating fees with your third party, always follow the money!

Don't Get Gouged

I've seen some clients get into a nice, cozy relationship with their IT service provider and not realize that they're being gouged for prices. They become complacent. They pay the same for a new computer that they paid two years before, even though prices have fallen. They accept at face value the service provider's rate per hour without questioning them or talking to the competition.

Keep your eye on the marketplace and challenge your service provider to always provide you the best deal.

Have a Direct Line to the Top

Remember that IT outsourcers are techno geeks. They may know everything there is to know about the latest gadgets and gizmos, but they might not be as adept at customer service and the business end of things. For this reason, insist on a direct line of communication to senior management.

Don't Be Overly Dependent on One Provider

I have a customer who out-sourced his e-mail, website, e-commerce site, and overall IT management to one firm. Guess what happened when there was a billing dispute? Suddenly all services were affected. Even if you're paying your bills on time, what if the firm suffers financial hardship, an Internet outage, or a scud missile attack on their offices? You go down with them. To avoid losing everything, spread the risk.

Have one firm do your e-mail, use another for your website, and a third company to worry about your network.

Always Consider Relationships

Before you outsource a major IT process, consider the reaction of your internal IT people. Make them part of the selection process. Have them help manage the service provider. This way competing interests won't get in the way of your goals.

Match Your Agendas

IT service providers sometimes think they know what's better for their clients than the clients themselves. Such thinking can lead to problems down the road, for instance, when the client tells the IT people what they want done, and the IT people do something else instead, thinking they have a better solution. Unless you're willing to pay for something you didn't ask for, make sure you and your service provider agree on the deliverables and outcomes of your relationship before proceeding with the relationship.

Outsourcing Insights

My company once had a big disaster when installing a sales force automation application for a client. They expected to better track forecasted sales, while we were intent on improving their quoting process. We had meetings and only heard what we wanted to hear. We believed we had the client's best interest in mind. Guess what happened? We were ultimately fired, and the client wasted a lot of time and money.

Avoid the Jack-of-All-Trades

Just because someone can build a computer doesn't mean he or she knows the first thing about website development, application programming, security, networking, clustering, data warehousing, telephony, or infrastructure management. These are a lot of big words, and they're all specialties. Don't fall into the trap of believing that one technology company can do it all. Never think that an IT outsourcer is going to be able to take care of all of your technology needs just because they "know computers."

Stay In Control

Sometimes technology people can be condescending when talking shop. It's as if they speak a different language and don't want to share that knowledge with anyone else. It's a control thing, and don't you fall for it. If you don't understand something, have them explain it. Don't agree to something unless you're absolutely clear why. This is your network, your computers, your applications, your business. An outside service provider is there to fill a need, not take control of your most important business assets.

The Least You Need to Know

- ◆ Application service providers, infrastructure management, programming, and website hosting are some of the more popular forms of IT outsourcing.

- ◆ IT outsourcing has become the most popular form of outsourcing because of its critical nature to many business and the explosion of the Internet.

- ◆ Security concerns, complexity, and the high cost of technology often lead companies to look for outsourcing solutions.

- ◆ A good IT service provider will supply competent people and consulting services to make sure you're making the best use of technology.

- ◆ Emphasizing security, anticipating the unanticipated, and avoiding inflexibility and price gouging are among the things to consider when entering into an IT outsourcing relationship.

16

Managing the Outsourcing Relationship

In This Chapter

- ◆ Challenges when managing outside service provider relationships
- ◆ Planning your outsourcing project
- ◆ Designing and implementing your project
- ◆ Terminating your relationship with the outside service provider
- ◆ Best practices when managing your outsourced project

ABC Home Mortgage needed a custom software application for tracking closed deals and payments. They contracted out the project to SoftEx, a firm that had done similar work in the past and that promised to deliver the software on time. As a matter of fact, the chief programmer on the project for SoftEx told his contacts at ABC that he thought they'd be able to deliver ahead of schedule.

ABC had a lot of confidence in SoftEx. After signing the contracts and making an initial payment to the software firm, they turned their attention to other pressing projects, assuming that SoftEx would come through on their end of the bargain by the deadline, if not sooner, and that the outsourcer would be in touch with them if they needed additional resources or information.

Fortunately for ABC Home Mortgage, SoftEx did come through on time. But ABC was taking a huge risk in not checking in with SoftEx regularly between the signing of the contracts and the delivery deadline.

Many things can go wrong between the time an outsourced service provider kicks off their outsourced project and the due date.

This chapter covers how to manage your outsourcing relationship to get the results you need. First, you need to detail the challenges you'll face as you begin the project, and then I offer some pointers for handling each individual phase of the typical outsourcing arrangement.

Before It Begins: The Management Challenges You'll Face

Congratulations. You've done a good job so far. You've selected the very best service provider. The contracts have been signed, and the people are in place. Now your relationship really begins. During the next few months, you're going to find out whether all those promises the outside service provider made are for real. You're going to face some unique challenges. Here are the most significant ones.

Supervision Challenges

You need to supervise your outside service provider's work on your project. You must check in with them frequently (sometimes daily, sometimes less) to make sure they remain focused on your job and they're on track to accomplish the project's objectives.

Even if the project is long-term you're still going to have to supervise the service provider. If you've permanently outsourced your call center, you'll probably need to discuss reports from your call center supervisors on at least a weekly basis.

Chemistry Challenges

You involved your key people during the selection process and introduced some of your employees to the people you'll be working with at the new outside service firm. Now that the project has started, you need to make sure that everyone is getting along. If there are corporate culture clashes or personality conflicts, you and your service provider must be prepared to resolve them so that they don't derail your project.

Communication Challenges

You need to have a reliable system of communications with your outside service provider. When are they available? How do you reach them? Who will you be talking to? What means of communications are best?

Competence Challenges

During the review process, you did all that you could to evaluate the outside service provider's competence. You assume that they're going to hit the ground running. If you've miscalculated, you need to be ready to jump into action. Do you fire the third party before it's too late? Do you have a backup lined up? Do you stick with the service provider and provide the necessary resources or training that they need?

Customer and Employee Perception Challenges

You may have prepared your customers and employees for the outsourcing relationship, but after you start working with them, are they responding as you hoped? Dell Computer's customers so disliked dealing with outsourced call centers that the company was forced to bring back some of its customer service operations to the United States. Other companies sometimes find that their employees, not just their customers, are unhappy with the new outsourcing arrangement, too.

Outsourcing Insights

If your outsourcing arrangement is big enough, you may want to consider creating a customer roundtable to give you feedback on what their needs are. Many customers would be happy to have a say in the things an important vendor is doing if it will affect their own business.

Scope Management Challenges

Contracts are made with the best of intentions. Everyone at the beginning of a relationship does their best to think of all the contingencies and work that a project will involve so that these items can be included in the agreement. But it almost goes without saying that extra work creeps up. More services are needed. Additional projects are heaped on the original. The original scope of your project expands. Your challenge is to keep these scope changes under control.

Time Management Challenges

Time is money, especially if your outside service provider is billing you by the hour. As the manager of this project, you want to keep track of what time is being spent and make sure it's being spent productively.

Budget Management Challenges

You need to manage other costs, too. Extra expenses such as supplies, travel, internal resources, tools, and maintenance should be part of your overall budget. You need to constantly track these costs against your budget to make sure nothing gets out of hand.

> **Knowledge Is Power**
>
> On average, organizations report that 4 percent of the outsourcing contract's value is spent on managing the relationship.

Stay Alert!

When it's time to pay your service provider, do so promptly. Holding up money for good reason, as long as it's stipulated in your contract, is fair enough. But not paying or delaying payment to your service provider will only put a large dent in your relationship and could come back to bite you in the long run.

Payment Challenges

Your service provider will want to get paid. You won't want to pay them if the results are not as you expected.

To effectively manage your relationship, you need to use payments as the incentive to make sure your third party is doing the job they promised.

Integration Challenges

Is your outside service provider affecting other areas of your company? Does the filing of financial statements by your reporting group depend on the outsourced accounting staff to complete their general ledger? Does the launch of your new website hinge on an outside network provider getting that new server up and running on time? You'll be challenged to manage everyone's expectations and deadlines, especially the ones that you're indirectly affecting.

Phase 1: Planning and Analysis

Now that I've covered the significant challenges you'll face when managing your outside service provider, let's talk about the specific phases of your relationship.

The planning and analysis phase will be the initial step you take to get the outsourcing arrangement under way.

Assignment of a Dedicated Project Manager

Make sure that a strong project manager, or leader, is assigned as soon as possible. One person should be accountable for the overall success (or failure) of this project.

Start Your Plan

Contracts are discussed in detail in Chapter 21, but I'll mention briefly that your contract should state the deliverables expected of both you and your service provider. Next, you need a plan of action that will document your method for getting there. To create this plan, sit with your service provider as soon as possible and agree on the individual steps to be taken to get to the end zone. During the next phase (discussed later in this chapter), this plan will be further fleshed out and finished.

> **Outsourcing Insights**
>
> When planning out the project, meet with the people whom you will be working with. Establishing a personal connection will help you work together, especially when problems occur.

Establish the Stakeholders

The stakeholders in an outsourcing project, whether short-term or long-term, are the ones who share the most interest and are most affected by the outcome of the relationship. It's essential that you identify all the stakeholders before you start your project so you know who your ultimate evaluators will be. For example, if you're outsourcing your telemarketing functions, the marketing manager may be acting as the project manager and will be ultimately responsible for the success of the project, but the individual sales managers and sales reps will suffer if the telemarketing service fails to generate enough leads.

Outsourcing Insights

Some people will always complain. They always tend to see life with the glass half-empty. Don't let these types get you down and don't let them call the shots.

Know Your Risks and Have a Backup Plan

If you're outsourcing your human resources department, what will you do if they turn out to be incompetent, or your people don't like them, or their promised cost savings don't materialize? What if they have too many personnel changes or their responsiveness is disappointing? Consider the risks you're facing and what you're doing to minimize them. Make sure you've got a plan of action in case things don't go as planned.

Phase 2: The Design

The design phase is where you're going to really hone the project plan into a good working document.

Nail Down the Details

During this phase you agree with the service provider on the timeline of your project. Here you set milestones and more specific deliverables than what had been laid out in Phase 1. You create a much more detailed list of tasks, responsibilities, and due dates. All of this will be put into writing in your project plan and updated as needed.

Build the Internal Team

During Phase 1, you decided on a leader/project manager and identified the stakeholders. Now it's time to build the team. If you're hiring an outside firm to help you implement the new manufacturing system, you need someone on staff to help them gather data, someone from IT to provide them with security codes and server access, and someone from operations to help coordinate training.

Provide Resources

Your third party may require resources. Perhaps they need to reserve conference rooms, buy computer equipment, hire specialists, or book time with senior management. During the design phase, identify and procure all the resources and make sure they will be available when needed.

Finalize Your Budget

When the plan is set and the people and resources have been assigned, have a solid idea of the total costs involved. It's time to finalize the amounts, get additional approval if necessary, and prepare to report to your management team on how well you're doing.

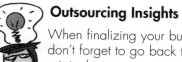

Outsourcing Insights

When finalizing your budget, don't forget to go back to your original return-on-investment calculations (see Chapter 8) and make sure that the amounts that you're budgeting are near to the numbers you used when evaluating your outsourcing decision. Differences should be investigated, explained, and resolved.

Set Up Strong Reporting Systems

Before moving forward, make sure your measurement metrics, both in terms of the formula and how things will be measured, are evaluated. If your service provider will be measured on the reduction in time to close a complaint call, do you have a system for tracking these calls? If your outside telemarketer is being paid on the number of leads they generate for you, do you have a means of recording these leads? If you're budgeted to spend $50,000 on travel during the course of this relationship, does everyone know how to properly document travel costs?

Approve Your Plan

Because circumstances change between Phases 1 and 2, it's essential to get your final plan approved by senior management (unless, of course, you *are* senior management!). Make sure you have buy-in from the highest level possible.

Set Up Administrative Duties

A lot of administrative details will be involved in the outsourcing relationship. You need to arrange to pay your outsourcer, for one thing. And certain activities, tasks, accomplishments, and assignments need to be tracked.

Someone must be responsible for handling these administrative tasks and, as the work progresses, this person will need supervision and support.

Communicate Effectively

During your relationship, make sure the right tools are in place to communicate quickly and effectively. If your service provider is managing your properties on the coast, you may want to employ cell phones, two-way phones, and beepers. You may want to communicate by e-mail, instant messaging, or calendaring. If the service provider is conducting clinical testing of your product across the country, you may find it more efficient to set up a web-based data-entry system.

Phase 3: Implementation and Operations

Phase 3 is the "get-to-work" phase. After all of your planning and analysis, you'll now be starting the project.

Finalization of the Design

Before you implement your project, you're going to need to go back to all the work you've done in the design phase. Certain facts may have changed (for example, a person who you expected to do training isn't available) or timelines may have shifted.

Outsourcing Insights

When you, as the outsourcer, begin to design and then implement a project, don't let anyone get away with telling you "we've never done it that way" or "that'll never fly here." Just because it hasn't been done before doesn't mean it won't work now. The best outsourcing relationships are where the service provider brings new ideas that stimulate their customers. Be open to change, and don't let your employees scare you away from doing something different just because it's never been done before.

System Testing

You need to test whatever setup work you did by doing a dry run. Make sure that sample transactions are put through the new system. Get a sample of the product from the service provider and make sure it's what you expected. Now's the time to make small changes so that everything's right to go live.

Transition to "Go Live"

By the time you go live, your design, development, and testing procedures should have been extensive enough to eliminate any surprises. Make sure you're personally involved in the "first" of everything. For example, if you're moving your website to a new service provider, the first sales transaction from this site should be yours.

Resolve Conflicts and Problems Quickly

What is the procedure for managing problems? If people are double-scheduled or overscheduled, who do they call? If a key material doesn't show up on time and your service provider is down, who should be notified? If your service provider and one of your employees aren't seeing eye to eye on an issue, who has the ultimate authority to resolve the situation?

Evaluate and Measure

You've agreed on the measurements and have set up good systems to track and report on the data. As your relationship progresses, you'll be looking at this information frequently. You'll be comparing actual costs to budgeted costs. You'll be tracking metrics against what was agreed. You'll be asking questions when the numbers aren't adding up to what you expected. You'll be making adjustments as necessary.

Keep Expectations in Line

The stakeholders in this relationship need to be informed of the project's progress. If they're expecting a significant jump in leads from the outside telemarketing firm, it is your job to make sure they're not surprised if the results are not as good as they were expecting. Stay in close contact with those people who depend the most on the outcome of this project.

> **Stay Alert!**
>
> Remember that it takes some time for a project to ramp up. Give yourself time to get up to speed.

Phase 4: Termination

After the project is complete, make sure you've fulfilled all the requirements as stated in your original contract. Check that there are no hidden liabilities or long-term commitments that could still come into play. Write a nice letter to the service provider and offer yourself as a reference. Good relationships often spawn other opportunities.

> **Outsourcing Insights**
>
> During your relationship, things will change. New people will be supplied by the service provider. Technical glitches will occur. Timelines will change. Other projects may take priority. You won't be able to predict everything that will happen. Prepare yourself to deal with these changes as they occur.

Outsourcing Insights

Remember that at the end of your outsourcing relationship, and assuming this isn't just a one-time job, you're only going to have four roads to take: renew with the service provider, replace the service provider, bring the functions back in-house, or drop the business because it's not profitable or necessary.

Outsourcing Insights

Never underestimate the power of leadership in an outsourcing relationship. When the customer and the service provider want to succeed, great things will happen. Leaders of both companies should remain involved and fully committed to the relationship from start to finish.

Best Practices in Managing Outsourcing Relationships

After participating in and/or observing hundreds of outsourced relationships, I've come up with a few best practices for making sure the relationship with your service provider goes as smoothly as possible from beginning to end. Ready?

Empower the People!

Make sure that the project manager has enough authority to make decisions to keep the project on track. Don't hamper him or her with overly excessive controls or bureaucracy. Also, if you have confidence in your service provider, let them "run with the ball," too.

Feel the Vibe!

Outsourcing relationships work great when people get along. You can help foster good relationships by arranging as many face-to-face encounters as possible. Keeping the service provider in the open and working with your employees should help solidify their relationship with the people that they're working with. Keeping them at bay will only widen any potential gap between your employees and them.

Communicate!

I've already mentioned this, but it's worth repeating: keep the lines of communication open. Provide the best tools possible to make communications quick and easy. Communication breakdown is a significant cause of outsourcing problems.

Form the Right Team!

Your project will need input from many areas of your organization. You want to choose people with the right attitude and influence to be the key members of the project. How the team behaves toward the outsourcing relationship will set the tone for the rest of the company.

Take Care of Your Service Provider!

Throughout the course of your relationship, make sure you're looking out for the interests of the service provider. Your relationship should not be adversarial. Both of you should be profiting together. Taking advantage of the service provider will only harm the long-term prospects for your relationship to grow.

Outta Here!

Always manage your relationship with the end result in mind. Avoid projects that go on and on, with no end in sight. As much as you love your service provider, you want to work toward showing them the door as soon as possible, as long as this means a successful termination to the relationship.

The Least You Need to Know

- ◆ Managing your outsourcing relationship will present managerial, cultural, and financial challenges.

- ◆ When you first begin your relationship, establish your stakeholders, evaluate your resources, finalize your budget, set up good reporting systems, and identify all of your risks.

- ◆ As you implement your relationship, nail down the details; build your internal team; and get your plan approved, tested, and ready to go live.

- ◆ As your relationship progresses, make sure you have a system for managing changes.

- ◆ Best practices for guiding your relationship include forming the right team, making sure your relationship is win-win, and focusing on the end result.

The Right Service Level Agreement for You

In This Chapter

- ◆ The pros and cons of service level agreements (SLAs)
- ◆ Defining the scope of your SLA
- ◆ Documenting problem management and business policies
- ◆ Compensating your contractors
- ◆ Using your SLA to measure the performance of your outside service provider

Feintool, a global leader in fine tool blanking, decided to outsource its entire ERP (Enterprise Resource Planning) system. This was not a decision to be taken lightly. Feintool has more than 1,500 employees worldwide who are dependent on this system. The company couldn't afford any downtime. They needed an outsourcer who could guarantee 24/7 access to the ERP system.

After a lengthy search, Feintool finally decided on a Swiss company called IN4U. The key reason Feintool chose IN4U was because of their service level agreement. IN4U promised, in writing, that Feintool's system would be up and running no less than 99.5 percent of the time. If they failed to meet this requirement, then IN4U would suffer significant financial penalties.

In the outsourcing business, service level agreements are generally associated with technology-based relationships, such as computer systems or call centers. But in fact, service level agreements, commonly referred to as SLAs, are a very important part of most outsourcing relationships.

This chapter explains their purpose and application and suggest ways you can create the right SLA for your company and the third parties you do business with.

What Is an SLA?

SLAs are contracts, in writing, that set out both parties' obligations under their outsourcing arrangement. The contract establishes the expectations between the two parties. It defines their business relationship and details the criteria that will be used to judge whether the outsourcing arrangement is working.

Service level agreements are most often used when entire processes are outsourced to a service provider. Most large outsourcing arrangements have a service level agreement in place, especially if a significant function is being outsourced. Sometimes SLAs are the only agreement between the service provider and their customer. Other times the SLA is part of an overall and more encompassing contract. (These contracts are discussed in more detail in Chapter 20.)

SLAs are agreed upon by both customer and service provider. Sometimes, as in IN4U's case, their service level commitment is established right up front and built into contracts. In other cases, SLAs are worked out by both parties based on the requirements at hand.

An SLA is essential for most outsourcing arrangements because …

- ◆ It will legally protect both you and your outside service provider.
- ◆ It documents both parties' responsibilities.
- ◆ It serves as a basis for compensation.
- ◆ It establishes a starting and ending point of your outsourcing relationship.

Do I Really Need a Service Level Agreement?

Think about it: you're outsourcing some important process or function to a third party. There's a lot riding on the decision. Wouldn't you feel better if your service provider's promises were in writing?

SLAs have become a popular way to minimize some of the risks associated with outsourcing. And they're not just for the customer.

Service providers have as much of an interest in a good SLA as you do. An Internet service provider wants to know from the very start of a relationship how quickly they need to respond to questions and what types of issues take priority over others. The company that is collecting receivables on your behalf wants to make sure you are satisfied with the methodology they'll be using.

Outsourcing Insights

It's always a good idea to include your business goals in your service level agreement. Apprising your service provider of your overall goals will help you to agree on deliverables, responsibilities, and metrics that are consistent with your goals.

The Risks of Not Having an SLA Agreement

Without a good service level agreement, you may be leaving too much up to chance.

The following sections outline some potential hazards of not having an SLA.

Anyone Home?

Suppose you outsource your deliveries to a transportation company. You put together a big order for a customer in Florida, and the driver picks it up from your warehouse and takes it away. One evening a few days later you get a call from the customer asking where the order is. You call the trucking company … no answer! Later you find out that the trucking company is only open during normal business hours.

Stay Alert!

Many vendors have standardized service level agreements that they ask their customers to sign. Remember that just because the agreement looks standardized, it doesn't mean that you can't change it. Read the agreement carefully and insist on corrections that are important for you.

Without a service level agreement in place, the trucking company has no obligation to help you whenever you need an answer. You haven't agreed on when they'll be available in case a problem arises.

The Bottomless Pit

Service level agreements can help both parties understand when services begin and end and what the costs are going to be if they continue.

Many years ago, MicroTech installed an accounting system for a client and left their ongoing service relationship open. That was a big mistake. The client called them day and night with computer-related questions, regardless of whether MicroTech's accounting application was involved! They thought all this extra service was part of the deal.

CAUTION

Stay Alert! _____

Don't rely on the service provider to monitor their performance under an SLA. Assume that your systems are better and keep track of as much information as you can internally.

MicroTech had to write this project off as a loss. But they learned not to make the same mistake again. All future projects had an SLA in place that defined what they were responsible for. This helped bring those bottomless pit projects under control.

Who's Responsible for What?

"I don't understand why we've been fired," cried Jamie. "I thought we were doing a great job!"

Jamie runs an outsourced investor relations firm, handling stockholder-related matters for dozens of public companies that don't want to fund their own internal investor relations departments. She was just told by a large customer that their relationship was being terminated.

"We answered all calls from their investors. We took care of their press releases. We made sure materials were mailed out when requested. We kept on top of all shareholder events. This just comes as a complete surprise."

Unfortunately, there was a misprint in the company's annual report. The customer believed that the annual report should have been reviewed more closely by Jamie's firm. There was no formal SLA between the two firms, and Jamie had no idea that she was responsible for reviewing her customer's annual report. The error was a glaring embarrassment. And it could have been avoided if both parties had thought to put an SLA in place.

No One To Cry To

Without a good service agreement in writing, when something goes wrong you might not have any legal recourse should your outsourcer not live up to its end of the bargain.

Maybe your outside public relations firm promised to send out six press releases a month. Or your outsourced quality assurance firm agreed to ship out your product with a 95 percent customer satisfaction rating. But what happens if they don't?

Service level agreements, like all contracts, get both parties' commitments down on paper. That means you'll have legal recourse if something goes wrong.

Outsourcing Insights

A recent survey of executives that rely on service level agreements found that dependable service is more important than being compensated when mistakes occur. If your Internet service goes out, do you really care whether you're compensated the $2 for a lost day?

Defining the Scope of Your SLA

For the most part, you shouldn't have to worry about creating an SLA from scratch. Most good service providers will already have one in place. You should, however, read it carefully and make changes where necessary. Initially, make sure the scope of your relationship is very clearly defined.

Get Examples and Do Your Research

Do a little research to make sure the service provider's SLA is consistent with the industry. You can find examples by searching the Internet or by asking friends and business partners who may already have SLAs in place. Get an attorney involved. In the end, this is a legal contract and will probably require the input of an experienced professional.

Match Cultures

Different industries and even different firms within a single industry define service differently. In the investment banking industry, things must happen quickly and on deadline. You need a service provider that is ready to react to your requests immediately. Similarly, if your business relies on orders placed over the Internet and you've outsourced this to an e-commerce service, you better make sure they understand the importance of being up and online all the time. However, if you run a little antiques store and get a couple of inquiries a month on the web, you can probably get away with a more relaxed, and therefore less expensive, level of service.

Stay Alert!

Some service providers like to defer setting up an SLA until a "baseline period" of activity has been established. The theory is that once this period has passed, the service provider can then come up with measurements against the baseline. Don't buy this line. Get your SLA in place as soon as possible and use estimates in lieu of any baselines.

Make sure that the culture and organization of the service provider and the SLA you sign respects your company's needs.

Nail Down the Details

"We will respond to your calls as quickly as possible." How quickly do you mean? "Our service technicians are experienced." Experienced in what? You can be experienced after one month on the job or one year on the job, yet the level of experience would certainly differ.

Avoid vague promises in your SLA. Nail down each commitment to the finest level of detail possible.

Define the Terms and Performance Levels

Definitions are very important in service level agreements. What constitutes an "error"? How do you define "best efforts"? What exactly is an "incident"? A good SLA will define all technical language and other important terms used throughout the agreement. In addition, a good SLA defines the metrics to be used to evaluate performance levels. (We discuss metrics and measuring your service level agreement later in this chapter.)

Name the Key People

When you make the decision to work with a new service provider, it might be because of specific people that you met during the evaluation process. Sometimes key persons give you that sense of comfort and make personal commitments that persuade you to sign on the dotted line. It would be lousy if, after you sign up with the company, you're suddenly assigned different people to work on your account.

Your level of service is going to depend on the people who are providing that service. Some people may think this is going overboard, but I recommend that your SLA state names, locations, contact information, and background of the key people you'll be working with. Both the company and its key people should stand behind the service level commitments that are being made. It's a given that people may change roles or leave the service provider, so you need to make sure the SLA can be updated as these changes happen.

Specify What Can Be Outsourced by the Outsourcer

In the world of outsourcing, even the outsourcers outsource! Your SLA should state whether your outsourcer will be using other outsourcers to provide work on your behalf. It should also specify any limitations to such practices that you believe should be in force.

Establish Start and End Dates

Your agreement should specify definitive start and end dates. The agreement should provide for how it gets renewed and set out the grounds for termination. No service provider wants to be stuck providing service forever without getting paid. And you don't want to be locked into any unnecessary service arrangements.

Managing Your Policies and Problems

In addition to defining the scope of your relationship, a good SLA lays out how services will be performed and what happens when the inevitable problems occur.

Accountability

Your SLA should clearly state who is responsible for what. For example, if you're hiring a company to install an accounting application for a client, the SLA will likely state that the contractor is responsible for the training and support of that specific application and that your own staff is responsible for backing up the database and making sure the system can be accessed by users.

Outsourcing Insights

Keep your SLAs simple and brief. Use plain language. Establish clear goals and easy-to-understand measurements.

Accessibility

Your SLA should also state who has permission to do certain things. For example, do you need to provide your contractor with any passwords or other security passes? If so, the SLA should stipulate who has access to the passwords and what they can use them for.

Processes

When the inevitable problems occur, your people need to know who to call for help and what information they need to have available so the service provider can fix the problem. These details should be spelled out in the SLA.

For example, if there's ever a database issue with software my company installed, we first have our clients call the software manufacturer for direct help while also notifying us so we're in the loop. If the vendor can fix the problem, great. Otherwise, the next level of support comes directly from us. We also define in our SLA the types of problems that would require an on-site visit and what the charges would be.

The whole reason why you've got an SLA is to make sure you're getting the right service when you need it. Knowing the exact steps to take will get you back to work in a hurry.

Stay Alert!

If you're based in New York, is it a problem that you're relying on an outside service provider who is located in California? Do you need someone to be local? Your SLA should spell out exactly where the service will be performed, and who will pay for any transportation costs.

Outsourcing Insights

According to a recent poll, only 26 percent of SLAs in effect had penalty clauses. Your SLA should include a clause that spells out what your recourse is in case something goes wrong.

Availability

I bought a computer game for my son a few months ago and had problems installing it. I called the technical support number and was told that their support "department"—I later found out this was an outsourced firm—was not open on the weekends. Aren't weekends the time when fathers and sons spend time together playing computer games? I bet the company who outsourced technical support for this game wishes they had specified in their SLA that the firm must be available on evenings and weekends.

Make sure your SLA agreement addresses when the service provider will be available for service.

Escalation

Working one's way through various levels of service technicians can be a frustrating experience for a customer. Many service providers nowadays offer SLAs with different levels or "classes." These levels define how quickly you'll get serviced and by whom. For instance, one level of service might escalate a customer's service call if the call remains open for more than two hours. A higher level of service might put the initial call immediately through to a senior technician. A good SLA documents what conditions trigger escalation of an issue.

Responsiveness

A customer catches you on your cell phone and tells you that she gets a strange tone when she calls your main business number. You try it yourself and experience the same problem. In a panic, you call up your outsourced telephony firm to find out what's going on. After waiting 20 minutes on hold, you're redirected to a general voicemail box to leave a message. Argh!

Your SLA should state how quickly you'll get an answer to your problems. Some SLAs include emergency phone numbers to call. A good outsourcer understands that when their service fails, it's potentially catastrophic for their customer.

Backup Plans and Downtime

Sometimes all else fails and it's time to turn to Plan B. You might want to include a section in your SLA that discusses what the procedure will be if a primary service fails. Is there a backup plan?

When to Pay and When Not to Pay

Unfortunately, sometimes the service you contracted for may not meet your expectations. Your SLA needs to address what your options are in case you're not getting what you expected.

A Change in Plan

I've already warned you of the perils of scope creep—the unchecked expansion of a project that eats up budgets *and* deadlines. Unfortunately, it's such a common occurrence that you should plan for some scope creep all the while you're taking steps to avoid it. For instance, let's say you sign a contract with an Internet service provider (ISP) for as many e-mail accounts as you have employees. If your business experiences a spurt of growth thanks to the new ISP arrangement, you'll need to hire more employees, and will then need more e-mail accounts. Does your SLA take these sorts of changes into consideration?

Here's another scenario: you contract with a firm to provide content and layout for a quarterly four-page newsletter for your company. However, by the third newsletter, you realize that you need to bump the length up to eight pages to accommodate all of the issues you need to cover. A good SLA has provisions for dealing with modifications and scope creep, including the costs associated with any changes. Planning in advance for changes in plans enables you to proceed with your project with fewer delays.

Give Me Credit

In many cases, you will have to pay up front for services to be rendered in the future. But what happens if something goes wrong or the services you paid for long ago aren't up to snuff? If your service level agreement provides for credits for future services in case of contractor error or underperformance, you will be covered without having to rewrite your original contract.

Show Me the Money

In the end, it all comes down to the money. SLAs should always include a section covering the costs associated with all contracted services. It should specify how much the service will cost and when payment is due. In addition, it should clearly identify what services cost extra and what services are included as part of the primary fee.

You Are Terminated

Somewhere else in your SLA, you need to address what happens when one of the parties fails to meet their obligations. Among the consequences, the contract should spell out what constitutes grounds for premature termination as well as each party's future liabilities and any open amounts due. Also as part of termination, it must be agreed who owns any tangible or intellectual property generated.

Measuring Your SLA's Success

So how effective is your service level agreement? Is your outsourced provider doing what they promised? Are you getting the level of support you expected? Are your people happy? Are your customers happy? You should have a plan for measuring the success of your SLA. I discuss various ways of getting these measurements in Chapter 18, but no matter what method you choose, make sure it is spelled out in the SLA.

What's the Period?

Don't forget to define the measurement period in the SLA. If your expectations are to reduce the number of customer complaints, you need to indicate the timeframe for those improvements.

Reporting

With all the promises being made, a good service provider will be anxious to show you just how well they're doing. Your SLA agreement should state what reports the third party will provide to you, what will be included on the reports, and how often they will be provided.

Put Teeth into the Deal

Service companies are in the business of making promises. If they don't live up to their promises, they shouldn't expect to be paid! A good system of measurement puts some teeth into the deal. Your SLA should have a provision that if certain metrics aren't obtained as promised, compensation will be affected.

The Changing SLA

If you stick with your service provider for any length of time, your relationship will evolve as your business grows and your needs change. You might find that some things you thought the third party would handle are better left to you. And maybe other responsibilities that you didn't think about are more suitable for the service provider to deal with. You may both come up with good ways to measure your progress and better methods for resolving problems. It should go without saying that as your relationship changes, so, too, should your SLA.

The Least You Need to Know

◆ Service level agreements (SLAs) define the relationship, expectations, and obligations with your outsourced service provider.

◆ Without an SLA, you're leaving to chance that services will be completed on time, on budget, and to your satisfaction.

◆ SLA agreements should define key terms, spell out who is responsible for what tasks, and match cultural requirements between the provider and the customer.

◆ Good service agreements should stipulate access requirements, location of service, availability of service, and response times.

◆ Compensation requirements also need to be spelled out in an SLA and matched to services performed.

◆ SLAs should include specific measurement and reporting criteria to determine how well the relationship is going.

Measuring the Success of Your Outsourced Project

In This Chapter

- ◆ The importance of measuring the results of your outsourcing project
- ◆ Typical metrics used to determine your success
- ◆ Popular approaches to measuring success or failure
- ◆ Compensation options for paying your contractor

Tony, VP of Administration at a mid-size service firm, decided to outsource the company's human resources to a Professional Employer Organization (PEO). About six months after doing this, he met with the company's CEO, and the PEO came up as a topic in conversation.

It was not a meeting that Tony would ever like to repeat again. The CEO asked some very reasonable questions, and he wasn't getting any answers. The CEO wanted to know if the company was saving as much money as expected. He asked if the company's human resources costs were now in line with their competitors. He reminded Tony about the PEO's promise, during the search process, to lower health insurance premiums and wanted to know if these savings had been achieved yet. Tony didn't have answers to any of his boss's questions.

The CEO was clearly frustrated with Tony, and asked him one final question: "How can I tell my board that outsourcing our entire human relations function was a good decision?"

Tony had failed to do one very important thing when establishing this outsourcing relationship: he didn't agree on metrics with the PEO. Without metrics, there was no way for him to know if his service provider was actually accomplishing what they had planned!

You're outsourcing a process or function to a service provider to achieve a certain benefit—cost savings, productivity gains, resource allocation, and so on. After a certain period you'll want to take a look back at what's been achieved and make sure that the relationship is working out as hoped.

This chapter examines the why's and how's of measuring (and paying for) the results of your outside service provider's work so that you can judge for yourself whether the decision to outsource was really worth it.

Why Measure?

If you don't measure how things are going, how do you know whether they're going well? Sometimes that gut feeling isn't enough. Every outsourcing project or relationship should have some type of measurement system in place.

Stay Alert!

It's very important to set up your system of measurement before starting your outsourcing project. Be prepared to invest in the people and tools necessary to collect and report on the data you'll need to help you realize the benefits of the arrangement.

An Ongoing Check of Progress

Measuring your project while it's still underway will help keep costs under control and your eye on the end goal. If you've hired an outside firm to help you with telemarketing and, after a realistic time-frame, you find that your lead generation is behind what you hoped, you can take corrective action or even terminate the arrangement before it gets too expensive.

A Basis for Sharing the Wealth

Some outsourcing arrangements include incentives and contingency payments to the service provider, based on the success of the project (discussed later in this chapter). You need to track these factors closely and accurately—your profitability depends on it.

A Continuous Exercise in Improvement

There's room for improvement in any outsourcing relationship. Reading your customer surveys may show you that your outsourced call center is doing well enough, but could still get better in certain areas. A good system to measure these results will help you and your service provider improve their work as it's happening.

A Way to Solve Problems as They Occur

A system of measurement may help you identify problems. For example, you may find that one customer service rep is responsible for the majority of the negative customer reviews. Helping her do her job better, or making sure your service provider replaces her, may solve this problem.

Another Round?

Measuring the results of your outsourcing arrangement will help you determine whether you would benefit from outsourcing the same task again, or if you want to change your service provider over the long term. If you decided to outsource the management of your most recent trade show, a comparison of costs of the service provider versus what it would have cost if you had managed the show yourself will help you decide whether it's worthwhile to outsource this task in the future.

> **Knowledge Is Power**
>
> According to an American Management Association study of 619 firms, fewer than 25 percent of those firms that outsourced finance and accounting functions fully achieved their goals of cost reduction, time reduction, or quality improvement. The reasons are numerous and are case-specific. Proper systems of measurement, however, can provide a warning signal before trouble really occurs.

What Gets Measured?

As touched on briefly in Chapter 8, when measuring results of a project, there are usually specific metrics, or values, you can measure. Choose those things that can be quantifiably calculated. Also set goals and measure these results against those goals.

Suppose that instead of hiring a west coast sales force, you decide to outsource this territory to a dealer channel. You'll want to establish a specific goal (such as a 50 percent increase in sales over a 12-month period of time) and then track the results. Or maybe you decide to outsource your sales management software to an outside provider. Here your goal may be to reduce the long-term cost of maintaining the software and increase the number of phone calls each rep makes. All of these goals are measurable.

Looking Forward and Backward

Metrics can be forward or backward looking.

Forward-looking metrics are called *proactive metrics*. Proactive metrics are used to evaluate conditions as they're happening and to help you take action before a serious problem occurs. For example, you outsource your help desk and you agree with the service provider that there should never be more than 20 callers on hold at the same time. At the point where 18 callers are on hold, the help desk system may send out an alert to inform you of the situation. Proactive metrics enable you and the outsourcer to take corrective action before the problem escalates.

> **Business Buzzwords**
>
> **Proactive metrics** is a system of measurement that acts in advance of a measurement goal.

> **Business Buzzwords**
>
> **Forensic metrics** looks at information from the past to help you evaluate a goal.

Backward-looking metrics are sometimes referred to as *forensic metrics*. If you were to use forensic metrics to evaluate the help desk outsourcing arrangement outlined in the previous example, you might have your outside help desk send you a report each week identifying the number of callers on hold by hour. Looking back, you can see that on two occasions there were more than 20 people on hold at the same time. Based on this information, you can take action to make sure that the same situation is avoided in the future.

Productivity and Cost Metrics

Some metrics may hinge on how quickly and efficiently things are being done. You may want to measure the effectiveness of your service provider based on how productive they are, or how they help you reduce your costs. Factors to consider would include the following:

◆ Time to complete

- Output per hour
- Labor costs per unit
- Overall costs per hour
- Overall costs per unit
- Volume of work completed
- Defect rates
- Backlog size
- Rework levels
- Decrease in absolute costs

Customer Service Metrics

Maybe you're outsourcing to improve customer service. If this is your intent, you probably will want to measure at least some of the following items:

- Time to acknowledge a problem
- Time to resolve a service call
- Accuracy of responses
- Number of customer complaints
- Survey results
- Nature of problems
- Number of problems resolved
- Product defect rates
- Product returns
- Product-specific complaints

Outsourcing Insights

Make sure you include whatever metrics you're using in your service level agreement (see Chapter 17) so that both you and your service provider know how their evaluation will be done.

Sales Metrics

If you're outsourcing some of your revenue stream to a service provider, such as a contractor or technician whose services are ultimately billed to your customer, you should track the following metrics:

◆ Increase in revenue

◆ Increase in net margin

◆ Profitability of the outsourced revenue stream

◆ Accounts receivable turnover

◆ Net increase in cash flow

Outsourcing Insights

You might want to hire an independent party to evaluate the results of an outsourcing project. An internal team may bring with it the politics of your organization. An external evaluator is paid to be far more objective.

Intangible Metrics

Some metrics are difficult to measure. Usually through a system of ratings (like 1 = best, 5 = worst, etc.) you can ask employees and customers to evaluate an outsourced service. This is not an exact science. Results will be subjective.

Nonetheless, by using this system, you may be able to measure things such as the following:

◆ Satisfaction levels

◆ Organizational commitment

◆ Teamwork

◆ Loyalty

◆ Areas for improvement

Systems of Measurement

After you've decided what you're going to measure and what your targets are, it's time to think about your measurement approach. The following sections describe some of the most common measurement methods.

Gain Sharing

Gain sharing is a bonus incentive system where everybody benefits as goals are achieved. In a gain-sharing system, your intent is to measure the improvements, or gains, that you've achieved over a certain period of time and then share the results of those gains with your service provider. For instance, if you're outsourcing your quality control process, you may agree with your third party that for every 1 percent decrease in rejects over a certain baseline, you'll compensate them *x* dollars.

Outsourcing Insights

In Chapter 8, I discussed the financial factors you must consider when deciding whether to outsource. In particular, I focused on whether outsourcing would provide a satisfactory ROI, or return on investment. Many of the metrics discussed in this chapter can be used in your initial calculation to help you decide to undertake the outsourcing project.

Balanced Scorecard

The balanced-scorecard system of measurement takes into consideration four factors: financial analysis (cost/benefit), customer service analysis, quality analysis, and learning/growth analysis. This method requires you to come up with criteria and parameters for each of these four areas.

Effectively using the balanced-scorecard approach involves many steps, including setting targets, establishing measures, allocating resources, and reporting.

Suppose, for example, that you want to use the balanced-scorecard approach to evaluate the success of an outsourced marketer's advertising campaign. You would probably evaluate sales (financial), brand recognition from a telephone survey (customer), creativity of the campaign (quality), and goals for the next campaign (learning/growth) as your scorecard factors.

Outsourcing Insights

Develop your balanced scorecard with your service provider. Together you should both agree on the factors needed to justify success of the relationship.

Knowledge Is Power

A good book about the Balanced Scorecard system of measurement is *Balanced Scorecard Step-by-Step: Maximizing Performance and Maintaining Results,* by Paul R. Niven (Wiley, 2002).

Zero-Based Sourcing

Using a zero-based outsourcing system means that at the end of each period the outsourcing decision is re-analyzed as if it were being evaluated for the first time. It's a rejustification of the decision from a base of zero. You don't look back at past factors; instead, you look ahead at the next period. Using a zero-based sourcing approach, a roofer may determine that outsourcing masonry work this quarter isn't necessary because the weather is expected to be cold and the number of backlogged jobs is fewer.

Customer Surveys

A very popular system of measurement is based on customer feedback. When I changed my cable TV to satellite, the satellite company sent in an outsourced technician to install the dish and set everything up. A few days later, the satellite company called and asked me for feedback on the service. My responses, I'm sure, were used to judge the effectiveness and performance of the technician.

Benchmarking

In college I once got 42 percent of the questions right on an exam and was awarded a B. This was called a "curve" by the professor—in effect, my results were benchmarked against others in the class and the grade adjusted accordingly. Many companies "grade" their outsourcers the same way. They make it a priority to perform well against their peers rather than in absolute terms. Your system of measurement may rely on benchmarking the performance of your service providers against the results of others in your industry.

Now What?

You've made a lot of progress. You've set up a system of measurement and identified the metrics that will be important in evaluating your outside service provider. As the results start coming in, what are you going to do with them? Assuming you decide to stay the course, you may want to incorporate into your ongoing service level agreement (see Chapter 17) a payment schedule that's based on the metrics.

Let's consider some of the most popular payment options.

Performance-Based Contracts

Under performance-based contracts (also referred to as incentive-based contracts), the client typically agrees to pay the service provider a certain baseline amount, with bonuses built in when agreed-upon goals are successfully reached. A performance-based contract can benefit both the customer and the service provider. The service provider can reap significant benefits if certain milestones are reached. The customer pays above and beyond the baseline amount only if the service provider lives up to its end of the bargain.

Performance-based contracts are used to motivate both the service provider and the customer to attain certain metrics. For example, an outsourced telemarketer may receive a minimum fee plus an extra fee for each qualified lead above a baseline that she provides to the customer.

Contingency-Based Contracts

A contingency-based contract is an agreement whereby the service provider gets paid *only* when their goals are met. They are usually more expensive than performance-based contacts because no compensation is provided during the term of the contract until successful. The service provider takes all of the risk, and in return reaps a bigger reward at the end. However, such contracts provide huge incentives to the service provider to meet the agreed-upon goals, because they don't get any money until they do so.

Outsourced accounts receivable collection companies often work under contingency-based contracts. These firms undertake all the collection work for no fee. If they do collect an outstanding bill on their client's behalf, they usually take a whopping 25 to 50 percent of the entire outstanding amount. It's a nice windfall for the agency, and a no-risk venture for their client.

Outsourcing Insights _____

Most contingency-based contracts require the customer to give the service provider exclusivity on the work. In other words, if you contract with a collection firm on a contingency basis, you more than likely will not be able to send out the same invoice for collection to two firms. Make sure that you include an expiration date on the contract so if your service provider doesn't reach their goal by a certain time, you are free to outsource the work elsewhere.

Fixed Fee

Fixed-fee contracts require the client to pay the service provider a set fee, or retainer, agreed upon in advance. You may agree to pay a fixed monthly fee to your outsourced legal firm that's doing immigration work for you, regardless of how much time they spend or the results they achieve.

Stay Alert! _____

Time and materials arrangements allow for the greatest flexibility with also the highest amount of risk. You want to keep a much closer eye on your service provider when you allow them to bill for every hour they incur.

Time and Materials

Your outsourcing agreement may be based solely on an hourly rate. Temporary workers, word processors, and office support often bill based on time and materials. As with fixed-fee arrangements, metrics play a part in determining your long-term relationship with the service provider.

Equity

Some outside service providers become insiders—especially when they get paid for their services through equity. An outside attorney may provide start-up help in return for a piece of the new venture. An outsourced chief financial officer may work by the hour for a time until he or she reaches an agreed-on milestone (such as securing a first round of financing) and then receive shares in return.

Equity compensation can be extremely expensive—giving up a piece of ownership for a service is a high price to pay. But it's also a great way to limit cash payments to a critical third party.

Bringing It Back Around

When the project is complete, compare the measured results with your original estimates. Was your ROI what you expected? Did you reap other measurable benefits, too? Figuring out what you did right and wrong in the initial calculation will help you make better outsourcing decisions in the future.

The Least You Need to Know

◆ By instituting a system of measurements for your outsourcing project, you're establishing an ongoing means of checking the progress of the project, a yardstick for calculating compensation, and a way to solve problems as they occur.

◆ Metrics can be forward focused (proactive metrics) or backward focused (forensic metrics).

◆ Popular measurements focus on productivity/cost, customer service, sales, and intangible factors.

◆ A good system of measurement supports compensating your service provider based on performance, milestones reached, and goals achieved.

Chapter 19

Going Global

In This Chapter

- ◆ Reasons for outsourcing work overseas
- ◆ The pitfalls of going global
- ◆ Things to consider before starting an outsourcing relationship with an overseas partner
- ◆ Best practices for offshore outsourcing

Wipro Technologies is a business process outsourcing firm headquartered in Bangalore. A few years ago, the company started a model for clinical process outsourcing (CPO) that has proved to be a tremendous help to hospitals in the United States and around the world.

Wipro's CPO services allows health-care facilities to electronically send scans of their patients to specially trained radiologists in India who, adhering to Western standards, analyze and determine the results of the scans. The data from the scans are then sent back to the originator with the results.

With this system, patients in the United States can get their results back quicker without sacrificing medical quality. And because of the lower cost of living in India, hospitals here can get the work done at a much lower cost than if it was done domestically. Because response time is lowered, the overall level of care is increased without increasing the overall cost of the care.

Shipping off work to be done overseas is not a new concept. But the practice has exploded in recent years. The offshore outsourcing revolution is underway.

Thanks to advances in technology, people can transfer data with ease. English has spread itself to all parts of the world. Telecommunications is cheaper. Air travel is easier. New tools enable people in far-flung places to see each other and share information. Because of these changes, companies now look in places they hadn't known existed to find qualified people to outsource their work.

In this chapter, I go over the very basics of outsourcing your work overseas. I focus on the practice of using foreign third-party firms to do the work for you.

Why Go Overseas?

Aren't there enough good people here at home? Do you have to go all the way to India to set up your call center? Is it really necessary to employ a contractor in China to assemble your furniture? Must you store your rolls of wire in an Eastern European warehouse? In many cases, businesses have found significant benefits in *offshore outsourcing*. Here are some reasons why.

Business Buzzwords

Offshore outsourcing is the exporting of work from the United States and other developed countries to other areas of the world.

Knowledge Is Power

The population under age 18 in China is larger than the combined total populations of the United States and the United Kingdom. Many more Chinese people will be looking for work over the next few decades, which is sure to keep offshore outsourcing costs under control.

A Reduction in Cost

The most popular reason why companies outsource their work overseas is to reduce their costs. Labor rates in many developing countries are often significantly lower than the rates here in the United States. Outsourcing with a company in a country with lower labor rates can improve your bottom line.

Location, Location, Location

Other companies outsource work overseas to satisfy logistical issues. Your warehouse in Eastern Europe can get products into the hands of your European customers more quickly than if the same products were shipped from your warehouse in Minneapolis.

Finding an inexpensive location for manufacturing your products before bringing the final product back into the United States may improve your efficiency.

Or maybe your products require special conditions, such as consistently warm or cold temperatures. Outsourcing the manufacturing and storage of these products to places in the world that are more suited to your needs might make a lot of sense. Sometimes companies even choose to outsource to a certain location because a key employee lives there and wants to be close to the action. Another reason might be that a resource required for the product is more readily available and cheaper in, say, Brazil than it is in the United States.

Following the Sun

Service doesn't stop when the sun goes down. Many companies now serve customers around the clock from around the world. A user in England doesn't want to find out that they can only get help during working hours on the east coast of the United States. Outsourcing some of your support services to an overseas provider solves this problem by spreading your capabilities around the clock from around the world.

An Educated and Specialized Work Force

With outsourcing, you're no longer limited to the expertise of the American work force. Many firms in China, India, Pakistan, and other far-flung places employ highly skilled programmers, scientists, writers, researchers, and engineers. Their employees speak English and have been educated in America or England. They may have special expertise in their field. And they want to work with you.

Less Regulation

Why are certain drugs legal in Canada but not in the United States? How come you can buy a Cuban cigar in London but not in New York? Even the European Union and Japan have protectionist policies against imports. For years, people have argued about the governmental constraints on trade. Some say these conditions are overkill, whereas others think there should be even more regulations in place. Because the rules in different countries vary, it may be easier to outsource work elsewhere to avoid red tape.

Localized Help

The Bangalore region of India has grown exponentially, both in population and in economic output, over the past decade. The pro-Western government has offered tax credits, low-interest financing, and employment grants to encourage foreign business to do business with their local companies. They've even set up special organizations to help non-Indian companies understand the culture and the work environment of the region and to assist them in finding partners and investors. Thanks in large part to this kind of assistance from local governments, outsourcing work to that part of the world has become easier.

Financial Wizardry

Think exchange rates. Think tax incentives. Think government grants. My father-in-law is British and no longer buys a CD in England, but spends a fortune at Tower Records whenever he visits us in America. Why? With the exchange rate so strong, it's 30 percent cheaper for him to buy his music in this country than back home. Overseas outsourcing has the same advantages. Many companies consider the work there to be part of a financial instrument—hedging exchange and tax rate fluctuations with what they'd pay if they do the work at home.

Look Before You Leap: The Downsides of Overseas Outsourcing

With all these great reasons to outsource overseas, you should jump into it, right? Well, not exactly. Like everything else, there's a negative side. Shipping off your next programming project or assembly job to Vietnam has its risks, as I explain in the following sections.

Knowledge Is Power
The Philippines graduates an estimated 15,000 technology students annually.

Communication Problems

Before you outsource your customer service operations to the company in Bangalore, be careful of language differences. Your American customers may sense the foreign accent and could be put off by it. If the phone operator turns out to be more than just a little difficult to understand, your customers will get frustrated.

And besides your customers, what about your employees? Shifting assembly work to a firm in China may make financial sense, until your production people in the United States try to communicate with their Chinese counterparts. If your outsourcer's English language skills are weak, you increase the risk of communication miscues and improperly performed work, turning a proposed cost savings into an expensive nightmare.

Time Zone Differences

The "follow-the-sun" customer service approach is great. But what if you've outsourced a research project to a Taiwanese firm who keeps just "regular" business hours? Timing your phone calls to match their day can be difficult. Even if you use an outside service provider in Europe, you're still looking at a five or six hour time difference from the east coast of the United States. This means you've got to get your calls done before noon or you'll have to wait until the next day. Consider time zones before you leap.

Cultural Clashes

Will cultural differences get in the way of your relationship with the foreign service provider? If you outsource work to another country, you have to deal with their holidays and cultural rules. GE Real Estate found this out when they outsourced a software development project to an affiliate in India. Problems went unnoticed because Indian workers, unlike their American counterparts, were reluctant to speak up when they thought something was going wrong. The Indian workers were culturally trained to take orders without asking questions, even if they thought the orders weren't the right thing to do. Holidays and religious festivals also impeded productivity.

> ### Knowledge Is Power
>
> Santiago, Chile's capital, is among the least-expensive cities in the world. The government there has recently created an English speakers' registry to assist American companies in outsourcing work. Chile, which has free trade agreements with the United States and the European Union, is considered by many to be a potential outsourcing hotspot in the years to come. More help can be found at www.chileus. org.

Financial Complications

When it's time to pay the outside payroll service that is based in Phoenix, you simply write them a check. But when it's time to pay the independent programmers you hired in Malaysia, how are you going to get them their money? Do you have any spare Malaysian ringgits lying around? Setting up a system for paying an overseas contractor may require you to open up a foreign bank account, establish letters of credit, or arrange wire transfers. Get ready for some high finance!

International Taxes

Operating in another country means learning that country's tax laws. Are you subject to local taxes because you're farming out work to a local company? Are there hidden duties and import/export taxes that will surprise you at the dock? Depending on the significance of your investment, you may find yourself hiring local tax experts to advise you.

Legal Complications

The United States has a fair (though far from perfect) system for settling disputes. Can you say the same for the country you're about to do business in? What would you do if an offshore outsourcer took advantage of your intellectual property in their own country? If your outsourcer violates the terms of your contract, what recourse do you have? If your contractor operates in violation of the law, could you be held liable, even if you weren't aware of his actions? (For more information on the liabilities involved in outsourcing, see Chapter 22.)

Oversight Difficulties

One thing's for sure in this great world of ours—no country has cornered the market on incompetent people! You'll find shoddy work anywhere. But it's a lot tougher to deal with poor quality or lack of reliability when your service provider is halfway around the world and isn't picking up the phone. I've known business managers to get on a plane and fly to any corner of the United States to berate a service provider. But would they do the same if the work were being done in Southeast Asia?

Infrastructure Challenges

Many foreign places have serious infrastructure problems. Your outsourcing partner might experience nagging problems with their water and electricity. They may not have the access to a highway system for delivering parts and products. They might not have regular access to basic services like mail and trash pickup. All of these problems put a damper on productivity and reduce or eliminate altogether the benefits of outsourcing. Get ready for uncontrollable delays and lack of services that you take for granted.

Bribery and Other Problems

In some countries, it's not at all unusual to be asked to pay corrupt politicians to carry on with your business. Many companies who have outsourced to India, the Ukraine, and parts of South American have complained of having to "take care of" a local customs agent or paying off government workers. Failure to do so may mean the shipment you're waiting to receive has been mysteriously held up for further review. If you're farming out work to a country with a less-than-reputable political system, you may find yourself incurring extra "duty tax" that you didn't count on.

Global Piracy

Many emerging Eastern European and Asian countries are struggling to establish, and then enforce, intellectual property laws. Microsoft has to contend with countless unlicensed copies of its Windows software being sold in plain view on street corners. A big contributor to this problem is their outsourcing of development and production work overseas. If you're concerned that someone outside of the United States may steal your ideas or your content, you may want to reconsider overseas outsourcing.

Political Instability

In 1959, when Fidel Castro came to power in Cuba and the government nationalized privately held property, many American companies lost millions of dollars in investments. And Russia recently nationalized Yukos, one of the country's largest energy companies, an action believed to have been taken because its owner was a staunch opponent of the government. As these examples illustrate, developing countries offer a lot of outsourcing opportunities, but they also often suffer from political instability. If there's a change in the political winds, you could end up losing all that you invested in the relationship, just like Michael Corleone did.

Before You Take the Plunge

Going into foreign markets may be a great outsourcing opportunity for your company, but it's not without its risks.

Before you move forward, though, keep a few guidelines in mind.

CAUTION

Stay Alert! _____

If you're outsourcing overseas, you should be aware of the Defending American Jobs Act of 2004. Sponsored by more than 50 legislators, the bill proposes to cut federal funding from companies that lay off workers at higher rates in the United States than abroad. The legislation would also require companies that apply for federal grants and loans to declare the salaries of employees in the United States and abroad. As of this writing, this bill has not become law.

Find the Experts

You'll want to line up professional help, among them consultants who specialize in outsourcing and attorneys familiar with the local tax and legal systems. Depending on the language skills of the people you're considering, you may want to secure an interpreter, too.

Hire a Local Agent

Consider hiring a local agent who knows the currency, customs, and language to represent your interests while you're evaluating overseas outsourcing candidates. The agent could serve as your guide when you visit the country and could also act as your eyes and ears when you're not around. Although an agent can't stop you from making a fool of yourself at the local festival, he can help you navigate the cultural waters more effectively than if you were on your own.

> **Knowledge Is Power**
>
> Most countries have business development agencies and many local regions have established chambers of commerce. These are great contacts when looking for a local agent. Also try that country's embassy.

Use U.S. Laws

Try to structure your agreements so they are subject to United States laws, not the laws of the service provider's home country. Your goal is to have as much legal protection as possible in case things go wrong. Navigating another country's legal system can be troublesome.

Contact the Local Chamber of Commerce

In regions where special efforts are made to attract foreign business, local chambers of commerce have sprung up. They will provide information about local laws, officials, taxes, transportation, the work force, and religious customs that will help smooth out your relationship with the local company.

> **CAUTION**
>
> **Stay Alert!**
>
> Experts at a recent Privacy and Data Security Summit warned that outsourcing work overseas can sharply increase data privacy risks and the complexity of managing that risk.

Follow the Leader

Some countries—China and India among them—have been dealing with Americans for a long time. Other countries are interested in opening up to American businesses, but they are still working out all of the kinks in the system. If you're outsourcing work overseas for the first time, consider starting with a place where people are used to working with foreigners. You can take comfort in the fact that someone has probably already laid much of the groundwork.

Establish Payment Terms Up Front

Depending on market conditions, you may want to try to pay in dollars so as to avoid exchange-rate fluctuations. Arrange for payments to be made via wire transfer to speed up delivery. Or, if you're sending money overseas to an outsourced supplier, find out whether the company can offer you a bank letter of credit so that you have a guarantee of payment. Alternatively, you could pay fees into an escrow account so you can release the monies when services or products have been satisfactorily delivered to you.

Changing Your Work Hours

Be prepared to change your schedule. Sending work overseas means grappling with different time zones, so get ready to change when you work.

Knowledge Is Power
According to a study by Global Insight, a private consulting firm, the cost savings and use of offshore resources lowers inflation, increases productivity, and lowers interest rates. The firm predicts that outsourcing will produce a total of 317,000 net new jobs in the United States through 2008. The study also calculated that outsourcing added some $33.6 billion to the U.S. gross domestic product (GDP) in 2003, and could add a total of $124.2 billion through 2008.

Go Forth and Prosper

Depending on the size of your investment, you may want to visit the outside service provider on his home turf. It's tempting to buy in to the pretty pictures on a website or the woman speaking to you in immaculate English. But before you ship 500 pallets of parts to a Chinese firm to assemble, you may want to take a look at their facility, their work force, and their management practices.

Use Technology

As mentioned previously, overseas outsourcing has exploded, due in no small part to the growth of technology. Documents, videos, photos, drawings, design plans, conferences … these can all be facilitated through the Internet without leaving your office. When possible, take advantage of this technology to make your outsourcing experience easier.

The Political Environment

As I write this, offshore outsourcing is a highly controversial topic. Not only are many American companies sending work out to be done overseas, they're also building their facilities in countries such as India and the Czech Republic and hiring the locals as employees at much lower rates.

Many Americans lament the loss of American jobs to foreign firms. Outsourcing proponents argue that outsourcing makes American businesses more profitable and efficient. Whatever your viewpoint is on the subject, be prepared to answer some tough questions should you decide to send some of your own work overseas.

Be prepared for customers and employees to express grave concerns about your company sending work away from this country. Depending on the size of your investment, or your company's visibility in its community, you could even get some unwanted attention in the press.

> **Knowledge Is Power**
>
> India's export revenues from software outsourcing have exceeded targets and will reach $17.3 billion in the fiscal year ending March 2005, according to the National Association of Software and Service Companies. In the year ending March 2004, India's software exports stood at $12.8 billion, and the industry employed 770,000 people.

Outsourcing your work overseas can certainly prove beneficial to your bottom line. Even with the risks involved, you could save a lot of money and change your business forever for the better.

The Least You Need to Know

- Reducing costs and improving customer service are some of the more significant reasons for outsourcing work overseas.

- Language barriers, distances, differences in time zones, and cultural differences are the kinds of challenges you'll face when working with a foreign service provider.

- Foreign laws and tax systems, government corruption, and piracy may become issues for you if you're working in certain parts of the world.

- When establishing an overseas outsourcing relationship, it's best to use consultants and local agents to help smooth the path.

◆ Expect to change your work hours and make better use of technology to succeed with a foreign service provider.

◆ Although offshore outsourcing may be a great thing for your business's bottom line, be prepared for the potential political fallout from this decision.

Part 4

Staying Out of Trouble

You're going to face many challenges during your outsourcing project. One of the biggest could be proving that the independent contractor you hired is really independent and shouldn't be classified as an employee. Fortunately, the IRS provides a lot of useful information for making this determination, and I help you make sense of it all.

You learned about the importance of service level agreements in Part 3, but your contractual commitments don't end there. You'll want contracts in place preventing your outside service provider from "poaching" your customers and disclosing your confidential information.

Also in this section, you'll become aware of other legal liabilities and ethical challenges you could face. Are you doing the right thing for your customers and employees by outsourcing? How can you conduct yourself profitably *and* ethically?

Chapter 20

Employee vs. Contractor: What the IRS Says

In This Chapter

- ◆ Identifying the different types of employment
- ◆ Defining the independent contractor
- ◆ The Internal Revenue Service's Common Law Rules
- ◆ What happens if the IRS says an independent contractor is really an employee
- ◆ Filing requirements when you outsource to an independent contractor
- ◆ Where to get more information

The bigger they are, the harder they fall. That's what Microsoft learned when the software giant outsourced a bunch of work to independent contractors.

To save taxes and other employment costs, Microsoft hired several independent contractors to help on certain projects and to do tasks such as editing, proofreading, and software testing. The contractors were paid an hourly amount that often exceeded what the company's employees were paid.

The problem was that Microsoft treated their independent contractors too much like employees. The contractors worked along with regular Microsoft employees, reported to the same people, and were even given security clearances and equipment similar to the work force.

The IRS wasn't happy. Upon auditing the company's payroll records, it uncovered the relationship and found that the company's independent contractor agreement wasn't satisfactory. Ultimately, Microsoft settled with the IRS and paid a boatload of back taxes and penalties. The company thought that their problems were over, but unfortunately this settlement only opened up the floodgates.

A group of these independents filed a class-action lawsuit against the company, claiming that if they were treated as employees in the eyes of the IRS, then they should be entitled to the benefits that all the other Microsoft employees were getting, such as participation in the company's stock option, health insurance, and pension plans.

Microsoft fought the case and lost. In the end, these independents weren't really independent at all. Microsoft ended up providing them with benefits and incurred significant legal fees to boot. Outsourcing their work was a good idea. Unfortunately, the company didn't take the time to establish a relationship with their service providers that was satisfactory to them or the government.

Microsoft's challenges with independent contractors is a well-documented case of the risks involved in outsourcing work to independent contractors. This chapter explains how to make sure you're minimizing the chance that your contractors do not inadvertently become part of your payroll.

When Is an Employee an Employee?

As mentioned in the first part of this book, the IRS has created specific definitions that spell out when a relationship is an employer/employee one. In the eyes of the IRS, there are three types of workers: common law, statutory, and nonstatutory. If a person doesn't fall into one of these three categories, he or she may be considered an independent contractor.

Common Law Employees

A common law employee is anyone who works for you where you control what that person does and how he or she does it. Even though the employee may have freedom in their job, if you're the person laying out the details of the work, you're probably an

employer. So if you're giving your bookkeeper her software, a desk, and a phone
extension, and you're telling her how the
books are to be kept and when she must do her
work, you're probably looking at an employee,
not an independent contractor. Companies
often mistakenly classify common-law employees as independent contractors.

Under common-law rules, anyone who performs services for you is your employee if you
can control what will be done and how it will
be done. This is so even when you give the
employee freedom of action. What matters is
that you have the right to control the details of
how the services are performed.

Stay Alert!

It's widely believed that
the IRS gets a big return on
investment when they find a business that's in violation of the independent contractor rules. One
business could yield dozens of
wrongly classified workers, which
could then result in thousands of
dollars in back taxes and interest.
This area has become a nice revenue generator for the IRS.

To determine whether an individual is an employee or independent contractor under
the common law, the relationship of the worker and the business must be examined.
All evidence of control and independence must be considered.

Statutory Employees

There are four types of statutory employees:

♦ A driver who distributes beverages (other than milk) or meat, vegetable, fruit,
or bakery products, or who picks up and delivers laundry or dry cleaning.

♦ A full-time life insurance sales agent whose principal business activity is selling
life insurance (or annuity contracts), primarily for one insurance company.

♦ An individual who works at home on materials or goods that you supply and
that must be returned to you or to a person you name, if you also furnish specifications for the work to be done.

♦ A full-time salesperson who works on your behalf and turns in orders to you
from wholesalers, retailers, contractors, or operators of hotels, restaurants, or
other similar establishments. The goods sold must be merchandise for resale or
supplies for use in the buyer's business operation. The work performed for you
must be the salesperson's principal business activity.

Statutory Non-Employees

According to the IRS, "there are two categories of statutory non-employees: *direct sellers* and *licensed real estate agents*. They are treated as self-employed for all federal tax purposes, including income and employment taxes, if:

♦ Substantially all payments for their services as direct sellers or real estate agents are directly related to their sales output, rather than to the number of hours worked and

♦ Their services are performed under a written contract providing that they will not be treated as employees for federal tax purposes."

Defining the Independent Contractor

Like the definition of a common law employee, the definition of an independent contractor is also all about control. Rather, I should say *lack* of control. When you outsource a job to someone where you agree on the output or result but where you take no part in getting the job done, you may have entered into an independent contractor relationship.

In the following sections, I dig into this issue a little deeper.

Independent Contractor or Employee? You Decide

The IRS has produced a very straightforward document titled "Publication 1779—Independent Contractor Or Employee," which you can use to determine the nature of your relationship with your outsourced service provider and whether that relationship should be classified as employment or as an independent. In this publication, the decision is based on three main factors: behavioral control, financial control, and your relationship. Let's look more closely at each of these factors.

Behavioral Control

The IRS wants you to determine exactly how much influence you have over how the person does his or her job. Influence is broken down into two factors:

- **Instructions.** If you are providing very detailed, thorough, and specific instructions to an outsourced service provider as to how their job should be done, it's suggested that your relationship is more that of an employer-employee.

- **Training.** The IRS doesn't like it when a company provides training to a worker, but then doesn't consider the worker to be an employee. If someone is truly independent, they shouldn't rely on their client for their training.

Financial Control

The IRS likes to judge just how much financial control a company has with its outsourced party. Financial control is generally divided into three categories:

- **Significant investment.** The more the third party has invested in himself or herself, through training, infrastructure, supplies, appearance, and so on, the more likely it is that the IRS would consider that person to be independent.

- **Expenses.** The more expenses that are absorbed by the contractor, the less chance there is that they will be thought of as an employee.

- **Opportunity for profit or loss.** If your outsourced service provider is exposed to suffering a loss on a project, they would appear to be more independent than an employee.

> **Knowledge Is Power**
>
> The Bureau of Labor Statistics reported that in February 2001, 8.6 million independent contractors (representing 6.4 percent of total employment) were used by businesses across the country.

Relationship of the Parties

Finally, the IRS will consider the overall relationship between you and your service provider. Among the issues up for consideration are …

- **Employee benefits.** If you're providing your contractor with the same or similar benefits that your employees are receiving, then bingo! This could tell you something! The IRS would not be able to differentiate between the compensation an employee is receiving and the compensation that your contractor is getting. They may therefore determine that it's an employer-employee relationship.

◆ **Written contracts.** Do you have a written contract (or service level agreement) that defines your relationship and that specifies, in detail, why your relationship is strictly arm's length? (We explore agreements and contracts in more detail in Chapters 17 and 21.)

The IRS's Common Law Rules

The IRS has come up with rules, sometimes referred to as the "common law rules," which can help the employer determine whether he or she has truly entered into an independent contract agreement or whether it's really an employer-employee relationship.

These rules are meant to be viewed as guidelines, and they are not set in stone. You don't have to comply with every single rule, but you should be able to address each one if asked. Your written agreements (for example, your service level agreement) should address these rules.

Your independent contractor may actually be considered to be an employee if he or she …

◆ Must comply with your work instructions.

◆ Receives training from or at the direction of you.

◆ Provides services that are an integral part of your business.

◆ Provides services that must be rendered personally.

◆ Hires, supervises, and pays workers on your behalf.

◆ Has an ongoing working relationship with you.

◆ Must follow set hours of work that you establish.

◆ Works full-time for you.

◆ Does your work on your premises.

◆ Must do their work in a sequence set by you.

◆ Must submit regular reports to you.

- ◆ Receives payments of regular amounts at set intervals.

- ◆ Receives payments for business and/or business expenses.

- ◆ Relies on you to provide tools and materials.

- ◆ Lacks a major investment in resources for providing services.

- ◆ Cannot make a profit or suffer a loss from their services.

- ◆ Works for one employer at a time.

- ◆ Does not offer their services to the general public.

- ◆ Can be fired by you.

- ◆ May quit work at any time without incurring liability.

If You Fail the Test

Okay, okay. So you goofed. You thought you had a nice little outsourcing thing going with an independent contractor and then you read the common law rules and discovered that you've actually got an employee on your hands. Who cares? Among the government agencies that take a serious interest in such things are …

- ◆ **The IRS.** You might owe back taxes, penalties, and have filed the wrong forms.

- ◆ **The Department of Labor.** You may have violated rules for hiring, against discrimination, and employment.

- ◆ **The Social Security Administration.** You probably didn't pay your share of Social Security and Medicare taxes, so you'll be liable for them, plus interest and penalties.

- ◆ **Your state's workmen's compensation bureau.** You probably didn't pay workmen's compensation premiums for these people, so the state's going to want the premiums, plus penalties and interest.

- ◆ **Your state's unemployment agency.** If your state requires a business to pay unemployment insurance premiums based on gross payroll, you may have to play catch-up here, too.

> **Knowledge Is Power**
>
> A February 2001 Bureau of Labor Statistics study found that independent contractors were more likely than workers in traditional arrangements to be over the age of 35, white, and male. They also were more likely to hold a Bachelor's degree.

◆ **The National Labor Relations Board.** You may have shortchanged your contractors of benefits they deserved. This organization may fight you on their behalf.

As this list makes all too clear, not calling an employee an employee could cost you a lot down the road. Honest mistakes aside, some wily characters don't properly classify their employees for the very purpose of avoiding these financial responsibilities. These organizations aren't very sympathetic to managers and owners who willfully ignore the independent contractors' guidelines.

Where Can I Get More Information?

The IRS (www.irs.gov) makes available plenty of resources to help you determine whether you're outsourcing arrangement is more employer-employee or that of an independent contractor. All of the following documents are available on the IRS website, www.irs.gov:

◆ Tax Topic 762—Independent contractor vs. Employee. A short article discussing the relationship between employers and businesses.

◆ Publication 1976, Section 530—Employment Tax Relief Requirements. An explanation about Section 530 regarding independent contractors and how a business can receive relief under the code.

◆ Publication 1779—Independent Contractor or Employee. A graphic, easy-to-read brochure that explains the independent contractor rules.

◆ Form SS-8—Determination of Worker Status for Purposes of Federal Employment Taxes and Income Tax Withholding. A form that you can complete that helps you determine whether a worker is an employee or an independent contractor.

◆ Publication 15-A—The Employer's Supplemental Tax Guide. A supplement to Circular E, the Employer's Tax Guide, which includes information about independent contractors among other employment tax–related issues.

The Independent Contractor Test

Courtesy of the IRS, the following examples give you real-life scenarios that you may find yourself facing. Can you determine which example is an independent contractor or an employee? The answers follow the examples.

Example 1

Jerry Jones has an agreement with Wilma White to supervise the remodeling of her house. She did not advance funds to help him carry on the work. She makes direct payments to the suppliers for all necessary materials. She carries liability and worker compensation insurance covering Jerry and others that he engaged to assist him. She pays them an hourly rate and exercises almost constant supervision over the work. Jerry is not free to transfer his assistants to other jobs. He may not work on other jobs while working for Wilma. He assumes no responsibility to complete the work and will incur no contractual liability if he fails to do so. He and his assistants perform personal services for hourly wages.

Example 2

Milton Manning, an experienced tilesetter, orally agreed with a corporation to perform full-time services at construction sites. He uses his own tools and performs services in the order designated by the corporation and according to its specifications. The corporation supplies all materials, makes frequent inspections of his work, pays him on a piecework basis, and carries worker compensation insurance on him. He does not have a place of business or hold himself out to perform similar services for others. Either party can end the services at any time.

Example 3

Wallace Black agreed with the Sawdust Co. to supply the construction labor for a group of houses. The company agreed to pay all construction costs. However, he supplies all the tools and equipment. He performs personal services as a carpenter and mechanic for an hourly wage. He also acts as superintendent and foreman and engages other individuals to assist him. The company has the right to select, approve, or discharge any helper. A company representative makes frequent inspections of the construction site. When a house is finished, Wallace is paid a certain percentage of its costs. He is not responsible for faults, defects of construction, or wasteful operation. At the end of each week, he presents the company with a statement of the amount of money that he has spent, including the payroll. The company gives him a check for that amount from which he pays the assistants, although he is not personally liable for their wages.

Example 4

Bill Plum contracted with Elm Corporation to complete the roofing on a housing complex. A signed contract established a flat amount for the services rendered by Bill Plum. Bill is a licensed roofer and carries workers' compensation and liability insurance under the business name, Plum Roofing. He hires his own roofers who are treated as employees for federal employment tax purposes. If there is a problem with the roofing work, Plum Roofing is responsible for paying for any repairs.

Example 5

Vera Elm, an electrician, submitted a job estimate to a housing complex for electrical work at $16 per hour for 400 hours. She is to receive $1,280 every 2 weeks for the next 10 weeks. This is not considered payment by the hour. Even if she works more or less than 400 hours to complete the work, Vera Elm will receive $6,400. She also performs additional electrical installations under contracts with other companies that she obtained through advertisements.

Example 6

Rose Trucking contracts to deliver material for Forest Inc. at $140 per ton. Rose Trucking is not paid for any articles that are not delivered. At times, Jan Rose, who operates as Rose Trucking, may also lease another truck and engage a driver to complete the contract. All operating expenses, including insurance coverage, are paid by Jan Rose. All equipment is owned or rented by Jan and she is responsible for all maintenance. None of the drivers are provided by Forest Inc.

Example 7

Steve Smith, a computer programmer, is laid off when Megabyte Inc. downsizes. Megabyte agrees to pay Steve a flat amount to complete a one-time project to create a certain product. It is not clear how long that it will take to complete the project, and Steve is not guaranteed any minimum payment for the hours spent on the program. Megabyte provides Steve with no instructions beyond the specifications for the product itself. Steve and Megabyte have a written contract, which provides that Steve is considered to be an independent contractor, is required to pay federal and state taxes, and receives no benefits from Megabyte. Megabyte will file a Form 1099-MISC. Steve does the work on a new high-end computer that cost him $7,000. Steve works at home and is not expected or allowed to attend meetings of the software development group.

Example 8

Donna Lee is a salesperson employed on a full-time basis by Bob Blue, an auto dealer. She works six days a week and is on duty in Bob's showroom on certain assigned days and times. She appraises trade-ins, but her appraisals are subject to the sales manager's approval. Lists of prospective customers belong to the dealer. She is required to develop leads and report results to the sales manager. Because of her experience, she requires only minimal assistance in closing and financing sales and in other phases of her work. She is paid a commission and is eligible for prizes and bonuses offered by Bob. Bob also pays the cost of health insurance and group-term life insurance for Donna.

Example 9

Sam Sparks performs auto repair services in the repair department of an auto sales company. He works regular hours and is paid on a percentage basis. He has no investment in the repair department. The sales company supplies all facilities, repair parts, and supplies; issues instructions on the amounts to be charged, parts to be used, and the time for completion of each job; and checks all estimates and repair orders.

Example 10

An auto sales agency furnishes space for Helen Bach to perform auto repair services. She provides her own tools, equipment, and supplies. She seeks out business from insurance adjusters and other individuals and does all of the body and paint work that comes to the agency. She hires and discharges her own helpers, determines her own and her helpers' working hours, quotes prices for repair work, makes all necessary adjustments, assumes all losses from uncollectible accounts, and receives, as compensation for her services, a large percentage of the gross collections from the auto repair shop.

Example 11

Donna Yuma is a sole practitioner who rents office space and pays for the following items: telephone, computer, online legal research linkup, fax machine, and photo-copier. Donna buys office supplies and pays bar dues and membership dues for three other professional organizations. Donna has a part-time receptionist who also does the bookkeeping. She pays the receptionist, withholds and pays federal and state employment taxes, and files a Form W-2 each year. For the past 2 years, Donna has had only three clients, corporations with which there have been long-standing rela-tionships. Donna charges the corporations an hourly rate for her services, sending monthly bills detailing the work performed for the prior month. The bills include charges for long-distance calls, online research time, fax charges, photocopies, postage, and travel, costs for which the corporations have agreed to reimburse her.

Example 12

Tom Spruce rents a cab from Taft Cab Company for $150 per day. He pays the costs of maintaining and operating the cab. Tom Spruce keeps all fares that he receives from customers. Although he receives the benefit of Taft's two-way radio communica-tion equipment, dispatcher, and advertising, these items benefit both Taft and Tom Spruce.

Answers

1. Jerry Jones and his assistants are employees of Wilma White.

2. Milton Manning is an employee of the corporation.

3. Wallace Black and his assistants are employees of the Sawdust Company.

4. Bill Plum, doing business as Plum Roofing, is an independent contractor.

5. Vera is an independent contractor.

6. Jan Rose, operating as Rose Trucking, is an independent contractor.

7. Steve is an independent contractor.

8. Donna is an employee of Bob Blue.

9. Sam is an employee of the sales company.

10. Helen is an independent contractor and the helpers are her employees.

11. Donna is an independent contractor.

12. Tom Spruce is an independent contractor.

The Least You Need to Know

◆ The IRS breaks down employees as common law, statutory, and nonstatutory.

◆ When determining whether a service provider is properly classified as an independent contractor, you must consider how much control you exert.

◆ The IRS has a list of common law rules, or guidelines, to help you determine whether a third party is properly classified as an independent contractor.

◆ If an independent contractor is improperly classified, you could be in hot water with the IRS, the Department of Labor, and various state agencies.

◆ Many resources are available for determining whether someone is an employee or an independent contractor.

Chapter **21**

Getting It in Writing

In This Chapter

- ◆ The importance of written contracts between you and your service provider
- ◆ Key components of your independent contractor's agreement
- ◆ What your confidentiality agreement should include
- ◆ Creating a strong noncompete agreement with your outside service provider

Mark had an outsourcing nightmare on his hands. He runs a company that installs and supports computer networks for small- and medium-size businesses. Certain work, especially when it came to setting up the network security, was highly specialized. For this work he outsourced to Tony. It turned out to be a big mistake.

Unfortunately, Tony stole away a bunch of Mark's clients and set up shop right down the street from him. Tony had kept track of who Mark's customers were and then went to them behind Mark's back and offered to do the same work for 20 percent less than what Mark was charging.

Not all the customers moved to Tony, but many did. Quite a few others forced Mark to lower his prices just to keep them as customers.

How did this happen?

In Mark's rush to get Tony out to work, he never had him sign a contractor or noncompete agreement. He was free to do what he wanted!

Mark's story is not an unusual one. Your outside service providers may be dealing with some confidential material. They could be working directly with your customers. They may have access to information that could be very valuable to your competition.

And there could be other issues, too, such as payment disputes or questions about scope and work locations. For most large-size projects, you never want to outsource a task to someone without a proper contract in place. We've already discussed the role that one of these contracts, the service level agreement, plays in Chapter 17. This chapter examines some other common contracts that are used in outsourcing arrangements and discusses how to use those contracts to protect yourself.

Why Have Agreements?

Mark didn't think he had the time to put together an agreement with Tony, and he paid the price for it. If Mark's experience hasn't convinced you of the importance of using contracts, maybe the following reasons will.

> **Outsourcing Insights**
>
> You should make at least three copies of each agreement with your outside service provider. Make sure all three copies should have original signatures. Keep one copy for yourself, give one copy to the service provider, and give the third copy to your attorney.

You Need to Document Your Relationship

If the IRS comes knocking, asking you to prove that your service provider is an independent contractor rather than an employee, you'll be glad you had an independent contractor agreement in place. Written correctly, and signed by both parties, it will go a long way to help you demonstrate to any regulatory agency that your relationship was arms length and not employer-employee.

You Want to Establish Deliverables, Scope, and Objectives

A contract, like a service level agreement (discussed in Chapter 17), between you and the service provider will spell out, in writing, the exact deliverables, scope, and objectives of your relationship. It may even include specific measurements, too, such as the number of new customers a public relations firm promises to land for you. Having it in writing will help to avoid miscommunications.

An Agreement Will Help Reduce Disputes When They Arise

A good contract can be used to resolve problems between the service provider and the customer. If either parties have any questions about payment terms, location of work, hours, and responsibilities, they should be able to look to the contract to see what they agreed upon.

You'll Be Protected by Law

If problems ever do occur, you'll be glad that you had an agreement in place. In the example at the beginning of this chapter, if Mark had solid confidentiality and non-compete agreements in place, he could have taken Tony to court. Tony would have had a tough time proving his innocence if he had signed a noncompete agreement.

Service Level Agreements

I explained the importance of using service level agreements (SLAs) in Chapter 17, but a few things are worth repeating here.

Service level agreements represent mutually agreed-on commitments, deliverables, and measurements. They are most often used when entire processes are outsourced to a service provider.

For example, if you outsource your call center to a third party, your service level agreement may include benchmarks for the number of calls handled and the length of time it takes to resolve trouble tickets. Or if you outsource your marketing functions to a professional firm, you may both agree on the number of qualified leads that you expect to be generated from the firm's efforts.

Most large outsourcing arrangements have a service level agreement in place, especially if a significant function is being outsourced.

Independent Contractor's Agreement

Most experts advise that an agreement should be signed between you and the independent contractor when you initiate an outsourcing relationship. This section summarizes the key sections that should be included in this agreement.

Independent contractor agreements are different from service level agreements. They are usually prepared to document an individual contractor's relationship with a company in order to satisfy the IRS's rules (see Chapter 20). There are usually no service level commitments made in this kind of agreement. I've included a sample independent contractor agreement in Appendix A.

Services

The services section should define exactly what services the independent contractor will be performing for you. Here is where you'll state the objectives, deliverables, and tasks.

For example, if you're outsourcing your bookkeeping to an independent contractor, state that the contractor is responsible for maintaining all of the company's books and records in accordance with Generally Accepted Accounting Principles (GAAP).

You may then go further to describe the types of records the contractor will be responsible for (i.e., payroll, accounts receivable, accounts payable, general ledger) and that the contractor will deliver an adjusted financial statement to you within five business days of the end of the month as your deliverable.

Term of Agreement

In this section, you'll define how long the agreement will last and the ways in which it can be terminated.

Some agreements are open ended. Others specifically state a starting and ending date. You might specify that the termination may be verbal or in writing, or that notification may be required by either party in advance of terminating the agreement. In addition, you might want to include valid reasons for termination, such as noncompliance with the contract, change of ownership of either party, or lack of payment.

Time Devoted

Here you will specify how much time you think the independent contractor should commit to your company. If you've outsourced your telemarketing to an independent contractor, you may have both agreed that the telemarketer will devote 10 hours per week under your contract. If you've outsourced the maintenance of your building, you might want the contractor there every day.

Outsourcing Insights

A fixed contract or a contract where payment is made based on deliverables may not require any commitment of time to the relationship, just a specific result.

Place Where Services Will Be Rendered

This section will state where the work will be done. If you're ever audited, the IRS may be particularly interested in this section. Take another look at the IRS's 20 rules (see Chapter 20) to make sure that where the work is performed does not breach the conditions of these rules.

Payment and Terms

All parties will take a great interest in what's written in this section. Here is where you'll agree on rates per hour, fixed payments, milestones reached, forms of payment, and payment dates.

Independent Contractor Relationship

In case the meaning is lost on the parties involved, some companies like to include in their contracts a clause stating that the service provider is an independent contractor and will be responsible for their own taxes, workplace, expenses, and other items that may be otherwise interpreted as an employer-employee relationship.

Unfortunately, this clause doesn't mean that the person you're working with can't be reclassified as an employee. The government is a little smarter than that. They'll look beyond what's in this contract to how the relationship is really working. So although it's nice to have this section in your agreement it's not going to shut the door on any allegations that your arrangement is not arms length.

Confidential Information

Most independent contracting agreements include wording about confidentiality and nondisclosure (discussed later in this chapter). Including them in your primary agreement saves having to create separate agreements.

Noncompete

You should include a noncompete clause in your contract. See the section on noncompete agreements later in this chapter to make sure you've got everything covered.

Stay Alert!

When contractors step into your building, you'll be liable if anything happens to them. Make sure all contractors have general liability insurance coverage and have named you as the insured on their policy. More about this in Chapter 22.

Employment of Others

Independent contractors often hire others to perform work for them and their customers. But what if those people get hurt while they are working on your job? What if they upset one of your clients or steal something from your company? This section should state that all legal and financial responsibilities for employees or subcontractors of the independent contractor remain with the independent contractor. You may also want to require the independent contractor to get your approval before bringing in any outside help.

Dispute Resolution

Here you'll agree where and how disputes will be settled. You may name a third party, decide to send all disputes to arbitration, or let your disagreements be decided by the courts. You should agree on where disputes will be handled, too—in your home state or in the contractor's.

Some independent contractor agreements go to great lengths documenting procedures for settling a dispute to avoid delays in the project and potential litigation. If you expect disputes to arise due to the nature of the project, you may want to both agree on specific steps that should be taken to get the issue resolved so that both parties can move on.

Complete Agreement

This section states that there are no other agreements between the two parties other than this one. If you have an SLA with your provider, you could include this clause in that agreement. You may also want to say here that any other agreements are superseded by the terms of this agreement.

Contact Information

Most contracts end with the contact information of the people who are responsible.

Nondisclosure/Confidentiality Agreement

Your contractor may be working with some pretty confidential information. Unlike your employees, your independent service provider will likely be serving other customers, perhaps even competitors of yours. Because of this, it's very common to require outside service providers to sign nondisclosure and confidentiality agreement before beginning their work.

As mentioned previously, you can include this information in your independent contractor agreement. However, you might want to keep it separate if you're doing other projects with the service provider; you want them all covered under a single confidentiality agreement. Also, if you share confidential information with the potential service providers during the interview phase, you should have them sign this agreement during the interview phase.

> **Outsourcing Insights**
>
> Some independent contractor agreements also include provisions about hiring each other's employees. Outside service providers are not exactly thrilled when their customers hire away the people working on their job—and vice versa. If this is a concern to you, you may want to include a provision that forbids the hiring of each other's employees for a period of time no less than six months, starting after the contract has terminated.

A sample nondisclosure and confidentiality clause is included in our sample agreement in Appendix A. For now, let's take a look at the key sections of any such agreement.

Agreement Not to Disclose Confidential Information

The first section of your agreement will put in writing that the independent contractor will not disclose any confidential or private information. You may want to specifically define what you consider to be confidential, such as employment records, payroll data, or customer information.

Return of Confidential Information

Here you will require the contractor to return any restricted information they use. You'll deny their right to copy or remove such information from your premises.

Right to an Injunction

> **Business Buzzwords**
>
> An **injunction** is a court order prohibiting a party from performing a certain action.

In this section, the contractor agrees to maintain confidentiality of information learned through communication with company employees. If the company suspects that the contractor is spreading information to the outside world based on these conversations, this section gives the company the ability to stop this action through a legal *injunction*.

Reasonableness

Maybe it's stating the obvious, but you want your independent contractor to agree in writing that you're not being unreasonable in asking for their best efforts to keep things private.

Survivability

Just because your agreement ends doesn't mean you want the contractor going out and blabbing your company's private details to the world. In this section, you state that the agreement survives the termination of your relationship forever and ever.

Entire Agreement

If this is the only agreement between you and the contractor, you may want to state this fact here. This is so there is no confusion if things ever get ugly. If this agreement complements your independent contractor's agreement, that agreement should be referenced in this section.

Successors and Assignees

If your bookkeeper retires and his son takes his place, you want to make sure he'll be held to the same confidentiality requirements as his dad. If your contractor is bought out by another company, you'll want to make sure your data is protected. This section makes sure that all the promises made by the contractor will also be honored by anyone who takes their place.

Outsourcing Insights

Some agreements make it clear that any change in ownership of either customer or service provider is grounds for re-evaluation or termination of the agreement. This protects both parties.

Noncompete Agreement

I think you would agree that Mark, from our example at the beginning of this chapter, wished he'd had a noncompete agreement in place before outsourcing his work to Tony. The noncompete agreement will help protect you from the nefarious service provider who tries to poach your customers. The terms of this agreement should be included in your independent contractor agreement or in a standalone contract.

Noncompete agreements are pretty short, usually no more than a page. A typical noncompete agreement includes the following:

- Name of contractor
- Type of services performed
- Statement that the contractor will not compete with the customer
- Term of the agreement
- Geographic area of the agreement
- Damages

Typical noncompete agreements last for three to five years after termination of the outsourcing arrangement. The geographic areas covered by the agreement vary widely, depending on the type of work that is done.

Noncompete agreements can be easily challenged. If a contractor finds out that others you worked with violated their noncompete contracts without a response from you, the contractor may be tempted to try the same. If the terms are too prohibitive or you breach your obligations under the agreement, a court of law may find in favor of the contractor.

Reality Check

Having independent contractor, confidentiality, and noncompete agreements in place with your outside service provider certainly protects your interests. But don't kid yourself thinking that just because you have an agreement in place nothing will go wrong.

Many independent contractors are small shops. Pursuing damages from them may be fruitless. Litigation can be expensive and time-consuming for both parties. Proving that they've disclosed confidential information or are violating your noncompete agreement may be very difficult. Finding them might be even harder.

The best thing you can do is to avoid this kind of trouble altogether. Doing your research beforehand, getting references, and thoroughly checking out the contractor's background will help you select someone who isn't going to let you down.

The Least You Need to Know

♦ Having a contract allows you to establish written deliverables, reduce disputes, and keep things consistent.

♦ Your independent contractor's agreement should address the services that will be performed, where work will be rendered, and how payment will be made.

♦ Your confidentiality agreement should state that the contractor agrees with the reasonableness of your request.

♦ A noncompete agreement can be easily challenged if it is too prohibitive or if you do not perform your obligations.

♦ When things get ugly between you and a service provider, agreements will help, but fighting in court will be time-consuming and expensive.

Chapter 22

Limiting Your Liabilities

In This Chapter

- ◆ Ways to reduce your legal liabilities before you begin an outsourcing relationship
- ◆ Typical legal liabilities you'll encounter when outsourcing
- ◆ Defending yourself when a problem occurs

What a mess the University of California, San Francisco Medical Center (UCSFMC) found itself in! They had outsourced the transcription of medical records to an outside service provider. This was certainly not an uncommon practice. Hospitals around the world outsource the transcription of medical data. Hundreds of companies provide this service on an outsourced basis.

Unfortunately, UCSFMC picked the wrong service provider. The hospital didn't know that the service provider was also outsourcing. And one of the service provider's outsourced people, a certified medical transcriber, was in the middle of a payment dispute with her employer.

Imagine the hospital's shock when the woman threatened to post sensitive information about one of UCSFMC's patients on the Internet unless she received the payment she claimed was due from her employer. To back up her threat, the woman e-mailed copies of the patient information to the hospital, making it clear that she had taken this sensitive material.

The hospital was in a very precarious position.

UCSFMC had outsourced this important task, and now they found themselves facing all kinds of liabilities. If this information were released, they could be sued not only by the patient's family, but also face penalties from the Health and Human Services Agency due to violations under the Health Insurance Portability and Accountability Act (HIPAA).

Was this an isolated incident? Not a chance. A year later, a few workers in Bangalore who were employed by another medical transcription firm threatened the very same thing.

Happily, both situations were eventually resolved without any medical information being improperly released. But what a scare!

So much can go wrong when you outsource. A service provider's employees may misbehave. An important quality test performed on your behalf might be substandard. Your outsourced payroll service might screw up your employees' tax withholdings. Your third-party support center could give the wrong advice to a customer.

No matter how much research you do beforehand or how well you manage your relationship with an outside service provider, things can still go wrong. Where does your responsibility end and the service provider's begin? The line is pretty tough to determine.

> **Stay Alert!**
> Always make sure you've got copies of all information that's being used by your service provider. Make sure you are backing up your data. Give your service provider only the data they need to do their job.

Many lawyers tell their clients who are putting together significant outsourcing arrangements to protect themselves in three main ways:

- Consider every potential exposure up front and put precautions against them into the contract.

- Prepare for any potential problems in advance and have a plan to react.

- Have an established procedure for settling disputes as quickly as possible.

In this chapter, I expand on these concepts so you can do everything you can to avoid getting into hot water!

Reducing Your Liabilities Before You Start

You'll never be able to avoid legal liability altogether, but that doesn't mean you can't be prepared. Every good outsourcing relationship has written agreements (see Chapters 17 and 21). These agreements should incorporate legal wording to help protect you against potential legal problems.

Outsourcing work does not exonerate you from liability. So before you begin an outsourcing relationship, take some steps to legally protect yourself.

Do Your Research

Don't walk into an outsourcing agreement blind. Review your potential risks with an attorney. Talk to others who have worked with the service provider and find out what kind of problems they've had. Ask them how they protect themselves against liabilities. Research similar arrangements. Read case studies. Get the worst-case scenario from as many people as you can.

> **Outsourcing Insights**
>
> Most outsourcing experts agree that doing the right amount of due diligence before you start your relationship is the best way to avoid any problems down the road. Take your time and don't rush through the evaluation process.

Consider the Implications of Vicarious Liability

Most state laws protect companies and individuals against *vicarious liability*. If you outsource work to a third party and, other than give them a deadline, relinquish control on how the work is to be done, you should be legally protected if the third party is negligent. Vicarious liability should be thought about and addressed early in the contract stage.

> **Business Buzzwords**
>
> **Vicarious liability** is when one person is liable for the negligent actions of another person, even though the first person was not directly responsible for these actions.

Consider Your Corporate Structure

Are you an S Corp? A sole proprietor? A C Corp? Your corporate structure may protect you in case of a problem. Again, consult an attorney to determine what's best for you.

One client of mine created a separate holding company that contracted with the service provider so that if there ever were a problem, any liability would pass through only to that entity. You can do lots of things to protect yourself from liability if you structure your organization correctly.

State the Limits of Your Liabilities

Most lawyers recommend stating a maximum liability right in the agreement with your service provider. For example, you may state that you're only liable for the amount paid and not for any losses incurred as a result of the service provider's negligence. This may help limit your exposure. By agreeing to this, the service provider would be taking responsibility for any financial risks over and above the amounts paid to them.

Understand Local Laws

Liability laws vary from state to state and from country to country. Familiarize yourself with the local laws regarding supplier/customer contracts. Outsourcing your call center to India? Find out what your rights are in that country (and local area). Often, local laws favor the local business. Hire a local lawyer if necessary, and research the applicable laws.

If possible, make sure your agreement states that the location of any dispute settlements be in your home state. This way, if there is a problem you don't have to travel halfway across the country (or world) to defend yourself.

Expecting the Worst: Typical Outsourcing Liability Issues

When preparing yourself for the worst, you need to know what the worst-case scenarios are. What kinds of problems can get you into legal trouble?

Intellectual Property Ownership

Intellectual property ownership is a complicated area. By intellectual property, I mean copyrights, patents, trademarks, trade secrets, and other special knowledge.

If you're a publisher and you contract with a writer to write an article about outsourcing, who owns the final work product? If you outsource the design of a software program, does the software company have the right to use the program elsewhere or is it entirely yours? What if you hired a bookkeeping firm and they use their proprietary software to do your accounting? Is the data yours or theirs?

If you intend your outside service provider to play a role in creating some type of intellectual property, you need to make it clear who owns the end product. This will avoid nasty arguments down the road.

Stay Alert!

There are no friends in outsourcing, only business partners. Maintain your relationship strictly on an arm's length basis. If things turn ugly, you may be surprised how that friendly service provider suddenly turns into an enemy.

Privacy and Confidentiality

No one wants to be in the hot water that the San Francisco Medical Center found themselves in. An outside service provider will very likely be dealing with a lot of sensitive information—information about your business, your customers, and even your employees. What if this information gets into the wrong hands? What if it is sold to your competition or used against you in some other way?

Clearly state what information is confidential. Agree in writing that any private or confidential information will not be disclosed to anyone not specifically mentioned in the contract. This should all be part of a confidentiality agreement (see Chapter 21). Take steps in advance to secure and control this information as much as you can.

Disaster Recovery

You hire a document management company to maintain your customers' files, and the company's backup system crashes, resulting in the loss of critical data. You outsource your network to a hosting company, and they go out of business. There's no shortage of potential disasters that could befall anyone you outsource work to. Are you preparing for this now?

Your customers will assume that you're doing everything necessary to secure and maintain their information. If your outside service

Stay Alert!

Make sure you have flexible options for exiting your outsourcing arrangement. Try to structure it so that termination is at your discretion with as little notice as possible. This will enable you to bail out if things really go bad and before potential liabilities are incurred.

provider fails, you fail. Your customers will point their finger at you first. With your outside service provider, make sure you've agreed on what disaster recovery procedures are in place to safeguard important information.

Negligence

If the service provider falls down on the job, what are you going to do? If your own customers are relying on this work to be done and you're not able to meet these commitments because of *negligence* on the part of your subcontractor, are you liable? Probably.

How would you feel if the general contractor who's building your new kitchen farmed out work to an electrician whose shoddy work caused an electrical fire? You'd probably go after the contractor and the electrician. Who's to say your own customer won't do the same? Bottom line: make sure to state what constitutes negligence in your service contract and who's responsible for a negligent act.

Business Buzzwords

Negligence is the failure to exercise the degree of care considered reasonable under the circumstances, resulting in an unintended injury to another party.

Outsourcing Insights

Outsourcing is a discipline, not an action. It's not a quick decision or an easy process. It takes commitment and a long-term outlook. Going into an outsourcing relationship with these thoughts in mind will help you avoid liabilities in the future.

Disruption of Operations

If you or your service provider don't do what you promise, you could cause the disruption of your customer's operations. The customer could then sue you for potential loss of business. It's essential that you establish who is responsible for a customer's disruption of operations.

Labor and Child Laws

Remember when Nike got into trouble when the media found out that one of their foreign subsidiaries was illegally employing children in their factory? Remember when Kathy Lee Gifford lent her name to a clothing line that was made by children under sweatshop conditions?

For all you know, the manufacturer in Thailand whom you've outsourced a key component to is flogging pregnant women and feeble old men to get your work done. Suddenly you've got human rights advocates picketing your front door and the press calling you for a statement. Both Nike and Kathy Lee suffered through months of abuse, not to mention lost profits, while sorting out their individual messes. Are you prepared to do the same?

Tax Planning

As discussed in Chapter 20, the IRS has very specific rules about whether a contractor is an employee. If you fail to meet these standards, you might end up having to pay back taxes and significant penalties. Make sure your relationship is in compliance now or you could face liabilities in the future.

Conflicts of Interest

Hooray! You found a great technical writing firm to create documentation for your products. They seem experienced and knowledgeable about your industry, too. Your joy turns to fear, though, when you discover, months later, that the firm does the same type of work for your arch-competitor. How much of your information is finding its way into their documents, and vice versa?

When a service provider gets experience with a certain industry, it's common for them to want to leverage that experience and resell that knowledge back to others in the industry. But there could be an overlap. Maybe you don't want your marketing consultant looking at your customer information, especially when you find out that the same consultant is working for two other firms competing against you.

If a service provider is accused of passing on confidential information to you because of a conflict of interest, are you also liable? This will be a matter for the courts to decide, but it's up to you and your service provider to state each other's responsibilities in writing beforehand.

Bankruptcy

A client of mine outsourced their corporate travel to a local agency. One day the agency shut its doors and the owners disappeared, filing for bankruptcy. All pending travel plans were thrown up in the air. My client's customers were waiting for people to arrive for important meetings. Projects got delayed. Shipments had to wait.

> ### Knowledge Is Power
>
> The Meta Group, a consultancy firm, finds that most corporations suffer up to a 20 percent decline in productivity the first year of an outsourcing arrangement due to "knowledge transfer."

Sure, you can sue the bankrupt firm, but how are you going to get pennies from a stone? If your service provider folds, you could be left holding the bag. Who's liable then?

When Things Go South: Your Defenses

No matter what kind of precautions you take, there's always going to be a chance that things will go wrong. What can you do? Fight back!

Have a Backup Plan

When union workers in Atlantic City, New Jersey, went on strike, management and salaried employees found themselves cleaning dishes, mopping floors, and manning the buffet lines. Unless you're prepared to don rubber gloves and start doing the grunt work, make sure you're prepared for these sorts of contingencies. Keep a list of potential service providers in reserve. Make sure your employees can pick up the slack if your outsourcing arrangement suddenly stops.

Get Insurance Coverage

Look at your liability insurance coverage carefully. Many of these policies exclude coverage of claims against you for work performed by an outside party. If possible, have this amended. Liability coverage is relatively inexpensive, with rates varying depending on the size of the organization. Most insurance companies will accommodate you, but it may come in the form of a special rider to your existing policy and may only be limited to named people or firms (i.e., the service provider).

> **Business Buzzwords**
>
> A **named insured** is an individual or entity (that means you) who would have the same rights and responsibilities as an individual or entity named (that means your service provider) as an insured in their own policy declarations. You get the same coverage as your service provider and the service provider's insurance carrier is the responsible party.

Also check that your outside service provider has liability coverage. Request a copy of their policy and make sure there are no specific exclusions that would affect you. Ask for your company to be added as a *named insured* on their policy. Ask your insurance carrier whether they will insure you if you're the subject of a lawsuit caused, in part, by a third party.

Beware of *waiver of subrogation* clauses. A typical waiver of subrogation clause reads as follows:

> The Owner and Contractor waive all rights against (1) each other and any of their subcontractors, sub-subcontractors, agents and employees, each of the other, and (2) the consultants, separate contractors ..., if any, and any of their subcontractors, sub-subcontractors, agents and employees, for damages or other causes of loss to the extent covered by property insurance.

Business Buzzwords

A waiver of subrogation is an agreement between you and your third party provider that one or both parties' respective insurance companies cannot recover against the party in the event of a loss.

If you have this kind of clause with your service provider, your hands will be tied if you try to go after them for compensation. Most attorneys recommend that you keep waiver of subrogation clauses out of your contracting agreement.

Have a Dispute-Resolution Clause

Your contract or your service level agreement should address how disputes will be resolved. Typical steps include the following:

- Face-to-face discussions
- Mediation
- Arbitration
- Litigation

Mediation is a nonbinding process where both parties can get together with an independent third party and try to agree on a resolution. This step is taken only when direct conversations don't progress. If mediation fails, both parties can agree in advance to seek a legally binding resolution made by an independent arbitrator. Only when all of these other methods are exhausted would the problem go to litigation. In many cases both parties agree to binding arbitration if disagreements arise, which means that many disputes never go to litigation.

Going On the Offensive

If one of your employees makes a mistake, you usually can't sue him or her. But if a third party makes a mistake, you've got legal options. If you're the subject of legal action because a customer is unhappy with your work product, you may want to consider instituting legal action against the service provider who did the work for you.

Litigation should always be the last course of action because it's the most expensive and time-consuming path to take. Unfortunately, however, you must be open to this option, especially if you're the subject of a lawsuit through the fault of a service provider you hired.

The Least You Need to Know

- ◆ You can head off liabilities in advance by doing your research and forming your corporate structure correctly.

- ◆ Before starting your outsourcing relationship, make sure to state the limits of your liability and check local laws.

- ◆ To limit your liabilities you need to put agreements in place to protect your intellectual property and confidential data.

- ◆ Negligence, a disruption in operations, and labor/child laws can also make you liable for damages.

- ◆ Be aware of unfavorable tax laws, conflicts of interest, and bankruptcy scenarios that can lay the liability of a problem squarely on your shoulders.

- ◆ The best defense to fighting liabilities is a good offense.

- ◆ Other defenses against outsourcing liabilities include having adequate insurance coverage and dispute-resolution procedures.

Chapter 23

Outsourcing Ethics

In This Chapter

- ◆ A look at typical outsourcing ethical dilemmas
- ◆ Characteristics of an ethical outsourcing relationship
- ◆ Tips for conducting an ethical relationship with your service provider

Monica, a 26-year-old Mexican worker, applied for a job at a company near where she lived.

During her interview, Monica was subjected to a humiliating strip-search examination and was made to take a pregnancy test. But because she needed the work, she didn't complain. Who could she complain to, anyway?

Unfortunately, the job wasn't any better. Monica was subject to compulsory overtime and pay below the Mexican minimum wage. She was also not entitled to basic benefits.

The company performed contract manufacturing for a large American computer firm. When word got out about these conditions, the American firm found themselves under fire.

"We are working with our suppliers on an ongoing basis to ensure that our suppliers' practices reflect our values and are consistent with our labor and environmental standards," sputtered the spokesman for the computer firm. "We have implemented a Supplier Code of Conduct that has been rolled out to our top 50 suppliers and we are working with those suppliers to ensure that their practices meet our code."

This incident did not happen 20 years ago. It was reported in January 2004. And human rights agencies continue to find dire working conditions at overseas facilities outsourced by large companies.

> **Business Buzzwords**
>
> **Ethics** is defined as a set of principles of right conduct. Ethical codes of conduct approach human behavior from a philosophical standpoint by stressing objectively defined, but essentially idealistic, standards (or laws) of right and wrong, good/evil, and virtue/vice.

As the computer firm just described found out, contracting their manufacturing with an outside party did not relieve them of certain ethical responsibilities. Many felt that the manufacturing firm, by not investigating the employment practices of its outsourcing partner more fully, was guilty of an ethical lapse. As outsourcing has grown in popularity, many other firms have seen similar dilemmas spring up.

This chapter examines the *ethics* of outsourcing and how they can impact your business.

Is This an Ethical Dilemma?

Let's take a look at a few situations that have tested the ethical boundaries of outsourcing relationships.

The Overseas Outsourcer

A manufacturer in Pennsylvania figures out that a key component can be made much cheaper by a company in Vietnam. A software development firm in Silicon Valley, California, can develop software at a fraction of the cost by employing a team of programmers in Bangalore, India.

These two firms move their work overseas. They do this to stay competitive. Jobs are lost here. That hurts, but not as much as going out of business.

Are they behaving ethically?

The Poacher

You're renovating your warehouse facility to make its operations more efficient. You've hired a large consulting firm to help you with a business process project. The firm has sent in a team of people to rearrange your racking, relabel areas, redistribute lighting, and open up pathways to move products in and out more quickly.

The guy in charge of the project is really, really good. He also confides in you that he's burned out from his job with the consulting firm. You figure that hiring him would boost your operations even more. You extend him an offer and he accepts.

Stay Alert!

Your service contract should contain a clause forbidding both parties from hiring away each other's employees for a certain period of time. More about this is in Chapter 22.

You hired a good employee away from your service provider. Some contracts specifically disallow this kind of action, but not theirs. Besides, the firm got paid for the project, right? It'd be a shame to let such a good person slip away.

Was this ethical?

Padding Your Hours

Your newly hired outsourced shipping and mailroom firm seems to be doing a great job. You are experiencing fewer mistakes and getting faster fulfillment. However, when you get their first progress bill, you have to sit down. How did they rack up so many hours in so short a time?

Outsourcing projects often take many hours to complete. And you probably don't have the time to keep a close eye on what these people are doing. Isn't that why you're outsourcing? Well, what's to keep them from padding a few hours here or there? If your service provider bumped up their time by just 5 percent, would you even know? Unfortunately, many unscrupulous firms try this trick, and get away with it.

No question about ethics here! Charging for time that wasn't spent is fraudulent.

Mr. Loose Lips

You outsource your human resources department to a service provider and they do a bang-up job. They manage to reduce administrative hours and improve the time it takes to respond to employees' questions.

The problem is that the service firm told everyone about the success they had with you. You receive calls from their prospective customers seeking a reference. "I hear you guys were really in bad shape until they arrived," one caller blabbed. "I understand you don't provide your employees with dental insurance," another stated bluntly.

Did the service provider do anything wrong? Was some ethical line crossed? No one wants their dirty laundry hung out for everyone to see. This was not only unethical, but unprofessional, too.

The Saboteur

You and your production manager are in a heated battle. You want to outsource the making of a specific component and he wants to keep it in-house. You're his boss, so you win. But did you really win?

The component gets outsourced, but within weeks you're seeing disappointing results. Shipment dates are missed, quality seems deficient. The contracted manufacturer complains of lack of communication with the production people. The production manager shrugs his shoulders, claiming innocence. You have your suspicions.

The Corner Cutter

To cut back on expenses, the company that's hosting your website is using a less-than-adequate server with less-than-adequate security. Your outsourced payroll service cuts back on employees without telling you, hoping to handle its customer base with fewer people. To save a few bucks, the firm that provides your building's security puts new guards on the job with less training than before, and they don't inform you of this change.

Are these firms doing anything wrong? Yes. They're doing their best to keep themselves profitable. They're making judgments that affect their customers. They're cutting corners on promised services and they're not communicating these changes. Their customers, who assume they're getting the best service possible, are not.

Guidelines for Outsourcing Ethically

The preceding examples show that ethical challenges can crop up in almost any kind of outsourcing relationship. However, for the relationship to be successful, both parties should follow good ethical practices.

Knowledge Is Power

Nicolo Machiavelli (1469–1527), an advisor to kings and author of *The Prince,* believed that the employment of mercenaries to defend a country's borders was "useless and dangerous." He went on to say: "He who holds his State by means of mercenary troops can never be solidly or securely seated. For such troops are disunited, ambitious, insubordinate, treacherous, insolent among friends, cowardly before foes, and without fear of God or faith with man. Whenever they are attacked defeat follows; so that in peace you are plundered by them, in war by your enemies. And this because they have no tie or motive to keep them in the field beyond their paltry pay." Ethical lapses challenged outsourcers even hundreds of years ago!

In the following sections, I offer ethical guidelines for any outsourcing relationship.

Obey the Law

Both you and your service provider should obey the law. If your service provider suggests anything that's clearly illegal, end the relationship as soon as you can. This is not a recipe for success.

Make Sure There's Full Disclosure Between You and Your Service Provider

Do not hold back important information from your service provider, and make it clear that you expect them to be equally as forthcoming with you. If a key person at the service provider leaves the company, you would expect to be told. Similarly, if your project timeline has changed, tell your service provider immediately. The same is true if the people on your staff who are working with the service provider have been given other priorities.

For an outsourcing relationship to work, everyone should be privy to the same information.

Be Honest with Your Customers

When you hire an employment lawyer to represent you in an important case, would you be upset if she outsourced her research and prep work to someone else? Is your accountant doing your tax return, or did he outsource this work to someone with less experience and fewer qualifications?

Many companies outsource work; in most cases, it would have little impact on the relationship. Nonetheless, it's important to disclose all such practices.

> **Knowledge Is Power**
>
> A recent user survey on the ethics and disclosure policies of outsourced technology research firms found a substantial 87 percent of 133 senior IT managers said they want "published, clearly stated ethics policies governing the vendor/client relationships."

Make Confidentiality a Priority

Ethical service providers should never discuss their customers' information with anyone outside of the company, unless instructed to do so. You want to hire a service provider that puts confidentiality among its top priorities.

Put the Best People on the Job

If you outsource your bank reconciliation, shipping, business planning, or technical writing, you expect that the outsourcer will put a competent person on the job. A principled service provider makes sure the best people are doing the work for their customers. They don't throw inexperienced people on a job just to bump up the billable hours. They don't risk their customers' confidence by sending someone who isn't qualified out to do work.

Employ Best Practices

Good companies conduct themselves responsibly. They have procedures in place. They keep their people up to date and trained. They take pride in their workplace. They value their customers. All of these are good business practices. If you sense that a prospective service provider doesn't value these practices, you're probably talking to the wrong person.

Have Your Service Provider's Interests at Heart

Put yourself in your service provider's predicament. How would you like to be treated? What would be your expectations if you were in their shoes? How do you think you would feel if someone poached one of your employees? How would you respond if you were being given unreasonable demands? Keep your service provider's best interests in mind when conducting business with them.

Follow Industry Standards

Many industries have professional organizations. If you're an accountant there's the American Institute of CPAs. Lawyers have their state bar associations. Help desk service companies may belong to the Help Desk Institute. Some of these associations are merely trade groups. Others are state-sanctioned entities. But most have some statement of ethics among their members. Use these ethics guidelines when working with your service provider. Make sure he or she follows these rules.

Avoid Conflicts of Interest

Conflicts of interest arise when a service provider has motivations other than just doing the right job for you.

For years this issue has raged among public companies and the auditors that examine their books. There was once a time when a company hired an independent accounting firm to perform an audit and certify their financial statements each year. Now these firms have grown into billion-dollar organizations with outsourced information technology, business process consulting, and management services fueling their growth.

Eyebrows were raised as these firms gave their clients "clean" audit opinions while reaping millions in fees from other outsourced services. Some of these firms spun off their consulting arms into separate companies to avoid potential conflict-of-interest issues.

Sometimes an outsourcing company has a relationship with you (or others) that may cause a conflict of interest in the minds of the public, the government, or your shareholders.

Establish a Code of Ethics

After the recent spate of corporate scandals, many companies adopted codes of ethics. It's a good practice for you to come up with your own written code and make sure your employees know that you stand by it. You may want to encourage your service provider to do the same.

MachroTech (www.machrotech.com), an offshore information technology outsourcing company based in Connecticut and India, distributes its code of ethics to their customers, suppliers, and employees. This is a great example of good ethics in action. It reads as follows:

◆ We will only engage in lawful and ethical activities with all customers and will only take on assignments for which we are qualified. If we are not qualified to handle some work, or it is out of our realm of expertise, we will refer the customer to a reputable and qualified source.

◆ We will cooperate fully with law enforcement in all instances of unlawful activity. We will only work with customers who agree to conduct business in a lawful and ethical manner.

◆ We will be honest, diligent, and professional in all activities carried out for the customer, and in our own activities.

◆ We will not overbill, append to time-tracking records, or otherwise alter time-tracking information.

◆ We will take extensive measures to safeguard our customers' interests and security.

◆ We will not use customer information for personal, financial, or other gain, and will not disclose customer information under any circumstances.

◆ We will not engage in activity that compromises the interests of our customers.

◆ We will uphold industry standards and do our part to represent the industry in its most positive light.

◆ We will keep our technical skills, knowledge, and competencies current, and will work to remedy any deficiencies before they can affect the quality of the services that we provide to our customers.

Hire a CEO (Chief Ethics Officer)

Some companies go so far as to hire senior managers whose sole job is to be responsible for the ethical behavior of both the organization and its suppliers. After all of the scandals at MCI, the company appointed a chief ethics officer in late 2003. MCI's decision to hire a chief ethics officer mirrors the actions of such Fortune 1,000 companies as Deloite & Touche, Tenet Health Systems, and Dell Computers.

A chief ethics officer's job often includes creating a code of ethics for the company, overseeing ethics training for their company's employees and contractors, and setting up procedures for handling ethics-related issues. The chief ethics officer is usually responsible for all aspects of ethics and compliance programs and deals with exceptions or problems. He or she also advises senior management as to the ethical or compliance aspects of their decisions.

> **Outsourcing Insights**
>
> Many consulting firms specialize in helping companies develop ethical codes, training manuals, and personnel policies. A good place to start is the Institute of Management Consultants' website (www.imcusa.org). The IMC has its own code of ethics that its members are required to adhere to.

Maybe you don't have the resources of a Fortune 1,000 company, but putting someone in charge of your business ethics can be an important step for your company.

Form an Ethics Committee

The Internet search engine Google formed an ethics committee to ensure that the algorithms used for their searches were fair. The American Institute of Certified Public Accountants formed an ethics committee to oversee behavior and act as a sounding board for its members. And don't forget the Brinks Company, the security experts—they also have an ethics committee to make sure the company's policies and procedures are completely above board.

An ethics committee can perform the same role as a chief ethics officer, but it gets more people involved in shaping a company's behavior, including its relationships with any outside service providers.

The Least You Need to Know

♦ Expect to face numerous ethical dilemmas when outsourcing any kind of work.

♦ An ethical relationship places an emphasis on confidentiality, competence, and good practices between the customer and the outside service provider.

♦ As an ethical company, you should have your service provider's best interests at heart, conduct your business according to industry standards, and do your best to avoid conflicts of interest.

♦ Consider hiring a chief ethics officer or forming an ethics committee to help oversee your relationship with an outside service provider. At a minimum, develop a code of ethics for your company, and stand by it.

Sample Independent Contractor Agreement

What follows is an example of an Independent Contractor's Agreement. It is included as a guide and would need to be tailored to your specific needs. Always have any agreement reviewed by an attorney before using it.

Independent Contractor Agreement

This agreement dated _____, is made By and Between _____, ("Company"), whose address is _____, AND _____, ("Independent Contractor"), whose address is _____.

1. Consultation Services. The Company hereby employs the Independent Contractor to perform the following services in accordance with the terms and conditions set forth in this agreement: _____.

2. Incorporation. The Independent Contractor is an incorporated business or has provided an EIN number or Social Security Number. The Independent Contractor will receive a 1099 for services payments received at the end of each calendar year.

3. Terms of Agreement. This agreement will begin _____ and will end at the discretion of the parties. Either party may cancel this agreement on thirty (30) days notice to the other party in writing, by certified mail or personal delivery.

4. Time Devoted by Independent Contractor. It is anticipated the Independent Contractor will spend approximately _____ hours per week in fulfilling its obligations under this contract. The particular amount of time may vary from day to day or week to week. However, the Independent Contractor shall devote a minimum of _____ per month to its duties in accordance with this agreement.

5. Place Where Services Will Be Rendered. The Independent Contractor will perform most services in accordance with this contract at a location of Independent Contractor's discretion. In addition the Independent Contractor will perform services on the telephone and at such other places as necessary to perform these services in accordance with this agreement.

6. Payment to Independent Contractor. The Independent Contractor will be paid as follows: _____. The Independent Contractor will submit an itemized statement setting forth the time spent and services rendered, and the Company will pay the Independent Contractor the amounts due as indicated by statements submitted by the Independent Contractor within ten (10) days of receipt.

7. Independent Contractor. Both the Company and the Independent Contractor agree that the Independent Contractor will act as an independent contractor in the performance of its duties under this contract. Accordingly, the Independent Contractor shall be responsible for payment of all taxes including Federal, State, and local taxes arising out of the Independent Contractor's activities in accordance with this contract, including by way of illustration but not limitation, Federal and State income tax, Social Security tax, Unemployment Insurance taxes, and any other taxes or business license fee as required.

8. Confidential Information. The Independent Contractor agrees that any information received by the Independent Contractor during any furtherance of the Independent Contractor's obligations in accordance with this contract, which concerns the personal, financial, or other affairs of the Company will be treated by the Independent Contractor in full confidence and will not be revealed to any other persons, firms or organizations.

9. Employment of Others. The Company may from time to time request that the Independent Contractor arrange for the services of others. All costs to the Independent Contractor for those services will be paid by the Company but in

no event shall the Independent Contractor employ others without the prior authorization of the Company.

10. Noncompete. No employee, related party, or any other affiliate of the Independent Contractor will do independent work for a customer of the Company or prospective customer unless approved by the Company. If this agreement is terminated for any reason, the Independent Contractor agrees not to do any work for a Company customer or prospective customer for a period of up to 3 years after termination.

Company

By: _____   _____

      Authorized Signature   Date

Independent Contractor

By: _____   _____

      Authorized Signature   Date

Sample Request for Proposal

What follows is a sample Request For Proposal that was prepared for a potential outsourced Customer Relationship Management system. The purpose of this RFP is to point you in the right direction when preparing your own RFP, though clearly you will need to tailor it to your own specific needs.

Request for Proposal (RFP)

Customer Relationship Management (CRM) Solution

Issued for Bid: October 10, 2006

For:

ABC Company
100 Main Street
AnyTown USA 10000

Phone: 800-555-1000
Fax: 800-555-100

The material included in this RFP is proprietary and confidential. It may not be shared or copied in any form without the prior written consent of ABC Company.

Section 1—Response Instructions

1.1—RFP Response Due Date

All responses must be submitted no later than **5:00 P.M.** eastern time on **October 10, 2006** to be eligible for consideration by ABC COMPANY. Vendor response on intent to bid is due by **September 26, 2006.**

1.2—Submission Format and Content Requirements

Acceptable responses will include two hard copies of the Vendor response and an electronic version in Microsoft Word. Vendor responses should include the following:

- ◆ Detailed capability statements for each identified requirement.

- ◆ Responses shall follow the order of the RFP and reference specified section numbers. All additional documentation shall be submitted as appendixes to the RFP response.

- ◆ Responses shall include any Vendor Contract Terms and Conditions applicable in the event Vendor Bid is accepted, including payment terms and options.

- ◆ Responses shall include an Executive Summary section, which is to provide an overview of the Vendor's understanding of the scope of the deployment and summary as to why the Vendor should be considered a strong candidate to providing ABC COMPANY with a CRM solution.

- ◆ The Vendor is expected to identify and describe all limitations or exceptions to the stated requirements of the proposed solution as completely as possible. Alternative solutions that meet ABC COMPANY's business objectives are acceptable.

- ◆ Line itemization of all project costs, including recommended hardware, software, operating systems, maintenance, and consulting fees including training services.

- ◆ Vendor contact information including name, address, telephone number, and e-mail addresses for the purpose of clarification and/or questions on the submitted response.

- ◆ Vendor will identify any subcontractors who will be contracted for delivery of any portion of the proposed solution.

- ◆ Vendor Company information, including:

  Years in business

  Ownership

  Number of similar installations

  Number of employees

  Financial Statements for the past three (3) years

  Sample Integration Project Plans/Case Studies for similar installations in scope

  Indication if Vendor is a distributor or developer of the proposed solution or its components

  > In the event the Vendor is an authorized reseller, provide documentation providing status of Authorized Distributorship.

  > For Developing Vendors, indicate number of development staff including years of experience, list of professional certifications and notice of any planned product releases or system upgrades with timelines.

  List of three References for similar installations completed within the past twelve (12) months, including Company Name, Contact Name, Telephone Number, and description of scope of deployment.

1.3—Vendor Contact

Questions and/or clarifications with regard to this Request for Proposal should be directed to:

Jane Smith
Phone: 800-555-1000
Email: jane@abccompany.com

Section 2—About ABC COMPANY

Section 2.1—Company Overview

ABC COMPANY is the leading unified collaboration services provider with an integrated services offering including videoconferencing, audioconferencing, webconferencing, video network management services, and streaming for the enterprise and mid markets. Through web-based self-service solutions, experienced full-service call centers and diversified global networks, ABC COMPANY enables customers to conduct electronic meetings, events, and training from anyplace at anytime.

ABC COMPANY provides services for more than 2,000 companies and its client roster includes more than one third of Fortune 100 companies.

Section 2.2—Current Systems and Capabilities Overview

ABC COMPANY currently uses a collection of independent systems to perform Customer Relationship Management within the organization. These systems consist of the following:

System	Version	Purpose
Software 1	V6.0	To provide internal and external Trouble Ticket Management capabilities.
Software 2	V5.2	To provide Sales Force Automation capabilities to internal Sales Management, Account Managers, and Customer Relationship Managers as well as to facilitate Marketing Campaign Management.
Software 3	V7.0	Customer Accounting, limited Invoices, Accounts Receivable, Accounts Payable, and Budget processing.
Software 4	N/A	Software 4 is an internally develop system that manages ABC COMPANY's core business operations surrounding reservations, scheduling, management, production data management for all of ABC COMPANY's Video-, Audio-, Webconferencing, and Streaming Services.

continues

continued

System	Version	Purpose
		Software 4 maintains the majority of customer Company information including contacts, sites, and device information as well as contains all Customer usage information for billing.
Software 5	V5.1.6	Provides ABC COMPANY internal and external customers with Web Portal access to online reporting. Software 5 is configured to access a data warehouse that pulls a subset of data elements to provide Trouble Ticket, Usage, Quality and as well as other reports to authenticated users.

Section 3–Summary of ABC COMPANY's CRM Objectives

ABC COMPANY is committed to deliver Quality of Experience at all customer touch points at all times. To meet this objective, ABC COMPANY must be able to provide complete, immediate and accurate information to its internal customers, external customers, partners and resellers. ABC COMPANY believes this level of service is required to acquire new customers as well as maintain existing customers and is committed to implementing services and support that make doing business with ABC COMPANY as effortless as possible for the customer.

ABC COMPANY is also highly devoted to delivering new and innovative products and services to meet and exceed customer requirements touching all aspects of their Conferencing experience. This requires ABC COMPANY's CRM systems to allow for extreme flexibility in configuration, access, data portability and reporting functions. With continual growth, improvement and expansion of ABC COMPANY's product mix it is mission critical that product information, contracts, pricing, marketing efforts, partner capabilities, reseller activity and customer account history data work seamlessly together to provide ABC COMPANY with the analytics to prioritize, price, market, sell and support exactly what our customers want, exactly how they want it.

Section 4–Implementation Scope

4.1–Locations and User Information

- Number of Customer Service Users: 35
- Number of Sales Users: 76
- Number of Marketing Users: 12
- Number of Internal Technical Support Users: 24
- Number of Office Locations: 3
- Number of Remote Sales Offices (connected via T1, Cable or DSL): 7
- Number of Custom Views: 10 to 12
- Estimated Number of External Users (Customers, Partners, Resellers): 500
- Number of System Interfaces and Types: 5

4.2–Data Migration Requirements

- Migration for any Trouble Ticket or Sales Force Automation Data currently residing in existing systems if to be upgraded and/or replaced by proposed solution.

4.3–System Integration Requirements

- ABC COMPANY requires a dedicated team and/or Project Manager supplied by the Vendor for the full duration of the implementation.
- ABC COMPANY requires a detailed project plan including delivery dates to be updated on a weekly basis by the Vendor and submitted to ABC COMPANY each Friday afternoon before 5:00 P.M. ET during the life of the project.
- ABC COMPANY reserves the right to reschedule or alter the submitted project plans to ensure the project has zero negative impact on production systems or customers at their sole discretion.

♦ ABC COMPANY reserves the right to require certain aspects of the project be completed during off hours (including evenings and weekends).

♦ ABC COMPANY reserves the right to conduct an internal system evaluation, inventory and test plan prior to authorizing vendor's final payment on project completion.

Section 5—Technical Requirements

5.1—Hardware/Operating System Standards

5.1.1—Intel Server Standards

Windows 2000 Server SP4, Windows Server 2003

Pentium 4 Processor

512 MB RAM or greater depending on performance

MS SQL if SQL is required

5.1.2—UNIX Server Standards

SUN OS Version   8.0

Sybase Database

5.1.3—Workstation Standards

Microsoft Windows2000 Professional SP4

Microsoft Office2000 & Office XP

Internet Explorer V   6.0

RAM—128 MB minimum

Processor—500 MHz minimum

Hard Drive—4 GB Minimum

5.2–Client Software Requirements

To best support ABC COMPANY's internal users, a fully functional Web client is the preferred user interface. ABC COMPANY has users spread across multiple Call Centers, Remote Sales Offices and requires access for remote workers via DSL, Cable, ISDN and dial-up connections.

ABC COMPANY also desires to allow customers access to the CRM system to allow for viewing of account status and historical information such as trouble tickets, order status, managed inventory via a portal on ABC COMPANY corporate Internet site. Future applications of this portal may include the implementation of self service features allowing customers to open, close and change status of trouble tickets; permitting additions, changes and deletions of other customer data such as site locations and managed inventory.

Please describe in detail the internal and external client interface capabilities of the Vendors proposed solution including any bandwidth requirements to support WAN or Remote users or any browser plug-in requirements for either internal or external users. Please also outline any functional or feature differences between a Web and Full Client if the Vendor offers both options.

Section 6–Training Requirements

In order to ensure a successful installation of any software application ABC COMPANY requires a formal training program be conducted. Training programs specifically designed to address the individual needs of users by job function is required as outlined in the Training Classifications section of this document.

6.1–Training Classifications

- ◆ Customer Support Representatives
- ◆ Customer Support Managers
- ◆ Internal Support Technicians
- ◆ Marketing Program/Product Managers
- ◆ Sales Representatives/Account Managers
- ◆ Sales Managers

◆ Senior Executives

◆ System Administrator Training

◆ Train the Trainer Session for ABC COMPANY in-house Training Department

6.2–Training Delivery Requirements

A successful training program will include:

◆ Flexibly scheduled instructor lead demonstrations.

◆ Instructor lead demonstrations shall not exceed 4 hours in any one session; however, multiple sessions for any given job class may be scheduled.

◆ A customized Users Manual providing instructions on the most common operations.

◆ A customized Administrative Manual including information on product versions, passwords, instructions on day to day system maintenance procedures and troubleshooting guidelines.

◆ Computer Based Training (CBT) for use as refresher courses and new employee training.

Please describe in detail any training programs and methodologies utilized by the Vendor to meet this project requirement.

Section 7–Support and Maintenance Requirements

7.1–External Support Requirements

ABC COMPANY delivers business critical service and support to its customers across the globe on a 7/24 basis 365 days a year. Describe in detail the support and maintenance program options including Vendor escalation procedures, Service Level Agreements and pricing available by the Vendor to ensure ABC COMPANY's success in meeting the service and support requirements of its customers.

7.2—Internal Support Requirements

ABC COMPANY is also committed to providing internal first tier support for all business critical systems. Describe in detail the Vendors recommendation for preparing ABC COMPANY to provide internal support to its users and customers, include number of estimated support personnel by based on user count and recommended training and/or technical knowledge prerequisites.

Section 8—Implementation Schedule

ABC COMPANY's expectation is that implementation would begin as immediately as possible after the award of the project to the selected Vendor. Please describe in detail the project kick off estimated timelines including product procurement, scheduling and any initial project consultation procedures employed by the Vendor with estimated number of days lapse after contract award.

Section 9—Documentation Requirements

Prior to completion of the project ABC COMPANY requires all documentation including but not limited to user manuals, license certificates, Vendor work orders or time reports, project status reports, change management documentation, maintenance and support documentation and system configuration specifications be delivered to the ABC COMPANY designee to ensure compliance with the documentation standards of this project. Please provide a description of the standard documentation provided by the Vendor for a CRM installation and describe the Vendor's process to ensure accurate, complete and timely delivery of project documentation to ABC COMPANY.

Section 10—Change Management Process

ABC COMPANY is aware that it is common for changes to occur during the life of a project, however, ABC COMPANY requires a formal management program to control all project changes. Please describe in detail the change management processes and controls utilized by the Vendor to ensure on time, on budget and to specification delivery of the contracted project to ABC COMPANY.

Section 11—Completion Approval Process

ABC COMPANY requires the completion of a formal project conclusion phase whereby the Vendor will supply a detailed walk-through of the project deliverables to ABC COMPANY designee(s). Project deliverables include all hardware, software, review of system functions, completion of training and all documentation as outlined above. ABC COMPANY will not authorize final payment with out completion of the project conclusion phase. Please outline in detail any processes and procedures utilized by the Vendor to satisfy this project requirement.

Appendix C

Business Buzzword Glossary

application development   The writing, testing, and implementation of custom software programs.

application service providers (ASPs)   Business that outsource servers or software, generally over the Internet, for a periodic fee.

asset management   An outsourcing service that involves the scanning and tracking of the ownership of physical assets (furniture and fixtures, machinery, equipment, and so on) and reporting any changes in configurations to the customer.

at will employment   A legal doctrine that describes the relationship of employees and employers; the doctrine gives the employers the right to terminate employees and employees the right to terminate their relationship with the employer.

balanced scorecard   For outsourcing arrangements, a system of measurement that takes into consideration four factors: financial analysis (cost/benefit), customer service analysis, quality analysis, and learning/growth analysis. This method will require you to come up with criteria and parameters for each of these four areas.

benchmarking   For outsourcing arrangements, a system of measurement that compares the results of a project against similar projects or other similar factors.

business process   A collection of related structural activities that produce a specific outcome for a particular customer.

business process outsourcing   Taking an entire process and farming it out elsewhere.

business service provider (BSP)   An entity that combines outsourcing and consulting services.

channel   A means for distributing products through a network of experienced and trained service providers.

code of ethics   A written document outlining a company's ethics policies.

co-employer   A relationship that involves sharing and allocating employer responsibilities between a third-party leasing firm and its customer.

contract worker   A nonemployee individual who performs specific tasks over a predetermined timeframe and in accordance with a written agreement.

commodity outsourcing   The farming out of simple business tasks that have become so common that the customer generally selects a service provider based solely on price.

common law employee   As defined by the IRS, anyone who works for you where you control what that person does and how he or she does it.

common law rules   Rules determined by the IRS (sometimes referred to as the "20 rules" or the "common rules") that can help an employer determine if he or she has truly entered into an independent contract agreement or an employer-employee relationship.

contingency-based contract   An agreement whereby the service provider gets paid only when their goals are met. The service provider usually takes all of the risk, and in return reaps a bigger reward at the end.

co-opetition   An outsourcing arrangement with a competitor.

co-sourcing   Outsourcing a function, but not all of the function. When you co-source, both you and the service provider contribute employees and other resources to the project.

data centers   Companies that provide external warehousing of data.

direct costs   Those expenditures that can be absolutely linked to a task or activity.

distributor   An individual or a company that markets merchandise to retail stores or acts as an intermediary between a store and a manufacturer. Distributors generally maintain inventory.

e-commerce service   A service that provides all the tools needed for selling something online, including credit card authorization, inventory management, billing, and customer data tracking.

employee leasing   An outsourcing arrangement that involves terminating your employees so that an outside firm can hire them and then "rent" them back to you under specific contractual terms. The outsourcing company takes responsibility for certain tasks and costs related to your employees.

equity compensation   A compensation method whereby a business gives up a piece of ownership to limit cash payments to a critical third party.

ethics   A set of principles of right conduct.

factoring   The purchasing of accounts receivable from a business by an individual or company who assumes the risk of loss in return for some agreed discount.

fiduciary   An individual who is often in a position of authority who obligates himself or herself to act on behalf of another and assumes a duty to act in good faith and with care, candor, and loyalty in fulfilling the obligation.

fixed-fee contracts   An agreement in which set payments are made to the service provider. Sometimes these payments are unrelated to whether milestones are achieved, other times the fees are dependent on milestones.

following the sun   A service arrangement whereby capabilities are spread throughout the world to provide services round the clock.

forensic metrics   A system of measurement that looks at information from the past to help you evaluate a goal.

gain sharing   A system designed to measure the improvements, or gains achieved over a certain period of time and then share the results of those gains with a service provider. Gain sharing is a bonus incentive system where everybody benefits as goals are achieved.

goodwill   In business, the excess that someone is willing to pay for a company over and above the market value of assets, net of liabilities.

help desk outsourcing   Providing resources for answering internal and external questions and fixing problems with the customer's products and/or assets.

incentive-based contract Also referred to as a performance-based contact. An agreement for payment of services based on the achievement of certain goals.

incubator An organization designed to assist start-up companies, generally with respect to providing shared office space, office services, knowledge and technical assistance.

independent contractor A contractor who is self-employed and has the right to control the means and methods of performing work. If you are an independent contractor, the person or company you work for controls *what* you do, not *how* you do it.

indirect costs Expenditures that are related to an activity, but not directly attributable to the activity.

information technology (IT) outsourcing An outsourcing arrangement in which an information technology function, process, or task is performed by an outside company.

infrastructure management An outsourcing arrangement whose goal is to reduce the size of internal IT staff. Infrastructure management service providers are usually responsible for the operation, stability, and security of a client's network.

injunction A court order prohibiting a party from taking certain actions.

logistics outsourcing A type of business process outsourcing. Logistics usually manes things like supply-chain management, procurement, purchasing, e-business—processes that require many steps and coordination with multiple parties.

managed service provider A company that manages clients' key technology assets, such as servers, over the Internet.

metric A value that's part of a system used to measure the results of a process or calculation. Using metrics involves the employment of mathematical and statistical analysis.

moonlight To work at another job, often at night, in addition to one's full-time job.

multiclient shared services Outsourcing arrangements that are more about sharing products or services instead of using them exclusively. In this type of arrangement, the service provider has something that can be rented out to many customers or clients at the same time. The customer can outsource a function by sharing a resource with someone else.

named insured   An individual or entity (for our purposes, usually a customer who hires a service provider) who has the same rights and responsibilities as an individual or entity named (typically a service provider) as an insured in their own policy declarations. The individual gets the same coverage as the service provider and the service provider's insurance carrier is the responsible party.

negligence   The failure to exercise the degree of care considered reasonable under the circumstances, resulting in an unintended injury to another party.

noncompete agreement   An agreement between a service provider and a client in which the service provider agrees not to poach customers from the client.

nondisclosure and confidentiality agreement   An agreement that protects private information between a customer and their outside service provider.

nonstatutory employees   Even though the federal government defines certain people as employees specifically by the type of job they do, they also have two types of jobs that are never considered to be employment:

- Substantially all payments for services to people acting as direct sellers or real estate agents that are directly related to sales or other output rather than to the number of hours worked.

- Services performed under a written contract providing that those performing the services will not be treated as employees for federal tax purposes.

offshore outsourcing   The exporting of work to other countries.

partner   One of two or more persons associated as joint principals in carrying on a business for the purpose of enjoying a joint profit. A partnership can be a legal arrangement involving equity, or merely just a sharing of revenues or profits from providing an end product to a customer. Many outsourcing arrangements follow the latter arrangement.

performance-based contracts   Also referred to as an incentive based contact. An agreement for payment of services based on the achievement of certain goals.

proactive metrics   A system of measurement that acts in advance of a measurement goal.

professional employer organization (PEO)   A company that leases employees to customers and also provides other employer related services, such as payroll processing and administration.

retailer　An entity that sells goods to the ultimate end user.

return on investment　A measure of how effectively you can use your capital to generate income.

RFI (Request for Information)　A document that precedes the Request for Proposal (RFP). It asks for data from prospective outsourcers so that the requestor can determine whether the outsourcer is qualified to receive a formal RFP.

RFP (Request for Proposal)　A document that formally asks a prospective service provider to propose a solution. It includes guidelines to help the service provider prepare their proposal.

scope creep　Additional changes made to an existing project that add to the cost and time of the project.

service level agreement (SLA)　A written contract that sets out both parties' obligations under their outsourcing arrangement. The contract establishes the expectations between the two parties. It defines their business relationship and confirms the criteria that will be used to judge whether the outsourcing arrangement is working.

stakeholder　Someone who will be held accountable if the outsourcing relationship fails.

statutory employees　Individuals who are employees because the law says that they are employees. There are four types of statutory employees:

- A driver who distributes beverages (other than milk) or meat, vegetable, fruit or baker products, or who picks up an delivers laundry or dry cleaning.

- A full-time life insurance sales agent whose principal business activity is selling life insurance or annuity contracts or both, primarily for one insurance company.

- An individual who works at home on materials or goods that you supply and that must be returned to you or to a person you name, if you also furnish specifications for the work to be done.

- A full-time salesperson who works on your behalf and turns in orders to you from wholesalers; retailers; contractors; or operators of hotels, restaurants, or other similar establishments. The goods sold must be merchandise for resale or supplies for use in the buyer's business operation. The work performed for you must be the salesperson's principal business activity.

telemarketing   A means of generating and qualifying sales leads by calling potential prospects by phone.

time and materials contract   An agreement for payment based on an hourly rate and cost of materials.

traditional outsourcing   The most common type of outsourcing. It generally involves taking a task you don't want to do or can't do and having someone other than your employees do it for you.

transformational outsourcing   A combination of outsourcing and consulting. Transformational outsourcers take responsibility for a specific area of a company for a period of time while they recommend and implement new systems. Then they hand back these functions to the company and move on.

vicarious liability   When one person is liable for the negligent actions of another person, even though the first person was not directly responsible for these actions.

waiver of subrogation   An agreement between a customer and their third-party provider that one or both parties' respective insurance companies cannot recover against the party in the event of a loss.

wholesaler   A person or firm who buys larger quantities of goods than a distributor and therefore at a lower price. Wholesalers then sell their goods to distributors, other wholesalers, and to retail outlets.

zero-based sourcing   A system that, at the end of each period, forces the outsourcing decision to be reanalyzed as if it were being evaluated for the first time.

Appendix D

Additional Resources

The following resources proved invaluable to me during my research for this book; they will also help you learn even more about the subject of outsourcing.

General Outsourcing Websites

The Offshore Outsourcing Benchmarking Association
www.obenchmarking.com

OBA is an association of outsourcing professionals and companies that conduct benchmarking studies to identify the practices that improve the overall operations of the members.

The Outsourcing Directory
www.outsourcing.org

A web-based business directory providing information and tools for suppliers and buyers of outsourcing services.

The Outsourcing Center
www.outsourcing-faq.com
www.outsourcing-best-practices.com
www.outsourcing-journal.com

Tbe Outsourcing Center hosts a wealth of free research, case studies, database directories, market intelligence, and ever-expanding content that organizational decision-makers seek on emerging trends and best practices in outsourcing as a strategic business solution. Outsourcing Center is the publishing and marketing channel of Everest Group, a management consulting firm.

United Business Media's Outsourcing Pipeline

www.outsourcingpipeline.com

Outsourcing Pipeline offers breaking news, research tools, expert advice and analysis, practical how-to features, and insights into industry trends.

Michael F. Corbett & Associates, Ltd.

www.corbettassociates.com
www.firmbuilder.com

Two informative websites from Michael F. Corbett & Associates, Ltd., a management education and research firm dedicated to advancing outsourcing as a powerful management discipline.

Business Publications Search Engine

www.bpubs.com

A directory-based Internet search engine covering a variety of business topics, including many articles on outsourcing.

The Outsourcing Management Zone

www.theoutsourcerzone.com

Information, guidance, and resources covering the whole gamut of outsourcing issues and topics. Included are articles, papers, a directory of suppliers, background information, and much more.

IT Outsourcing Websites

Computerworld Magazine Online

www.computerworld.com/managementtopics/outsourcing

From the popular industry trade magazine, a website featuring outsourcing editorials and columns, features and news analysis, product info and reviews, white papers and vendor info, and research links on the web.

CIO Magazine

www.cio.com/research/outsourcing

Here you'll find articles about how outsourcing affects senior management.

The IT Outsourcing Essentials Guide and The IT Outsourcing Toolkit
www.OvitzTaylorGates.com

IT Outsourcing tools created by Ovitz Taylor Gates, a global management consulting and technology services company.

National Association Of Professional Employer Organizations
www.napeo.org

The largest PEO trade association representing more than 325 professional employer organizations nationwide.

Books

The Outsourcing Revolution: Why It Makes Sense and How to Do It Right by Michael F. Corbett (Dearborn Trade, a Kaplan Professional Company, 2004)

Strategic Outsourcing: A Structured Approach to Outsourcing Decisions and Initiatives by Maurice F. Greaver (American Management Association, 1999)

Offshore Outsourcing: Business Models, ROI and Best Practices, Second Edition, by Marcia Robinson, Ravi Kalakota (Mivar Pr Inc, 2004)

The IT Outsourcing Guide by Rob Aalders (John Wiley & Sons, 2001)

Outsourcing for Radical Change: A Bold Approach to Enterprise Transformation by Jane C. Linder (AMACOM, 2004)

Index

X–Y–Z